NGO IN THE HUMAN RIGHTS MANAGEMENT

NGO IN THE HUMAN RIGHTS MANAGEMENT

B.S. Aswal

CYBER TECH PUBLICATIONS
4264/3, Ansari Road, Daryaganj, New Delhi-110002 (India)
Ph.: 011-23244078, 011-43559448 Fax: 011-23280028
E-Mail: cyberpublicationsdelhi@yahoo.com
Website: www.cybertechpublications.com

NGO IN THE HUMAN RIGHTS MANAGEMENT

B.S. Aswal

First Edition 2010

Published by : Asian Offset Printers

G.S. Rawat for **Cyber Tech Publications**
4264/3, Ansari Road, Daryaganj, New Delhi-110002 (India)
Ph.: 011-23244078, 011-43559448 Fax: 011-23280028
E-Mail: cyberpublicationsdelhi@yahoo.com
Website: www.cybertechpublications.com

Preface

The presented book NGOs in the Human Rights Movement has been brought into being in view of mammoth demand across the country. The book especially throws light on NGOs and its increasing significance in the Human Rights Movement. The book comprises comprehensive treatment about NGOs and Human Rights, Human Rights NGO capacity building programme, approaches of organizational changes in the adoption of RBAs etc.

At the end of World War II, the phrase "human rights" was virtually unknown, whether in the media, in standard textbooks, or as a guideline for state conduct in the emerging international community. It was nongovernmental organizations (NGOs) that made the phrase a core element of the United Nations Charter in 1944, even as they pressed for the Universal Declaration of Human Rights, adopted three years later. This was but the beginning of a historic effort to make the Declaration a fundamental standard for measuring progress in civilized society. If the principal motivation was the prevention of another Holocaust, NGOs would fulfill the indispensable function, projected by Eleanor Roosevelt, of serving as the "curious grapevine" that would enlighten everyone about their rights and channel information about human rights violations to the world community.

The right to join a free trade union is a necessary condition of a free society and economy. Thus the reports assess key internationally recognized worker rights, including the right of association; the right to organize and bargain collectively; prohibition of forced or compulsory labor; minimum age for employment of children; and acceptable work conditions.

—Author

CONTENTS

1

Introduction

This chapter provides an outline of the general steps needed for starting and incorporating a NGO/NPO. Detailed instructions for each of these steps can typically be obtained from local governments or a designated government agency/board, an attorney, or a local nonprofit management support organization.

The issues covered here are of a very general nature, and actual situations will, of course, vary from country to country. Starting an NGO/NPO may only require a strong vision, or a need, for people to come together as a group and work to satisfy that need. NGOs can range from 1-2 persons working on a single local issue to an international NGO network with thousands of members working globally on a range of issues.

This feature is primarily based on the work of GDRC, itself an NGO, and the interaction it has had with other NGOs via its programme, the "NGO Café". The key ingredients that make or break an NGO/NPO, of course, are its programmes and projects. It covers the issues and themes that the NGO/NPO addresses, the target areas or communities that it works in, funding available and the activity's partners.

These are influenced by, among other things:

- the felt needs of target community (what are the real problems faced by the target community? How can the NGO/NPO identify them, or create a forum where it can be expressed by the community?)
- staff expertise available (what expertise and skills do the NGO/NPO staff posess? Are they full-time or part-

time staff? How can external human resources be mobilized?)

- funding strategy (what sources of funding can the NGO/NPO tap into? Which of these are local and international? How can funds for short-term and long-term activities be mobilized?)

While it is critical that a new NGO/NPO ensure that it is properly registered with the public authorities of the country, it is of even more importance to 'register' with its target community-in terms of ensuring acceptability, building trust, programme and project effectiveness, and bringing about real change.

ESTABLISH THE NGO'S BOARD OF DIRECTORS

Prior to incorporating or registering, an organization should first establish a Board of Directors or an Advisory Board and develop the organization's mission. The members of the board, as a group, have trustee and legal responsibility for the actions and operation of the organization. There are minimum levels of involvement required of board members in organizational and operational management:

- financial management
- planning
- programme
- resource development (fund raising)
- human resource management
- information management
- marketing and public relations
- governance (board affairs)

One of the steps in incorporating is filing the NGO's bye-laws (also called articles of association or incorporation) and many authorities require multiple officer and board member signatures.

DEVELOP THE NGO'S BYE-LAWS

Bylaws are the set of rules under which the organization will operate. They typically include such items as (a) number of members, term length, nomination process, committees, and meetings; (b) fiscal year/accounting cycles, committees, and officers' responsibilities; (c) methodologies, tools, and strategies, monitoring and evaluation etc.; and (d) how to amend the bylaws themselves.

Note that Bye-laws can also be called the NGO's "constitution" , "article of association" or "statues", depending on the law of a particular country.

Typical bye-laws of an NGO will contain the following information:

- Preamble
- Organization name and acronym
- Organizational logo
- Basic aim and purpose of organization
- Mission statement
- Functions
- Membership (types, conditions/qualifications of members, status, length of service, procedure to become members, rights and obligations, termination)
- Advisory board (role and functions, qualifications of board members, authority, elections, members)
- Organizational structure
- Asset management (Finance and property, membership fees)
- Legal status
- Contact address
- Dissolution of NGO
- Amendments, modifications, revisions of bye-laws

REGISTER THE NGO

- The NGO's name: Check to see if the proposed name of the organization is already in use. Check with the local government registry or similar agency/board to see if your proposed name is already taken. It may be necessary to provide two or three optional names for the

NGO/NPO! This also applies to the logo of the NGO, if you plan to use one.

- Registering or incorporating within your local government. It will be necessary to incorporate the organization within its given local government/agency by writing and filing the necessary forms. In most countries, there are specialized departments or officers within local governments that deal with registering an NGO (which may also be called by other different names: non-profit organization, voluntary organization, people's organization, etc.)

There are several documents that need to be submitted, and these differ from country to country. Information on the NGO/NPO Board, its mission statement, programmes and projects info, staff members, funding sources, etc. will be necessary.

A typical set of documents to be submitted to the appropriate authority for registering an NGO includes-Memorandum of Association or Bye-laws, including applicable rules and regulations; report of annual activities, financial reports/audit reports; sources and pattern of income and expenditure; minutes of the Executive Board or General Assembly that endorses the setting up of the NGO; letters of support (references) etc.

FUND-RAISING

- Funding and Fund raising: Remember money does not grow on trees. Even if a 'donation' is made to a programme or activity, it is done with an objective in mind-sometimes simply to get good karma. This is critical to understand when we approach a potential sponsor-why is he donating? What advantages can they obtain? What PR milage can they receive from the act?

It is equally important to maintain professionalism, within the NGO, to build adequate trust with the potential sponsor or donor. Transparency, accountability, communication etc. should be an integral part of the NGO. A good strategy is to create a working advisory group for each project or activity.

This group will have two types of members-strategic members, who will give weight and legitimacy, (and will also bring in key non-financial resources) to the activity, and financial members who will make the actual contribution, based on the strength of the strategic members! Do not always depend on external or large sources of funding-sometimes, it can come from surprising sources in your own backyard.

- Tax exemption: File for tax exemption with the national tax authority (where available). Now that you have formed your board, incorporated your organization, and developed your bylaws you are ready to file with the tax authorities for tax-exemption. The national tax authority may require a number of forms for this process. Be prepared to have the following information ready:
  - o A description of the organizations purpose and programs, including: who the organization serves and why, constituency demographics, examples of training materials, workshops, and other services, etc.
  - o Financial information: sources of funding; financial statements (revenue and expense statement and a balance sheet) for three prior or two projected years.

OFFICE MANAGEMENT

- Seek staff and office supplies. Volunteers, staff secondments, retired advisors etc. help in reducing personnel costs. Bulk purchases, surplus sales, voluntary donations, are ways to reduce costs. Some common forms of support include:
  - o Consulting services (management, advertising, marketing, promotion, legal, taxation, financial, strategic planning, project design, system development etc.)
  - o Financial support (capital costs, feasibility studies, small business start-up costs, credit facilities for purchase of assets, sponsorships, travel grants, deficit finance etc.)

- o Donate equipments (machinery, furniture, computers, office equipment and other infrastructure)
- o Donate products (educational, health care, construction, raw materials etc.)
- o In-kind gifts (could be any products other than the company's line of business)
- o Loaned talent/executive sabbatical (paid time off to perform volunteerwork)
- o Public relations services (NGO branding through corporate approaches)
- o Technical assistance
- o Use of corporate services/facilities (financial and administrative support services, meeting space, mailing services, computer services, printing and duplicating etc.)
- o Extend dealerships of products to NGOs, have a marketing partnerships for NGO products
- o Sponsor salaries of NGO professionals for a certain period

- Applying for a nonprofit bulk mail permit. NGO/NPOs receive additional discounts on bulk mailings. To receive these discounts, an organization must apply for a nonprofit bulk mail permit. Contact a local post office and request the necessary information packet for this permit.
- Insure the organization. Basic insurance coverage for the organization, its directors, and officers is critical when forming an effective and responsible organization. Many associations of NGO/NPOs offer group purchasing programs for insurance and other services such as supplies, employee benefits, and banking services. Basic insurance coverage should include the following policies:
  - o Worker's Compensation
  - o General Liability
  - o Director's and Officer's Liability

NETWORKING AND PROJECT MANAGEMENT

- Networking and Partnership: Networking-getting in touch with institutions, organizations, and individuals-anyone and everyone-who can be of help to the policies and programmes is a very critical aspect of an NGO's functioning.
- Private sector: Do not hesitate to partner with the private sector-a company, a business, a supermarket chain etc. This partnership should not be for funding purposes alone. Private sector actors can bring many other resources too.

Remember that-(a) NGOs stand to gain by being efficient and productive, engaging the commercial environment in their outreach and influencing companies to be socially responsible, and (b) Companies stand to gain by being seen as socially responsible, actively participating in social development and nation building, enlightened self-interest-poverty eradication benefits the corporate sector in the long run, and also raising employee morale.

The past decade has witnessed an erosion of belief in the capacity of democratic institutions to intervene effectively in shaping social and economic life and help solve our most pressing problems. A common refrain is that government is part of the problem, not the solution.... Deregulation, privatization, reduction of social services, curtailments of state spending-these have been the watch words, rather than participation, greater responsiveness and more creative and effective forms of democratic state intervention.

In the context of these global political developments, rethinking a wide range of questions about democratic institutions is a matter of urgency (Wright, 1995).

The dramatic changes of the late 1980s and early 1990s produced political and economic shifts in the relationship between the state, civil society and markets worldwide. Many academics and practitioners vigorously debate the social implications of these changes. Three central theoretical approaches explore these trends:

(1) states are large bureaucracies disconnected from the constituencies they were meant to represent-this view, accordingly, supports a shift in responsibilities and resources from ineffective state institutions to nongovernmental organizations;

(2) NGOs may have merits, but it is unclear whether they can maintain autonomy and legitimacy;

(3) the state is a dominant force which reflects and reinforces power relations found in the market and the market. in turn, controls NGOs.

To acknowledge changes in large social processes, and in the interest of tracking the trends and analyzing the results of these changes, Teachers College organized a symposium in 1998. That symposium at the Comparative and International Education Society (CIES) annual conference examined the roles and responsibilities of NGOs in the shifting political arena. It was designed to respond to a provocative article by Michael Edwards and David Hulme, also posted here, courtesy of World Development. The following five articles featured in this issue are based on the authors' presentations during that symposium.

Governments, bilateral and multilateral agencies and local actors have promoted NGOs for many of the reasons you will find discussed in this issue of CICE. Strengthening nongovernmental organizations is a key element in the building of civil society.

Therefore international agencies have launched large initiatives to create free-markets and build civil society on the assumption that democracy would follow. Educators and social advocates proclaim the virtues of local NGOs in promoting social change. The authors express varied concerns regarding the simultaneous proliferation and vulnerability of local NGOs around the world.

The title of this issue, "Are NGOs Overrated?" is deliberately broad to provoke debate on the purpose, significance and activities of various types of NGOs.

Mark Ginsburg's article NGOs-What's in an acronym? highlights some of the problems inherent in the characterization and evaluation of NGOs. He notes that the heterogeneity of NGOs, (in terms of sectors they serve, their scope, and their level and sources of funding), the varying theoretical approaches used to analyze NGOs, and different conceptions of democracy, often result in contradictory depiction of NGOs.

Gita Steiner-Khamsi highlights the "crisis in NGO legitimacy." In Too far from home? 'Modulitis' and 'NGOs' role in transferring pre-packaged reform, she observes that critiquing NGOs for moving from "state-independent to state-dependent entities" does not apply to post-socialist countries. She calls attention to the changing relations between NGOs and the state, and the role NGOs play in the transfer of educational modules and models of school reform.

Perhaps NGOs and state forces would be better served in reaching their goals if they worked more closely together. Robert Arnove and Rachel Christina's NGO-State relations: An argument in favour of the State and complementary of efforts, provides excellent examples of case studies in Palestine, Papua New Guinea and Nicaragua in which "increased complementarity of NGO-state relations" could have been and sometimes were accomplished with significant success.

Steven Klees and Lynn Ilon share a concern for market forces dominating NGOs' agendas. In Can NGOs provide alternative development in a market-based system of global economics?, Ilon explains that market demands compromise the service delivery goals of many NGOs. Klees comments in NGOs: Progressive tool or neoliberal force?, on the pressure on NGOs to take on responsibility for projects that were not part of their original objectives. Although Klees observes that "the NGO sector has been...part of a system that reinforces unequal development," both authors believe that NGOs offer promise for social change.

In this issue Nelly Stromquist and Michael Edwards are discussants of the previous five articles. In NGOs in a new paradigm of civil society, Stromquist reflects on the emergence of NGOs since the 1970s as a force "making claims on the polity and for the polity." She acknowledges and responds to the specific arguments made by the other authors. She observes that NGOs risk co-optation and misuse, but believes their presence guarantees that "new spaces for reflection and creative action permeate civil society."

It is fitting that Michael Edwards offer a response to the debate. In his article, Are NGOs overrated? Why and how to say "no", he reviews some of the reasons for the criticisms levelled at NGOs and proposes that there must be "room-to-manoeuvre" to allow agencies to profit from opportunities and manage threats. He urges NGOs and researchers to collaborate to create "environments for learning that nurture both reflective practitioners and engaged academics."

As political shifts have affected our institutions, we are fortunate to have technological innovations that have made it possible for CICE to debate these shifts. This is a continuing discussion. We hope that internet resources will allow global citizens to imagine a new kind of community. This inaugural issue signifies our hope that wide discussion will stimulate social and educational creativity.

Why are we Always here and What do we Want?

Non-Governmental Organisations have an important role to play in international decision-making. The participation of civil society in shaping our world and guarding its most precious ideas and values is vital. While governments remain the ultimate decision-makers, it is NGOs that allow citizens across the globe to partake in the political process and make their voices heard. Together with the Mayors, from whom you have already heard, we represent millions of people worldwide. Opinion polls show that these people want to live without the scourge of nuclear weapons, in a world where governments are mature enough to resolve conflicts with more effective, non-lethal methods. This is why we endorse the Mayor's campaign "2020 Vision".

NGOs working for nuclear disarmament have, year after year, participated in the Nuclear Non-Proliferation Treaty Conferences in order to promote the transition to a nuclear weapon-free world with three obligations of non-proliferation, disarmament and the abolition of nuclear weapons. The treaty contains all three obligations and does not make a hierarchy of them. We consider them all equally important to the survival of our world.

Some say we should not admit that the NPT is in crisis for fear of undermining it. We disagree. In order to make the Treaty work as it was intended, we must recognise that it has long been in crisis. Secretary-General Annan's High-level Panel on Threats, Challenges and Change did just that. In its recent report, it stated that "the nuclear nonproliferation regime is now at risk because of lack of compliance with existing commitments, withdrawal or threats of withdrawal from the Treaty on the Non-Proliferation of Nuclear Weapons to escape those commitments, a changing international security environment and the diffusion of technology." The Panel's final conclusion is especially alarming: "We are approaching a point at which the erosion of the non-proliferation regime could become irreversible and result in a cascade of proliferation."

We consider it our common responsibility at this Conference to stop the further erosion of the NPT and to strengthen the Treaty. Even though the NPT is in crisis, it remains a fundamental stepping-stone on the way towards a safer, nuclear weapon-free world. The NPT has set the global norms for non-proliferation and disarmament for 35 years, and the vast majority of its members continue to comply with its obligations without question. We commend these countries and appeal to all NPT member states to work tirelessly toward the preservation and strengthening of the Treaty.

This opening statement is a collective product of all NGOs participating in this Conference. It sets out, simply, our reasons why we believe that nuclear weapons in today's world are of no use at all, to anyone, for any reason. Later you will hear our main recommendations. We urge you to consider these reasons and recommendations in your deliberations about the future of the NPT.

2

The Character and Criticism

This research paper seeks to understand the phenomenon of non-governmental organizations (NGOs) participating in the human rights movement-at a global level, as well as in India. NGOs play an important role as actors in civil society by creating a link between individual citizens and the government. The significance of human rights NGOs has increased tremendously, with growing awareness about human rights. Human rights NGOs are recognized as legitimate players in civil society and their role to put pressure on governments has come to be widely accepted. The United Nations Charter too discusses them in Article 71. Human rights NGOs carry out a variety of functions, such as advocacy, human rights education, publication of matter relating to human rights, exposing instances of human rights violations, and putting pressure on governments to implement human rights.

They are also important for the role they play in creating and expanding the human rights discourse, by taking into consideration the various types of human rights violations the world over. International Human Rights Organizations (INGOs) have made their presence felt the world over, by being able to apply sufficient pressure on governments the world over. Amnesty International and Human Rights, two of the most prominent INGOs in the world today, have been discussed in this paper. NGOs in India act in a more localized manner, but they too deal with a wide variety of human rights issues, and take into account the idiosyncrasies of the Indian scenario. Although INGOs and NGOs have made achievements of note in the human rights movements, critics have pointed out several shortcomings in their manner of functioning. Possibly the two most severe types of criticisms levelled against them relate to an undemocratic manner of functioning, and a lack of transparency and accountability. This research paper delves into the manner of functioning of human rights INGOs and NGOs, the criticisms that they face and provides a brief comparison between INGOs and Indian NGOs in the human rights movement.

A BRIEF INTRODUCTION TO ROLE OF NGO

At the beginning of this study, it is essential to understand the fundamental purpose for the existence of non-governmental organizations (NGOs) and understand their significance in the human rights movement.

AIMS AND OBJECTIVES OF NGOS

NGOs constitute an important agent in what is known as 'civil society', which refers to the totality of players acting outside the state to achieve certain goals. NGOs exist in addition to other institutions, such as the media, trade unions, consumer organizations, etc. However, according to a more critical view, civil society includes only actors who are critical of the government, and not merely non-governmental. The role of the civil society has been seen as that of limiting untrammelled use of power by the state through the institutionalization of political and civil rights. This is done by creating a realm of actors, who function in a manner autonomous of state regulation in groups smaller than the state.

In this manner, the role of NGOs becomes to prevent states from becoming dictatorial and also to form a link between individual citizens and the state. Indeed, one of the most important roles played by NGOs is to constitute an effective 'pressure group' and constantly attempt to make the state accountable for its actions. Neera Chandhoke talks about civil society actors such as NGOs becoming "the site for the production of a critical rational discourse, which possesses the potential to interrogate the state".

It is for this reason that it has been argued that NGOs should be seen only in relation to the state.

NGOS AND THE HUMAN RIGHTS MOVEMENT

The United Nations has given recognition to the concept of non-governmental organizations under

Article 71 of the UN Charter, which states:

"The Economic and Social Council may make suitable arrangements for consultation with non-governmental organizations which are concerned with matters within its competence. Such arrangements may be made with international organizations and, where appropriate, with national organizations after consultation with the Member of the United Nations concerned."

Article 71 falls under Chapter X of the United Nations Charter, which pertains to the Economic and Social Council (ECOSOC). The of NGO sector played an important role in the ECOSOC, particularly as far as natural disasters and refugees are concerned. Moreover, NGOs have made significant contributions during the sessions that have been arranged by the Security Council to consult them, in the past.

The view that a public interest group qualifies as a 'human rights NGO' if it "bases its criticism of state conduct on international human rights law", on the basis of the states' adherence to principles laid down in the Universal Declaration of Human Rights, the Civil-Political Rights Covenant and other such instruments containing principles of international human rights law. Although several countries are parties to these instruments, the governments in these countries fail to implement human rights and it is for this reason that human rights NGOs have a role in making them accountable.

The view that human rights NGOs must base their functioning on whether the governments in their home countries are complying with international instruments on human rights has been rejected by several authorities, since it is restricted to the formal source of the norms, which are invoked to criticize state conduct.

It is submitted that a more favourable definition of 'human rights NGOs' would be one that takes into account the context of human rights violations in every state and one that incorporates a broad construction of the term. Steiner points out the importance of using domestic standards of human rights in the classification of NGOs into the said category, for it provides for holding those countries accountable, which may not have ratified such covenants.

The functioning of human rights NGOs must constantly respond to changes in human rights issues, new forms of abuse, new methods of addressing abuses and new manners of intervention.

This may often call for human rights NGOs to make serious choices about modifications in their methodology. Hence, it is important for human rights NGOs to keep in constant touch with the changing requirements in their field and reinvent themselves in accordance with the same.

Upendra Baxi, in a discussion on the tasks and missions of human rights NGOs, names the following functions:

Future Inventing: This refers to the process of constantly reinventing human consciousness and organization to shatter dominant discourses, which may not favour certain groups, such as racism, colonialism and discrimination against women.

Agenda Setting: Several NGOs create an agenda of political and social action, which arises out of their conception of a better future for human beings.

Norm-Creative: NGOs are often faced with the task of opposing developments that pose a threat to the normativity of human rights.

Implementational: Human rights NGOs carry out an array of functions relating to the implementation of human rights, such as investigation to expose human rights violators, and the process of lobbying. The performance of these functions often involves close collaboration with the media.

Solidarity: The duty of creating a global culture of empathy and a network that connects national and local level rights activists from the world over. Upendra Baxi also identifies four principles that human rights INGOs are characterized by, namely the primacy of human rights; non-retrogression; the right to effective remedies and the right to participation. Baxi is of the view that none of these characteristics are free from debate.

POLITICS OF NAMING

Baxi discusses the process of labelling human rights NGOs in terms of the nature of their work. NGOs may be labelled "non-human rights" or "anti-human rights", indicating that right to interpret human rights is a basic human right in itself.

He gives the example of two different NGOs advocating the right to life of unborn children and the right to pursue scientific research and experimentation as part of the right to freedom of speech and expression, respectively; neither of these NGOs can be said to be fundamentally anti-human rights, yet they pursue goals, which conflict. It is submitted that the method of labelling arises from the expansion of activity among human rights NGOs. This can be said to be true of NGOs India as well, where the number of NGOs and the diversity in the goals pursued by them are noteworthy.

HUMAN RIGHTS INGOS-CHARACTERISTICS AND CRITICISMS

Before delving into a study of the nature of INGOs, a word must be said about the role of the United Nations in introducing the concept of human rights through the Universal Declaration of Human Rights, which has become a starting point for virtually all INGOs and NGOs in understanding the core values of the inalienable rights of human beings.

The Universal Declaration of Human Rights, 1948

The Universal Declaration of Human Rights was adopted by the UN General Assembly on 10 December, 1948. The concept of Human Rights emerged from the Declaration, with Article 1 of the Declaration emphasizing the equality of all human beings, with respect to dignity and rights. It further emphasized on each person's entitlement to all the rights and freedoms laid down in the Declaration without there being any distinction of race, colour, sex, language, religion, etc.

It prohibits slavery and declares cruel, inhuman or degrading treatment or punishment to be violations of human rights. Arbitrary arrest and detention constitute a violation of essential human rights, as per the Declaration. These are some of the key features of the United Nations Declaration of Human Rights and also comprise some of the main concerns of human rights INGOs and NGOs.

A BRIEF HISTORY OF INGOS

The International Committee of the Red Cross, which was established in the year 1863 by Henri Dunant, a physician of Swiss origin is known to be the first INGO. There was a tremendous increase in the number of INGOs in the twentieth century, particularly due to the fact that the United Nations Charter had extended recognition to NGOs, under Article 71. Some of the prominent INGOs that came up were the International Commission of Jurists, Amnesty International, the Anti-Slavery Society, the Lawyers Committee for Human Rights, etc.

THE ROLE OF INGOS IN THE HUMAN RIGHTS MOVEMENT

Human Rights INGOs perform a range of functions, some of which are: the preparation of reports of human rights violations in countries across the world, distribution of such reports, creating awareness among the media about issues of human rights by distributing information to them, carrying out the tasks of lobbying and advocacy, with respect to human rights.

They also engage in drafting the model legislation, which incorporates the human rights discourse, providing education on human rights, organizing protests and demonstrations. Some of the prominent issues that human rights INGOs are concerned with are the rights of women and minorities, indigenous peoples, opposition to censorship, economic and social rights, rights of prisoners, children's rights etc. This research paper will briefly look at the working of two prominent INGOs, namely Amnesty International and Human Rights Watch.

Amnesty International: Amnesty International stands as one of the biggest and most active human rights INGO in the world. In the year 1999, Amnesty International had more than a million members in over 160 countries. It had national sections in 56 of these countries. 320 officials and 95 volunteers work in the Amnesty International International Secretariat, London. Every two years, an International Council constituted by representatives of the Amnesty International movement elects an International Executive Committee, comprising nine members.

Amnesty International also has consultative status at the United Nations, and was awarded for its achievements by the United Nations, on the 30 anniversary of the Universal Declaration of Human Rights. It was the recipient of the Nobel Peace Prize in 1977.

Amnesty International states its mission as the following:

> *"AI's vision is of a world in which every person enjoys all of the human rights enshrined in the Universal Declaration of Human Rights and other international human rights standards. In pursuit of this vision, AI's mission is to undertake research and action focused on preventing and ending grave abuses of the rights to physical and mental integrity, freedom of conscience and expression, and freedom from discrimination, within the context of its work to promote all human rights."*

Some of the specific violations of human rights that Amnesty International aims to redress are freeing of prisoners detained on the basis of their beliefs, ethnic origin, sex, colour, language, etc., ensuring free and fair trials for political prisoners, the abolition of the death penalty and putting an end to the torture meted out to prisoners.

Human Rights Watch: Human Rights Watch is a USA-based INGO, with its headquarters in New York. It is organized on the basis of divisions, which are categorized not on membership, but on region and the theme of work carried out by that particular division. Some of these specific themes of work carried out are women's rights, children's rights, arms. In the past, the INGO has also looked into academic freedom, drugs and human rights and prison conditions.

Its mandate is described as follows:

"Human Rights Watch researchers conduct fact-finding investigations into human rights abuses in all regions of the world... publishes those findings in dozens of books and reports every year, generating extensive coverage in local and international media. Human Rights Watch then meets with government officials to urge changes in policy and practice--at the United Nations, the European Union, in Washington and in capitals around the world. In extreme circumstances, Human Rights Watch presses for the withdrawal of military and economic support from governments that egregiously violate the rights of their people. In moments of crisis, Human Rights Watch provides up-to-the-minute information about conflicts while they are underway."

CONTRIBUTIONS OF HUMAN RIGHTS INGOS

Human rights NGOs play an important role in upholding human rights, as envisaged under the United Nations Declaration of Human Rights and other human rights instruments. They also perform the task of creating awareness about these human rights. Through their activities, they are also successful in setting human rights standards.

INGOs are often very large and influential bodies, capable of exercising international pressure. Due to this characteristic, they compel the governments of countries across the world to enforce human rights in their respective countries and be vigilant in order to prevent infringement of these rights. Since these INGOs are autonomous of the government, they are often useful owing to the fact that they can resort to the use of informal channels to disseminate information about human rights even in countries where the government regime is repressive.

CRITICISMS OF HUMAN RIGHTS INGOS

Legitimacy: It has been alleged that human rights INGOs do not have the legitimacy that they require, in order to carry out the tasks carried on by them. Kenneth Roth feels that "international organizations have volunteered and been volunteered for a variety of tasks that, in a word, require forms of legitimacy that international organizations never had." He claims that there is a "democracy deficit", for INGOs have assigned themselves the power and authority that they yield.

Elitist Bias: Another major criticism that INGOs face is that of having an elitist bias. Since the membership of most INGOs is constituted largely by educated middle class individuals from affluent western countries, it has been said on several occasions that INGOs lack any real connection with the "masses". Hence, the scope and participants in the dialogue relating to human rights is restricted to opinions and people from the North.

Chindi Odinkalu sums up the problem with respect to the activities of human rights INGOs in Africa: "while exhorting national human rights groups in Africa to think globally and act locally, these agencies think locally and act globally".

It is submitted that the framework in which INGOs formulate their policies are based on the conception of human rights as envisaged in international instruments relating to human rights, which often reflect a western bias. As a result, INGOs fail to appreciate the nature of the specific nature of human rights violations that developing countries face.

Ritualistic Pattern of Reports: Stanley Cohen expresses his distaste for human rights INGOs using a standard pattern in composing their reports. He is of the opinion that the format used by human rights INGOs-which involves, in the following order, the INGO expressing concern and condemnation for the objectionable practice in question, stating the problem, setting the context of the problem, describing the sources and methods of information obtained by the organization, allegations in greater detail, a statement of the relevant international instruments and lastly, calling upon the government to undertake some action-has become ritualistic. He calls for a change in this pattern. It is submitted that the following such a pattern in a mechanical pattern is likely to portray the INGO in bad light, for it shows a lack of innovation on their part. It is also indicative of the fact that the same format may be applied to dissimilar situations in the world.

Selection Bias: Critics point out that INGOs such as Amnesty International report extensively on human rights violations in relatively democratic and open countries-for example, there are likely to be more reports on human rights violations in Israel as opposed to those in Cambodia.

Amnesty International defends its position by stating that its mandate is to document any available information and pressurize governments on the basis of this information.

It is submitted, however, that the information ultimately presented by such INGOs is distorted and often biased against governments where information is easier to obtain.

HUMAN RIGHTS NGOS IN INDIA: CHARACTERISTICS AND CRITICISMS

Before entering into a discussion on the characteristics of human rights NGOs in India, it is essential to understand the evolution of the concept of human rights in India.

The Influence of the Universal Declaration of Human Rights, 1948 on the Definition of Human Rights in India

The impact that the Universal Declaration of Human Rights, 1948 has had on international non-governmental organizations been discussed previously in this research paper. The concept of human rights in India too has been modelled upon the definition given in the Declaration.

Section 2(d) of the Protection of Human Rights Act, 1993 in India lays down the definition of Human Rights:

> *"'Human Rights' means the rights relating to life, liberty, equality and non-disparity of the individual, guaranteed by the Constitution or embodied in the International Covenants and enforceable by courts in India."*

The influence that the UN Declaration on Human Rights as well as other Human Rights Covenants have had on the Indian statute on human rights cannot be overlooked. Hence, it may be said that this basic definition of human rights forms a guiding light for human rights NGOs in India, as it does for human rights NGOs at an international level.

CHARACTER OF HUMAN RIGHTS NGOS IN INDIA

The narrative of the human rights movement in India and its historical origins has always been contextualized in the post-colonial democratic era.

The turning point with respect to human rights activism in India was undoubtedly the Emergency period during the reign of Indira Gandhi. The Emergency was a period characterized by the curtailment of civil liberties through amendments to the Constitution to clamp down on the right to enjoy the fundamental rights enshrined within it, the promulgation of ordinances that legitimized the government's actions, such as arresting people on the pretext of 'preventive detention' as well as the establishment of new intelligence outfits, such as the CBI and RAW, which assisted the government with its agenda.

As a result of the severe repression of civil liberties by the government, several individuals and organizations came to the forefront, as champions of basic human rights. The most prominent among these was Jayaprakash Narayan's 'People's Union for Civil Rights'. A similar organization that was established was the 'People's Union for Democratic Rights'. The importance of these organizations was that they were autonomous of the government and critical of its actions.

Since then, the human rights movement in India has progressed with the establishment of other human rights NGOs, fighting for a variety of causes: The Human Rights Organization of Manipur, Civil Liberties Committee of Andhra Pradesh, Naga People's Movement for Human Rights of Nagaland, etc. are NGOs dealing with the human rights of minority groups in India; The Other Media works with human rights in Kashmir, the National Centre for the Protection of Human Rights coordinates several human rights activities; NGOs such as the Indian Association of Lawyers, the Lawyers Collective, the Human Rights Trust deal with human rights in their publications; the South Asian Human Rights Documentation Centre deals with documentation, research as well as implementation of human rights; the Punjab Human Rights Organization works with Amnesty International and the UN Human Rights Commission; the National Campaign on Dalit Human Rights works with Dalits, whose rights have been violated.

K. S. Krishnaswamy identifies six functions performed by human rights NGOs, namely:

- Gathering, evaluating and disseminating human rights,
- Advocating human rights,
- Lobbying and mobilizing public opinion,
- Providing legal aid,
- Providing humanitarian relief,
- Developing human rights norms.

It is submitted that in a developing country like India, it is important to equip citizens with the proper awareness about human rights, such that they do not remain distant concepts and the government does not take advantage of marginalized groups. However, in addition to creating awareness and aiding the formulation of public opinion, providing assistance in terms of physical resources may often be of tremendous importance.

The human rights movement has come a long way since the Emergency, with the proliferation of human rights NGOs ever since. Human rights violations in India have been manifested in different forms in India even after the Emergency, often with the state being a party to these violations or showing indifference to the plight of the victims. According to many writers, the human rights movement has expanded itself ever since its origin during the period of Emergency. It now focuses on a wider range of issues, with economic and social rights (in addition to civil and political rights), problems relating to inter-community tension, the struggle for natural resources and women's rights being some key illustrations.

These changes have been attributed to a variety of factors, such as the change in the way development is viewed, the nature of government programmes and the priorities of donor agencies.

Some examples of human rights violations in India may be enumerated here: the implementation of draconian legislation such as the Prevention of Terrorist Activities Act, human rights violations during communal riots in Gujarat, atrocities carried out by the Indian army in Kashmir, minorities such as transgendered individuals and Dalits being denied human rights, etc.

As is evident, human rights NGOs in India have constantly had to mould themselves according to the specific nature of human rights violations that they are dealing with. Aswini Ray points out that this is a challenge that the human rights movement has not been able to deal with sufficient ease: "They are periodically called upon to respond to them with indigenous theoretical and conceptual innovations in view of the paucity of comparable resources in the asymmetrical western liberal democratic experience.

This challenge still remains inadequately responded because of the limited empirical base of political theory within the western experience"

CONTRIBUTIONS OF HUMAN RIGHTS NGOS IN INDIA

Expansion of the Rights Discourse: Human rights NGOs have been instrumental in expanding the rights discourse to include certain rights, which were previously not part of the human rights discourse, due to the limited sense in which the state projected rights. As a natural consequence of this development, the state has been compelled to take steps for the implementation of human rights.

These NGOs have created awareness about the state being a human rights violator, by carrying out atrocities in Gujarat and Kashmir, for example, and through the passage of draconian law. In order to formulate an effective defence against these accusations, the state has had to bring about reform in its policies and actions.

Recognition of the Rights of Marginalized Groups: Human Rights NGOs in India have played a significant role by taking steps to guarantee human rights to marginalized groups, such as women and members of oppressed classes. It is due to the efforts undertaken by these NGOs that the rights of these groups have been taken cognizance of, by the state, and have also been widely recognized in society.

CRITICISMS OF HUMAN RIGHTS NGOS IN INDIA

Lack of A Comprehensive Approach: One criticism levelled against human rights NGOs in India has been that their approach is not a comprehensive one due to the rather rigid manner in which they focus only on a single issue. For example, the NGOs dealing with providing human rights to women may not engage with the problems of the peasantry. This would lead to issues such as those of women's exploitation in the farmers' movement being neglected.

Neera Chandhoke points out the perils of such an approach: "if each discourse occupies its own space and fights its battles independently from other discourses of resistance, the fragmented arena resulting from these particularistic practices is peculiarly vulnerable to being occupied by the state and by the dominant classes".

It is submitted that the NGOs must pursue a more flexible approach, for concentrating on single issues without thinking about inter-related rights of other groups may prove to be myopic.

Isolation of Human Rights NGOs: It is the view of several experts that with human rights NGOs isolating itself from other actors in civil society and the masses, they are plagued by a fundamental structural problem and as a result, they are rendered ineffective.

Guha argues that due to their restricted social base, NGOs do not enjoy popular support, to the extent that their exclusivity lends them the character of powerful class-based movements, often the kind that they are opposed to. Moreover, the media and the middle classes begin to view them as groups pursuing their vested interests and working as per the whims of their donors.

The Issue of Funding: Possibly the biggest criticism that human rights NGOs in India face is related to the issue of funding. It is alleged that many human rights NGOs formulate their programmes, such that the interests of their donors are given priority to. As a result, many of the areas of human rights that NGOs focus on, such as women's rights, are in fact, a product of the manipulation that their donor agencies exercise.

As per one report, foreign donors donated to the tune of Rs. 4,871.9 crore to Indian NGOs in the year 2001-2002.

NGOs carrying out rehabilitative activities after the tsunami floods came under suspicion when it was reported that these NGOs were quite affluent and that there was no transparency or accountability as regards the manner in which they utilized the funds that were provided to them by their donors for the specific purpose of rehabilitating those affected by the tsunami floods. Little is known about where the funds are utilized by the NGOs and which groups have been provided shelter.

In another instance, a UK-based organization, Enable, accused an NGO in India, to which it had donated money, of misappropriating aid worth Rs. 6 crore in the course of five years.

In fact, many human rights NGOs are run, not by the councils that they claim to have, but by individuals, who are in control of the funds granted to the NGOs. The situation is such that there are no means of keeping a strict watch over the flow of foreign funds and ascertaining who their real beneficiaries are.

Strident critics of NGOs in India believe that when NGOs fail to be accountable to the citizens they claim to be working in the interest of, they have no right to try to hold the government accountable for its actions. Often, NGOs have been found to be funded to a large extent by the government. Hence, the concept of funding can shake the very foundations on which an NGO is based, that is, the idea of critically assessing the government.

Some governments have made moves to pass legislation that would bind NGOs to comply with norms that would make sure that they worked in a manner that was transparent. NGOs have protested against such moves, on the ground that they should remain in a sphere free from the government.

One of the recommendations to improve the situation has been to structure the functioning of NGOs along the lines of the functioning of corporate bodies. Taking measures, such as establishing strict accounting standards, carrying out regular audits through the setting up of an Audit Committee, separation of the Chairman and the Chief Executive, restricting the service contracts of executive directors to three years, the pay of officers to be regulated by a remuneration committee, etc. would bring about some measure of transparency to the functioning of NGOs.

It is submitted that this is a natural outcome of the fact that human rights NGOs in India are likely to pursue goals that may be unique to their home country, owing to the peculiar nature of the problems that they are protesting against. Several NGOs identify their goals in terms of protest against specific policies of the governments of their respective countries, which result in human rights violations of citizens of that country. It follows that it may often be difficult to generate global awareness or solidarity about causes that are specific to the countries of origin of many local NGOs, and hence the solidarity expressed at a global level pertains to global issues of human rights. Further, most of these NGOs may not even possess the resources to bring their local cause into the global space, given the limited space that they operate in.

Resources and Power: Another point of difference between INGOs and NGOs is the quantum of resources at their disposal, and as a result, the number of people they seek to target. It is noteworthy that INGOs, such as Amnesty International, OXFAM and Greenpeace have more members than citizens in small countries, such as Fiji, Nauru and San Marino. Hence, it cannot be doubted that in the scope of their organization, and manner of operation, INGOs are far larger than NGOs. Often, NGOs in India may be small organizations, which take up a particular cause and deliberately aim at targeting a very small section of people.

For example, an NGO in India may take up the issue of trying to guarantee tribals residing in a particular region their human rights. The localized presence of many human rights NGOs can be seen in contrast to the massive scale at which some INGOs operate.

Moreover, the small-scale operation of an NGO may be due to a lack of greater resources, but it is also often a matter of choice, with domestic NGOs finding that effectiveness would be best guaranteed by local projects.

The Importance of Associationalism: Putnam, in his discussion on the fragility of civil society, records the observation that there is a considerable deal of anxiety revolving around the 'collapse' of civil society in the United States owing to a decline of associationalism. Hence, the view held in the west is that the scarce resource of "social capital" has been lost. It is of note that INGOs that operate in the world today are of western origin.

On the other hand, the idea of civil society in India seems to be flourishing, with the rapid expansion of the human rights discourse and the simultaneous increase in number of human rights NGOs. Contrary to the trend in the west, where INGOs could well be diminishing in number, the culture of associationalism is thriving in India, which is evident from the proliferation of human rights NGOs.

CONCLUSION

The human rights movement today would be incomplete without the contribution of civil society, particularly non-governmental organizations, which have been indispensable in the human rights movement, not merely for redressing the wrongs done to victims of human rights violators but also for successfully creating a comprehensive discourse on human rights.

Without NGOs contributing to the field of human rights at the international level and the domestic level in various countries, the state would exist without having any specific agencies to be accountable to, for the violation of specific human rights.

Further, these organizations have helped in bringing instances of human rights violations to the notice of the state, so that they can take action in that regard. The protection of human rights has become an issue of prestige in the current day scenario, with no state being able to afford complacency on its part. NGOs have also been instrumental in equipping marginalized groups-women, children, indigenous peoples, to name a few-with the ability to demand their rights.

However, the functioning of these agencies has, by no means, been without its share of criticism. The issue of funding has come up time and again, in the international as well as Indian context. There is no doubt about the fact that NGOs need to bring about more transparency in the manner in which they conduct their work, for anything short of that would make their credibility in the human rights movement suspect.

There is also a growing realization that the human rights discourse must be expanded-both at the international as well as Indian level. At the international level, INGOs must ensure that their definition of human rights does not reflect a bias towards the North.

At the domestic level in India, NGOs would gain by developing an inter-related approach to human rights, one that would take into account the human rights of groups that may be related to the ones whose cause they are advocating. Creating such alliances may lead to better mobilization of the victims of human rights violations. It would also make the human rights movement more effective, since it would reduce the fragmentation that currently exists therein.

Another constructive suggestion that can be made at this juncture would be to encourage NGOs and states to enter into a relationship that could lead to better cooperation. Although the goal of NGOs to apply pressure upon the government should not be lost sight of at any cost, it may be more beneficial for the state and non-state actors to enter into a non-confrontational relationship, one that could lead to an improved implementation of human rights.

Lastly, it must be said that the human rights movement is in a state of constant change, with new doctrines and ideas being added everyday to the human rights discourse. This will doubtless affect the working of the human rights NGOs. Whether it will assist them in developing a more comprehensive mandate or whether it would lead to constant disagreement between them resulting in a weakening of the human rights movement remains to be seen.

3

Guiding Principles on NGOs

Recognizing that non-governmental organizations (NGOs)* are essential to the development and success of free societies and that they play a vital role in ensuring accountable, democratic government. And recalling the right to freedom of expression, peaceful assembly and association enshrined in the UN Universal Declaration of Human Rights, the International Covenant on Civil and Political Rights and the UN Declaration on Human Rights Defenders. We hereby pledge our commitment to the following principles and our determination to work for their full implementation throughout the world:

1. Individuals should be permitted to form, join and participate in NGOs of their choosing in the exercise of the rights to freedom of expression, peaceful assembly and association.
2. Any restrictions which may be placed on the exercise by members of NGOs of the rights to freedom of expression, peaceful assembly and association must be consistent with international legal obligations.
3. NGOs should be permitted to carry out their peaceful work in a hospitable environment free from fear of harassment, reprisal, intimidation and discrimination.
4. Acknowledging governments' authority to regulate entities within their territory to promote the public welfare, such laws and administrative measures should protect--not impede--the peaceful operation of NGOs and be enforced in an apolitical, fair, transparent and consistent manner.

5. Criminal and civil legal actions brought by governments against NGOs, like those brought against all individuals and organizations, should be based on tenets of due process and equality before the law.
6. NGOs should be permitted to seek, receive, manage and administer for their peaceful activities financial support from domestic, foreign and international entities.
7. NGOs should be free to seek, receive and impart information and ideas, including advocating their opinions to governments and the public within and outside the countries in which they are based.
8. Governments should not interfere with NGOs' access to domestic-and foreign-based media.
9. NGOs should be free to maintain contact and cooperate with their own members and other elements of civil society within and outside the countries in which they are based, as well as with governments and international bodies.
10. Whenever the aforementioned NGO principles are violated, it is imperative that democratic nations act in their defense.

HUMAN RIGHTS NGO CAPACITY—BUILDING PROGRAMME

TRAINING AS AN ON-GOING PROCESS

In the last years in the global NGO community, an emphasis on workshops has taken root as if workshops were an end in themselves-instead of a means to an end. It is rare that a training workshop followed-up to ensure that it has had an impact. Workshops have been known to divert time, energy and funding away from other means which could be more effective in stimulating human rights change.

To be effective, training is best designed as an on-going process. A key part of that process can be a well-planned workshop. A more effective approach is often a series of workshops, with practical support to applying what is learned in between such workshops. This encourages learning through experience-the most effective manner for an adult to learn. This document provides a set of ideas which should be adapted by the trainers to suit their particular needs. The purpose of this document is help trainer's focus on the important role a workshop can play in training for human rights work if:

(a) Prepared with adequate lead-in time to ensure the content is tailored to the actual needs of the participants; with

(b) Principles of adult education applied e.g using highly participatory techniques.

If they are followed through with on-going accompaniment to support participants in applying what they have learned.

The administrative details so essential to workshop organisation are included-as well as guidance for facilitators in training methodology. The sections of this chapter broadly follow the stages: before, during and after a training workshop.

BEFORE THE WORKSHOP: PLAN AND DESIGN

As will be seen, by far the most extensive work is needed at the planning stage.

Target Participants

Several different aims can be accommodated in the selection of participants. Key criteria, depending on the aim of the workshop, might include:

(a) Priority for committed personnel who will stay in the NGO and apply in practice what is learned.

(b) The need of an individual to apply new knowledge and skills on this topic. It is sometimes the case that NGOs send their most experienced/most senior staff member-who may have been to many previous workshops, and need this one least.

(c) *Networking-cross-sectoral Participants*: A workshop can encourage day to day cooperation among human rights actors if they are together in an effective learning environment.

This might mean increasing awareness among local journalists by inviting them to be part of some/all of the workshop; or local officials or politicians; other partner NGOs etc. This can help enrich discussion, and increase awareness of the roles of the various actors (state and nonstate) in achieving the protection of a particular human right. The networking importance of workshops should not be underestimated. The advantages and disadvantages of including state officials should be considered (e.g making frank discussion more difficult; or helping to open doors to communication between NGOs and state officials, as well as working towards mutual understanding of the human rights framework or their work).

If a roundtable discussion as part of the workshop is envisaged, participation by any guests should be planned with the advocacy objective clearly understood by participants, and planning done so that the means of conducting the roundtable achieve that goal. It can easily occur that state officials come along and deliver a prepared speech about their ministry or institution. If it was a more interactive discussion that was planned, particular attention is needed to the issue of chairing the discussion to ensure that it remains coherent and focused.

(d) *Strengthen NGO Collaboration*: There is often competition among human rights NGOs for scarce donor funding. This can undermine practical cooperation among colleagues. In contrast, colleagues who come together for training can use the opportunity to develop or strengthen a coalition for advocacy.

Ensure Commitment by Participants

Any workshop must have a maximum number of participants. Above 30 or so, the level of interaction is lessened.

As part of selecting participants, a real commitment by participants to apply what is learned in practice in their work is essential if the workshop is to be worthwhile. Generally, the currency of workshops in the NGO community has been devalued because of overreliance on workshops by NGOs and by donors as workshops are relatively straightforward activities to define and fund.

Professional NGOs will be aware of the need to value their time, to ensure that the management of their organisation does not suffer from trying to attend endless workshops. Similarly, donors will need to be more rigorous in seeking impact from training, beyond the mere fact that a number of people have sat in a room together for a number of days. It sometimes occurs that participants are paid to participate in workshops-even for those who are in employment and paid (e.g as public servants) to be present anyway. This not only inflates the cost of workshops-but it is an indication of lack of real commitment to learning.

It also sometimes occurs that:

(a) Invited participants only confirm participation at the last minute; or

(b) After confirming they will attend, fail to show up. This wastes a place that could have been allocated to another person, or

(c) Participants attend some but not all sessions in a workshop. This undermines the utility of the workshop not only for the individual, but also for the group. This is because an effective workshop builds knowledge in steps, module by module. If you miss one part of the foundation, a participant may not grasp later stages of the workshop, or may delay the group by asking questions which have already been dealt with.

This is also disruptive to the group, as team-building is an essential element of effective group learning (see below). If the number of participants in any session is unpredictable, trainers may not be able to use their planned roleplay, and so forth.

How can workshops be taken more seriously, and valued, by participants? One way is to focus on improving the relevance of the workshop to the needs of the participants, through steps such as those set out in this chapter. However, additional steps may also be needed which involve a change of attitude to workshops.

One suggestion raised is to charge participants a fee for the workshop-even a nominal one: The cost of a workshop is generally greater than most participants realise.

A well-prepared workshop will have been planned perhaps for months in advance and a great deal of person-hours will have been invested. The overall cost per place in a workshop can be calculated in advance, and stated in the invitation to participants. Invitees can be allocated a nominal, or more substantial, part of that cost to pay to reflect their commitment to learning from the course, and applying that learning in their work.

This sum would need to be paid in advance by the participants to reserve their place. In another suggestion received, participants were provided with pre-reading material, and then tested on it (through multiple choice). If they do not pass, showing they have not read the material, their commitment to learning is in doubt, and their place should be re-allocated.

As part of this process of ensuring commitment by participants, consideration may be given to issuing certificates of participation for workshop participants. Similarly, facilitators should seek to identify participants who might be developed as future facilitators perhaps by giving them some experience by having them lead a session at a subsequent workshop.

Participants Prepare

Another aspect of the commitment to learn is: preparation for a workshop by participants. Lead-in time for preparation is essential so that pre-reading can be disseminated and studied by participants (as discussed above).

Pre-reading serves several purposes:

(a) To help ensure that participants are already empowered with basic knowledge so everyone is able to participate in discussions/ask questions from the outset of the workshop

(b) To try to establish a common minimum standard of knowledge among participants who may otherwise vary in their familiarity with the workshop topic.

However, the pre-reading should be carefully chosen:

(a) The number of pages to be read should be kept manageable.

(b) Pre-reading should be tailored to the participant's needs e.g if a basic introduction to human rights concepts is needed, a text that is clear, concise and simple should be chosen.

(c) A cover note with table of contents should distinguish between those documents to be closely studied, and those with are texts for reference only (e.g treaty texts).

(d) Participants should be asked to bring those materials to the workshop to be inserted in their workshop packs to save copying costs for the organisers.

Tailor the Content to the Needs of the Target Participants

It is essential that facilitators are provided with a clear profile of the participants well in advance. This is necessary

(a) So that the skills and experience of the participants can be drawn upon in planning case studies or sample scenarios to discuss;

(b) To increase the participant's sense of responsibility for their own learning by engaging with the facilitators to prepare the workshop in advance e.g by providing real case studies from their own experience to be used in discussion. These should be requested by the facilitator so that the workshop illustrations used come from the participant's day to day reality of human rights issues; and

(c) So that the level and nature of the content of the workshop can be tailored to the needs of the participants.

One useful way to obtain this information is to provide a short questionnaire to participants, such as the one below, and to ensure it is fully completed and returned to the facilitators in good time for their preparation of the content of the workshop. Prepare for follow-up to ensure the completion of the questionnaire. The purpose of the questions should be carefully explained, i.e. to help the facilitators plan the workshop to meet their needs-and not to 'judge' the participants. For example, in the section "position in organization/profession" people may not complete this part if they do not realise its importance. The practice of tailoring workshops to the needs of participants will hopefully become more widespread among human rights NGOs. In the meantime, it should be expected that the administrative support team of the workshop will need to call the participants for several times in order to receive the completed questionnaire.

Sample questions for invited participants:

1 Name:

2 Sex:

3 Age:

4 Contact details/organisation:

5 Position within the NGO (also if relevant profession/job):

6 NGO/human rights experience

7 Human Rights experience + any training (please give details, how long, by whom etc.)

8 Your specific human rights interests:

(a) As an individual and

(b) As part of your organisation

Create a Workshop Team

The preparation of a workshop depends on good communication and teamwork among the key actors:

the lead trainer; guest facilitators; the participants; the administrative support team, as well as the staff of the venue (e.g if it is a hotel).

Clarity of Roles: it is essential that each of the team involved in preparing a workshop know exactly where their responsibilities begin and end, and that this division of labour- and deadlines for the different stages of preparation are clear and respected. It should also be clear who has authority to ensure that the responsibilities are met by each member of the team-i.e. who reports to whom. The overall objective is to create a workshop that everyone involved is proud to say they were part of.

Select Facilitators

Of equal importance to the selection and preparation of participants, is the selection and preparation of facilitators. Those who will facilitate the workshop should be selected to form a well-balanced team.

The Anchor: Lead Facilitator

It is important to have a 'lead trainer' who is skilled in adult education techniques in the area of human rights. Their role is to act throughout the workshop as an 'anchor' pulling the various modules together. They provide introductions to modules which set out the objective and which relate it back to work already done by the group. The lead trainer should be responsible for briefing in advance each of the other trainers who will provide input. This is to ensure that each module is prepared to cover precisely what is needed in that module-to avoid gaps or duplication with other modules.

The lead trainer should therefore have the profile and skills of a trainer: ability to communicate simply and clearly to a non-specialist audience; experience of training methods (beyond presentations or lectures) such as roleplays; and most importantly they need to have the commitment to inspire and energise the workshop learning process.

A lead trainer needs to have in addition, some knowledge of international human rights law and practice-but they do not need to be a subject-matter specialist in all the topics of the workshop, as that is the role of guest facilitators. A well-balanced team of facilitators is one in which skills complement each other.

Local or International Facilitators

When considering whether to engage a local or international consultant as part of the training team:

Survey the Resources Available:

(a) Within your own NGO

(b) Seek training support from other regional NGOs who may be more specialised in the topic, or who may have a particular staff member who has experience as a trainer or subject-matter specialist. This can be an effective form of networking with other NGOs

(c) Check whether there are appropriate trainers who are staff members of international bodies present in the region, or in the capital. If a workshop is seen to be well-planned, a member of the UN family such as Unicef is more likely to respond positively to an invitation to contribute to a training session (e.g on their area of expertise e.g the human rights of the child)

If there is funding available to engage a consultant as lead trainer, or as a guest trainer, this allocation of scarce NGO resources will need to be carefully planned so that value for money is received. A written contract with clear division of labour can help ensure that expectations are met. At a minimum, an outline of the consultant's contribution should be produced in advance for the lead trainer to see if any adjustments are needed as to the material covered. If a consultant produces material for the NGO, the issue of copyright should be settled in advance so that the NGO knows whether it can replicate/ disseminate the material in the future.

Criteria for Selecting Facilitators

The concept of expert for workshop training requires some consideration. An 'expert' in a substantive area may not necessarily have expertise transmitting that knowledge etc. This has practical implications for workshops:

(a) Substantive experts are not always the most effective communicators: there can be pressure to use a particular 'expert' as a facilitator, if they hold a high official position in the public service or academia. Yet the real issue is whether they can communicate in the context of training adults (see participation below)

(b) It is important that even 'experts' be accountable for the quality of their preparation, and the impact of their module in terms of learning. Misperceptions among human rights 'experts' should be borne in mind when seeking to ensure accurate content for a training workshop. For example, there are widespread misperceptions among the human rights and legal community regarding:

(a) The nature of legal obligations undertaken by Russia on the international level (especially the commitment to bring the Constitution and all other laws, budgets, practices, whether federal or regional into full compliance)

(b) The binding, and sometimes immediate nature of the obligations in relation to economic, social and cultural rights and

(c) The role of a non-governmental human rights organisation in a democracy.

Interpretation/translation

If an international guest is to be part of the workshop team, the issue of translation and interpretation may arise.

For translation of their pre-reading materials, the necessary lead-in time will be needed to allow for that. The quality of translation is a major issue not only for NGOs but also inter-governmental organisations: quality control is essential to ensure accuracy of translation. Interpretation in a workshop may also be needed. This raises issues of cost, but also quality of communication. Interpretation can be a very costly addition to the workshop budget, and experienced professional interpreters will be needed. The terminology of human rights training can be quite specialised, and the quality of interpretation can enhance or undermine training. Quality standards vary, and recommendations should be sought from colleagues who have used the service-provider before.

If consecutive interpretation is chosen (i.e. an interpreter interprets after each section of speech delivered) this can slow down the workshop discussion. If simultaneous interpretation is used, the necessary equipment, the technicians to set it up, and the space for it in the room will need to be planned for. Either way, a team of interpreters is needed to ensure they received adequate breaks.

Gender

A criteria that should be always part of planning an effective workshop is the effective participation of women as both participants and trainers.

As a minimum, the role of the lead trainer will include identifying, and planning to bring out in discussion, the gender perspectives which a particular human rights topic, or skill, involves.

It goes without saying that, applying human rights principles to training itself requires that active steps are taken to ensure that discrimination is not a factor in the way the workshop is organised. (This is considered in more detail below: Applying human rights principles to training).

Administrative support

The success of a workshop also depends on the administration team. The logistics of organising effective training can be time-consuming, and should be the responsibility of an administrative team. The kind of tasks to plan for, include:

- Copy and disseminating pre-reading (asking participants to confirm not only safe receipt, but also that all emailed documents can be opened etc.)
- Preparing packs of materials for during the workshop
- Negotiate and book the venue well in advance (see below)
- Follow-up with participants who have not confirmed participation; or who have not received prereading materials; or who have not completed their participant profile questionnaires
- Organising travel arrangements for participants/ facilitators (where applicable)

- Compile final list of the participants in the form of a table containing, for example, the following:

  Name of participant

  Organisation Position/responsibility in the organisation

  Contact information(postal address, phone number, fax, e-mail address) etc.

- If the budget covers it, arrange social event as farewell for participants at end of workshop e.g group dinner.
- For longer workshops (from seven days upwards) a social event may be organised for the group's day off. Outdoor exercise where feasible will refresh participants, for continuing the workshop the following day, and help teambuilding and networking.
- List and obtain the necessary stationery: It's important to have several flip-charts, paper for them, markers, block-notes and pens for each participant, folders for handouts.
- Distribute information about the venue, usually a hotel (how to get to it, and the facilities which are covered)
- At the day of departure for the venue pack all the necessary stationery: markers, paper puncher, counting machine, a flip-chart, overheads for the projector.

Select the Venue

Cost will always be a factor to consider when choosing a venue for a workshop. However, a careful balance will be needed to ensure the impact of the training is not undermined by a venue that is mainly chosen because it is cheap.

The importance of the choice of venue increases with the length of the planned workshop.

To effectively learn, participants must be comfortable. The main teaching room should have:

- Adequate fresh air for the number of participants
- Natural light
- Comfortable temperature (warm/cool)

- No outside noise or other disturbance
- Open space allowing e.g a table in 'U' formation for all participants, so that everyone can see each other and the facilitator
- Space for subgroup work, so that chairs/tables can be moved around
- Seats that are comfortable-but not sleep-inducing
- Smaller rooms/spaces nearby, so that sub-groups can move to a new atmosphere for training exercises, so that the full day is not spent sitting in one place F or live-in workshops of more than one day, the following can enhance effective learning
- Hotel in quiet location, for a good night's sleep. Also, a location that is far from the participant's own office can help ensure that daily work demands do not intrude on the workshop (e.g with participants disappearing back to their office for parts of the workshop)
- Fresh, healthy food with plenty of choice to cater for participant needs
- Space for exercise/sport facilities, especially allowing participants to relax together in group games
- Business-centre with access to internet for cross-checking queries which arise during the workshop, fax and copier.
- If needed, seek the equipment for simultaneous translation in workshop town or city; otherwise the capital may be the only source. Agree a contract with the firm providing the equipment.
- Negotiate with restaurant of the hotel about menu and coffee-breaks, order drinking water for the workshop.

For a hotel, hosting workshops can be big business, and organisers should be prepared to negotiate on price, and other factors. To check on the quality of the service, they can ask the hotel for the details of previous workshops the hotel has recently nosted, and contact those organisers as a 'reference' by asking if they were satisfied with the service. Other NGOs will also be a valuable source of information regarding their experience with particular venues.

Plan to Evaluate the Workshop

The organiser of a workshop should update their own planning checklist after a workshop-so that through experience they create one most suited to their own organisation for the next time. If this is not to be forgotten, it should be planned in advance, and the responsibility for gathering lessons by the team, and suggestions for improving next time, should be clearly allocated.

Many great ideas for 'next time' are lost if they are not captured by the workshop team in a debriefing meeting soon after the workshop itself. This debrief encourages all the team to identify lessons for next time, and to applaud things which went well Evaluating the substance of the workshop can involve several steps. As a minimum, the first step is to:

Prepare an evaluation form for participants and trainers to complete and return to the organisers. This should be done anonymously, to ensure frank replies. The form should be carefully drafted to ask questions which will be helpful to the organisers for the future, and also to allow space for miscellaneous comments. The topics to cover include feedback on each module, as well as any topics which the participants would need to cover in the future. One example of an evaluation for will be used for the Amman Programme. In addition, two questions can be useful to stimulate reflection:

Q. What has been learned:

1. Based on what you have learned about yourself and the many possibilities for change presented by this module (or workshop), what two or three things do you intend to do differently in your role as advocate for human rights?

2. What obstacles in yourself or in your work environment do you expect to experience during your efforts to implement these changes? What will you do to minimise these obstacles?

Obstacles: Action to remove the obstacle:

a)

b)

c)

An evaluation form should be distributed to participants on Day 1 of the workshop, so that they can be encouraged to complete the form day by day, when their recollection is fresh.

At a closing session at the end of the workshop, the completed forms should be gathered. Some participants will have completed the form day by day, and others may need some time to be allocated on the last day. To encourage people to complete the form, any travel reimbursement etc. should be held back pending the handing over of the form.

Generally, feedback received in the evaluation forms is very positive. Participants enjoy a congenial atmosphere, perhaps met new people, and enjoyed the change of pace from routine work. However, the real test of the effectiveness of the workshop will come in the following months: Have the participants changed their behaviour, attitude, practices etc. and become more effective in their work to stimulate human rights change?

This question will usually be asked in an evaluation of a programme, particularly if funded by an international agency, to ensure the goals have been achieved. Regardless of whether the funder plans an evaluation, the NGO organising the training should wish to discover for themselves whether their goals were met, and how they might improve for the future. To answer the question of impact requires on-going contact with participants, and a structured process of feedback regarding:

(a) Whether and how the workshop achieved its aims;

(b) What do the participants now identify as their own training needs; and

(c) What they would recommend for any future workshops on that topic or for that group, etc.

Structured follow-up of this kind can help maximise the impact of the workshop with participants exchanging ideas/experiences with other participants on an on-going basis. Planning to evaluate training through for such a process of feedback will vary with the scale of the training, and the degree to which the organisers intend to learn and improve for the future.

DURING THE WORKSHOP: TRAINING METHODS

Before outlining options for training methods, the importance of effective administration during the workshop is emphasised.

Checklist for Administration during the Workshop

The administration team of the workshop may need to arrive at the workshop venue (if they are not already nearby) one day before the participants arrive, and may need to plan on departing one day after the workshop, after loose ends (such as hotel bills) are wrapped up.

- Final check of the reservation in the hotel, restaurant, examination of the hall and venue for administrative assistant.
- Make the acquaintance of the main service providers of the hotel (e.g managers of administration, the restaurant and business-centre). Issues of concern are often best raised with management, rather than staff of the hotel, to save time.
- Set up a table at the workshop venue for participating NGOs to bring materials about their activities.
- If necessary, reach agreement about the smoking area that should not be far from the coffeebreak venue and the main training room. Sometimes smoking is prohibited within the hotel but exceptions may be feasible if necessary for the workshop group. In some cases, there are several staff shifts in the hotel (usually 3 or 4) and it may be necessary to inform each shift about the workshop and its needs (e.g light in a particular room).
- Make a poster sign to guide participants to the training room, time of the beginning of the workshop, location of restaurant and catering schedule.
- Hire of the safety deposit box (to keep money and other valuables) On a daily basis:
- Specify to the hotel management the final number of meals to be ordered in advance (generally one hour

ahead, with the number of breakfasts ordered the night before).

- Notify the staff of the window of time within which the coffee break will be needed
- Prepare the training hall: On arrival, facilitators inspect the hall so that chairs and tables are placed as required. If necessary additional furniture is arranged with the hotel.
- Check the documents to be handed out (a packs for each participant, and cross-check the contents).
- Check the technical equipment (PC, fax, copier) and stationery. Note: Installation of equipment for simultaneous translation can take two hours, so access to the workshop room may need to be arranged early in the morning of Day 1.
- On the first day the hall will need to be opened one hour before the workshop (or more if equipment is to be installed). On the following days the hall can be opened 30 minutes before.
- The hall needs to be aired, with water and glasses provided for participants and facilitators. At the end of each day the hall is cleaned. Usually the hall is closed by the administrator on duty.
- Administrative assistants prepare the register, badges, block-notes, pens
- Registration of the participants. Participants may be given a folder of new materials (they will have been asked to bring the pre-reading materials they received in advance), a badge, a block-note and a pen. Each participant should sign in the register for each day of the workshop. When the equipment for simultaneous translation is used each participant gets ear-phones and put the number of the earphone in the register.
- The administrative assistant reimburses travel expenses of the participants. The assistants provide the participants with the necessary documents (e.g business trip order, business trip certification and cooperation

agreement).The participants may need to complete the forms in their organizations and send them to the headquarters of your NGO.

- Taxi or other transport is arranged to meet and to see off the lecturers and facilitators.. Similarly, transportation is arranged for the office equipment and translation equipment.
- The administrative team gathers financial documentation from all hotel services: bills for accommodations, for catering.

Choose Training Methods

Regarding the training content itself, facilitators prepare by choosing methods best suited to communicate with that particular group of participants. The idea of using a pre-workshop questionnaire was mentioned in section above to help the facilitators tailor their work to the specific needs of the participants. Choices will need to be made regarding the best means to communicate and facilitate learning.

Regarding dissemination of materials during the workshop, it is important that the lead facilitator control the content of the workshop pack so that only those materials consistent with the workshop are included.

Regarding volume of materials, a balance is needed to ensure participants do not feel overwhelmed by material, but also know they have reference material for further study if they choose to study the topic in more detail.

As was mentioned at the outset, this section outlines some guidelines for facilitators in training methodology. Additional resource materials on training methodology can be found in a variety of human rights training manuals that exist (some in Arabic) e.g. UN Training manual on Human Rights Monitoring.

To Begin: Clarify Expectations and Agree Rules for Interaction

The opening session of the first day of the workshop involves:

- Welcome of the participants
- Introduction of facilitators and of participants to each other. For introductions, often a game, such as the warm-ups listed as examples below, can be helpful to create an informal atmosphere which is a helpful foundation for the learning process. Expectations: The next session focuses on gathering and discussing together the range of expectations which participants will often have of a workshop.

  To ensure frank responses, it is helpful to have participants answer this question anonymously. This can be done by distributing coloured cards for people to write on, gathering them all before reading them out and listing them on flipcharts. Any major issues that arise concerning expectations should be addressed in that discussion.
- Outline the aim of the workshop and provide an overview of the whole programme: In the first substantive session, it is important to give participants an overview of the sequence of the workshop, and how each module will build on the previous ones. This map of the journey:
  * Gives a sense of security as each participant knows where the workshop is going, and where to slot in their particular concerns/questions later
  * Emphasises the importance of consistent participation throughout by the participants.
  * Allows the facilitator to show how the plan for the workshop does/does not match the expectations expressed, and clarify this.
  * Allows participants to plan their evening reading, so they get the most benefit from the following day's discussion etc.

Rules of Interaction: Invite the new group to propose rules which will govern their interaction. It is helpful for a group to agree, if possible by consensus, how they will behave in their discussions. Included in the norms agreed should generally be:

- People should not talk at the same time, but wait for each other to finish
- Respect time schedule (e.g returning from coffee breaks on time, all sessions start on time and finish on time etc.)
- Keep interventions short and to the point
- Everyone must attend all sessions
- Responsibility for sharing knowledge, resources, skills with each other

Warm up the Group

To start the day, as well as when the participants return after lunch, it can be very helpful to spend some few minutes playing a light-hearted game to 'warm-up'. The aim is to relax participants, create a sense of teamwork and informality, and help people to focus their minds and be truly present in the room after the distractions of breakfast/lunch. This can be a very important step to ensure that people are not intimidated by each other, as may occur where there is a variety of experience/age in the group and to enhance teamwork. Both facilitators and participants should take part, to ensure no unhelpful hierarchy is implied.

A facilitator can start with a warm-up exercise that has not been used with this group previously. Once participants become familiar with some examples the task of developing a new warm-up can be delegated to participants, taking it in turns to rotate the task among the sub-groups. This involves the participants more actively, and relieves the lead trainer of one task which can be delegated.

The following is a selection of some quite brief warm-up exercises developed by a Russian NGO activist Svetlana Velikoredchanina which might be replicated or adapted for future workshops-or form the basis for new ideas. Different ones will work better at different stages of a workshop. Timekeeping should be observed and warm-ups not get out of control. The best warm-ups are short. The names of different human rights are written on pieces of paper in a box and the team demonstrates it visually-through mime. This can be very brief and works well as the group tries to identify which right is in issue.

One by one participants watch each other walking from one side of the room to sit at their table. The people who follow, copy the sequence of actions of all the people in front, i.e. imitating the way that they walked and at the end add a little variation of their own.

Form a circle of standing participants, with hands outstretched, shake fingers, close eyes and then walk inwards together to make contact with the persons on the other side of the circle. Hands then join one by one in the middle, with eyes remaining closed. The challenge is for participants to unravel themselves to form one or more circles again.

Invite participants to think of a creature they 'feel' like and to walk to the end of the room at the end of the session imitating it (e.g a crab, giraffe)

Form a circle of standing participants; everyone turns to the right and picks each other on the back as if a woman in stilettos is walking on their back, then a horse, then an elephant, then thunder and lightening, then a snake....

Form a circle of standing participants "Who would you like to take to the mountain?" So everybody names somebody else and says why they would like to take them to the mountain and then the circle is formed. This works best when it is brief.

Seated in a circle, each participant passes a sheet of paper with own name at the bottom corner around the circle. Each writes good wishes for you, fold over the sheet and passes it on to the next person and so on, so that everybody gets a list of good wishes. This requires time.

Principles of Adult Education

General Principles of Adult education:

- Individuals are unique, particularly in the way they learn. Thus, a training workshop must use a variety of learning approaches in order to accommodate the different ways in which people learn.

- Learning does not mean information being "injected" into people through provision of facts-it emerges from their own experience. For this reason, participation is the key to adult education. The passive format of lectures is the least effective means of training for human rights work-there must be interaction, and the more participants are active the more they learn. For this reason, this chapter focuses on participatory techniques for facilitators, such as roleplays, case studies etc. Reflecting this, the term 'facilitator' is preferred to that of 'trainer.'
- Learning is most effective when the objectives have relevance and meaning for the participants in terms of their own lives, what they already know, as well as their personal goals. For this reason, section above emphasised the importance of participant selection: try to form a group that will have common goals and learn from each other. For example, include a range of disciplines all working on or affecting one issue.
- Learning is meaningless if it is limited to the acquisition of facts and figures. Information must be supplemented by an understanding of why it is important, and how it can be used to stimulate human rights change. Effective training facilitates this process.

Applying the Principles

Applying these principles involves the 'Trainer' being primarily a 'facilitator':

The aim is to facilitate learning and not merely to provide information. The aim is not academic, such as providing interesting facts, nor is to impress participants with the quantity of complex data the 'teacher' can display. The priority here is the opposite: to render the complex simple. Communication is the priority. This sometimes requires a cultural shift from a focus on 'teaching' by 'experts.' A facilitator creates an effective learning environment and an active learning process.

Encouraging the active involvement of all the participants (not only in discussions but also, for example, having a subgroup take responsibility for timekeeping by all the participants during one day). This helps to encourage participants to take responsibility for their own learning, as does their preparation by studying the preworkshop material Encouraging participants to work through a problem in training, and enhance their confidence in conducting various human rights activities.

Acting as resource to the participants not as an 'expert' who has all the answers e.g directing the participants to the materials and resources they need Promoting an atmosphere of cooperation. This includes investing time at the outset in games for "getting to know you", see below, on warm-up exercises; and creating an informal, non-hierarchical atmosphere so people are free to speak their mind Adapting the training and exercises to the specific needs of participants. This includes linking the training content with other training which the participants have received, as well as encouraging participants to constantly relate the training to their 'real life' experiences Reviewing regularly and wrapping-up: The facilitator re-summarises the material learned from each activity when it is appropriate and practical. This helps the participants be clear about their learning progress and skills development. Also, it gives them time to discuss what they have learned and integrate it in their own behaviour.

Closure: This is a very important part of the training process. The facilitator reviews all of the experiences of the session or the workshop so far, and sums up what has been learned so far. The wrap-up can provide an application of the session content to the daily work setting of the participants to which they will return. A link is made between the current session and the material previously covered-as well as to that material which will be addressed in future sessions.

Using a variety of educational methods and a variety of visual aids in:

Role plays

Case studies

Small/large group discussions

Brainstorming

Mini-lectures

Power relations analysis.

The main methods which can be useful are considered in turn in the sections which follow. Beforehand, regardless of which training methods are chosen, two general hints can help make the trainer's role easier, and better organised:

Rehearse Instructions: Clear instructions are essential. Giving step-by-step instructions is preferable to giving a list of instructions all at once. It is important not to overload the participants with instructions-give them directions as needed at the start of each day or each session.

Arrange the Room: For the training to proceed smoothly, it is important to have the room arranged effectively. Easels, flipcharts etc. should be placed where all the participants can see them easily. Chairs, tables, etc. should be arranged in a manner that allows for easy interaction among the participants, and good eye contact with the trainer/other group members.

Role-plays

This is a training technique which allows a large number of issues to be raised with participants all at once-this is how issues arise in real life. Role-playing can be used to examine problems, investigate facts, predict responses to advocacy approaches, and generally provide insights into attitudes which are different from those of the participants.

Role plays may involve participants acting out a situation in front of other participants e.g preparing the arguments they would use on a set of facts to take a case to the European Court of Human Rights. The 'actors' are given a detailed description of a situation and are assigned a specific role in it. Roles might be assigned to a team to represent the judges of the Court as well as the applicant and respondent. Roleplays such as this involve learning through doing, observing and providing feedback and analysis.

How to Develop a Role-play

Choose a situation that is realistic to the participants and which reflects the training goal of the module

Define the problem to be addressed in the role-play

Determine the number of 'actors' needed

Develop the specific roles for each person by answering these questions:

i. What is the person like

ii. What is important about the person's background

iii. How does the person feel about the other role player(s)

iv. How does the person feel about the situation

These questions should be written and reinforced orally to the 'actors'.

How to Introduce a Role Play

Regardless of the number of role plays and the types of participation, the facilitator should start the roleplay in the same way:

- Describe the purpose of the role-play for all workshop participants
- Describe the situation briefly and clearly for all workshop participants, even if prepared written roles are used
- Ensure 'actors' are allocated roles which do not reflect what they do in real life, and that they have not faced this problem in reality. Allocate roles in a sensitive manner and to avoid embarrassing a participant.
- Brief the 'actors' (without the rest of the participants). Allow enough time to understand their roles If it is an elaborate role play, brief and instruct the 'actors' the day before, so they have time to 'get into character' and even to dress up if they choose-which all adds to the fun-and the learning experience.
- Tell actors to add facts/information if necessary during the role-play (the facilitator can adjust the actors' briefing notes to fill gaps identified in this way for the next time). Tell the actors to try to give a realistic portrayal and not to overreact.
- Recall the learning objective of the session, and brief the observers as to what they should be looking for.

- Set the scene, e.g by arranging chairs.
- Give a final reminder to actors as to the time allocated.

How to Facilitate a Role-play

- Start the action by telling the actors to begin
- Observe quietly on the sidelines, do not interrupt. Note any issues that will need to be discussed in the plenary discussion analysisng the role-play
- Monitor the time and stop the role-play at the appropriate point.
- Thank the 'actors' using their real names, and invite participants to clap. It is important in this way to remove the 'actors' from their roles and to provide a transition for the discussion which follows

How to Draw Together the Learning Points

- Allow the 'actors' to comment on the experience before those who observed (reserving any planned 'surprise' for the observers to later in the discussion)
- Among the actors, ask for comments from the person who had responsibility for 'solving the problem' first
- Ask for comments/feedback from the observers. Review the way the situation; why the 'actors' behaved the way they did; how it might have been planned/done differently to achieve better results
- Encourage the observers to describe their own feelings as events occurred, rather than only analysing the behaviour of the role players.
- Summarise the major issues related to the purpose of the role-play-ensure the discussion does not focus on the acting abilities of the role-players. Keep the focus on what the role players contributed to the understanding/resolution of the problem in the situation.

Group Discussions

Communication is a two-way process. Lectures are never as satisfying as learning exercises in which everyone is participating. Discussion is an important way for participants to involve themselves in training.

They measure the success of a workshop by their own involvement in it, and the satisfaction they received from participating in meaningful discussions.

How to Facilitate Group Discussion

In large-group discussion, the facilitator will need to prepare in advance the questions, and the learning points they want to emphasise.

The facilitator's role is to:

- Keep the discussion moving, ask questions, provoke different views, promote a lively exchange of ideas,
- Ensure the discussion stays on the subject
- Get as many of the participants involved in the discussion as possible
- Provide facts, policy, law as needed (or from other participants or facilitators); and distil the key messages as planned from the session.

In essence, the facilitator is a catalyst-stimulating and guiding discussion, serving as a resource to the participants' own exploration of the topic. One of the challenges is to establish an environment in which participants feel free to disagree, try out new ideas, discuss their own experiences and propose solutions, conclusions or strategies.

When it comes to discussion in smaller sub-groups, the facilitator's role is to make the instructions clear and let the group work on their own.

Where the workshop is over several days, the facilitator should ensure the same groups are not formed all the time, to keep the interaction lively within them.

The facilitator should arrange the groups e.g to reflect diverse backgrounds and experiences. The facilitator should move quietly among the groups to ensure the assignment is understood and is being done correctly and involving all members of the group. At the end of a subgroup discussion, the conclusion or ideas from each group are usually reported to the full group. The facilitator should invite the small groups to choose their own 'rapporteur'.

This 'rapporteur' role should be rotated in the subgroup each time with a new voice presenting to the plenary. This is to ensure that some participants do not sit back and let others do all the work, and to minimise the risk that a group is dominated by one person's ideas.

At the end of the plenary feedback from each group, the facilitator will have prepared questions to ask the group as a whole. By listening carefully to the responses, the facilitator then helps the group draw conclusions about what they learned.

It is important to ask open-ended questions that make people think about their responses rather than questions which prompt 'yes' or 'no' answers.

How to Ask Questions of a Group

More generally, questions should be used to direct the group's attention to issues they have not considered. Ask questions that are:

- Open-ended
- Describe processes or procedures
- Require thoughtfulness
- Focus on feelings/reactions, and are perceived by the participants as helpful.

Examples follow:

- If all available information has not been given-you want to encourage the participants to think more: "I wonder if we have received all the information needed to reach a decision?"
- The discussion is wandering from the topic-you want to bring it back on track:

"What point are we now considering?"

- A summary of group consensus is needed before continuing: "I wonder if someone could summarise the points where we agree and disagree"

- Checking for clarity, participants tend to be more motivated to learn when they feel they the facilitator understands them and using the following phrases can be helpful:
- "If I understand you correctly, you're saying that...
- "Lets make sure everyone understands the point x is making. Would one of you summarise it for us?
- "What you're saying raises a question in my mind. For example, do you...
- "How do the rest of you feel about x's comments"

Brainstorming

Brainstorming, in training, has two purposes:

a) To teach participants not to make judgements until a maximum number of ideas have been developed.

b) To train participants to listen positively to the ideas of others, without making negative comments that discourage creativity Brainstorming is a structured discussion which is mainly used to solve problems. An example might be how to conduct effective advocacy on a particular human rights issue. It is based on the idea that a group can develop more ideas than an individual thinking alone. The process of brainstorming can be most effective when it has three steps: development of ideas, analysis and action planning:

Step 1: Development of Ideas:

In brainstorming, quantity is the goal: the more ideas the better. Generate ideas without evaluating them-there will be time for that later in the process.

This does not mean that quality is unimportant-only that when people stop to challenge quality during the creative process, it inhibits creativity. Put all the suggestions on a flipchart in front of the room during the exercise. This encourages participants to develop ideas.

Create new ideas by offering alternatives e.g adding, deleting, reversing, consolidating those already suggested.

Step 2: Analysis of the Ideas:

In the discussion, participants should be encouraged to ask for explanation of unfamiliar ideas.

The group establishes criteria for selecting the best ideas, then tests the ideas against the criteria.

As ideas are rejected because they don't meet the criteria, the group is left with a list of workable options. From these they can select the "best" solution.

Step 3: Action Planning

Finally, the group moves to the final phase, action planning: This consists of outlining the steps needed to put the adopted solution into operation.

A variation on the above process of brainstorming is useful if the topic is a sensitive one.

An example might be discussing barriers to human rights progress and their causes-particularly if there are state officials in the group.

Another issue that can be sensitive is asking participants to select the priority human rights issue they feel most needs to be addressed.

In this type of situation, the discussion can be started by first asking people to privately write one idea on a coloured card.

The cards are then collected and mixed up by the facilitator. They are read out, and stuck onto a board with the group suggesting how the ideas might be clustered (the cards can be fixed on a wall/a board which has been earlier covered in paper for this purpose by the facilitator).

In this way, views are not attributed to anyone-often a more frank and realistic discussion can then take place.

AFTER THE WORKSHOP: EVALUATE AND LEARN FROM THE PROCESS

As workshop organisers, it can be very helpful to adapt and update the checklists used, so that you learn from experience and ensure that future workshop training is more effective than what has gone before. This is also the time to consider the feedback from the evaluation forms gathered during the workshop.

On the administrative side, the post-workshop tasks may include the following: Assist in the preparation of financial report on the workshop Remind the participants to send the administrative forms (e.g for reimbursement of expenses) to head office.

Translate the feedback received as well as any international trainer's reports, if translation is needed. Disseminate and follow-up. Update any documents developed in, or for, the workshop, and translate for the future, if necessary.

Follow-up with any potential future facilitators identified among the workshop participants.

4

Role of the Transnational NGOs

INTRODUCTION

The questions to be addressed here-about the weakness or incompleteness of the existing United Nations Organization-raise three loosely related sets of issues.

(1) Some of these call for comparisons between the different parts of the UN: the regular staff of the Secretariat, the political core and the technical agencies, the Security Council or the General Assembly, peacekeeping or peacemaking, and the relative efficacy of such peripheral institutions as the International Court of Justice. Which programs, agencies and organs of the United Nations work best?; Which of them work least well?; How far is the weakness of some parts inherent in the tasks they have been given?; Or do they perform worse than they might, in ways that can be remedied by better organization and management?

(2) With the present constitution and structure of the United Nations, is there reason to think that these weaknesses are too deep-seated to be corrigible? If so, which parts of the Organization are most gravely compromised, which are open to correction? More important: What most seriously compromises the efficacy or the authority of the United Nations? And are there systematic differences in this respect, as between (e.g.) its technical and political branches?

(3) *Finally:* Do other organizations, whose operations parallel those of the UN, perform better some of tasks

that the UN itself is least good with? What legal status do these organizations have, and how do they stand in comparison with the UN's august claims? Or are the efficacy of the United Nations and its agencies undelmined by the very grandiosity of its Charter? Is the UN, as a result, open to criticism for a "democratic deficit"-i.e., its distance from the People of the World whose interests it exists to protect?

This chapter will say little about the first group of issues, except to comment on the relative success of the professional (or professionalized) agencies, in contrast to those whose functions are purely political and diplomatic: this contrast will point toward the deficiencies that are most deep seated and hardest to correct. Rather, the essay focuses on the problems that result from the dominance within the Organization of Nation State Governments (NSGs)-institutions whose motives are too often suspect-as compared to the apparent weakness of those other Non-Governmental Organizations (or NGOs), whose actual influence is out of proportion to their seeming power. Later, we shall have occasion to notice how the NGOS compensate for their weakness by judicious collaboration with the staff of the Secretariat, and how the Secretariat in turn forwards its own transnational agenda by drawing NGOs into the preparation and execution of their policy proposals.

We will start by making preliminary remarks about deepseated constitutional problems inherent to the UN as it stands. Historically, the title of the Organization is a misnomer: it is not a Union of Nations so much as a Cartel of Nation State Governments. Nations and States do not coincide. Some Governments rule countries that are homelands to people of many Nations: Russia and the USA both fall into this category. Conversely, the homelands of many Nations overlap territories governed by several Governments: the most vexed case is the Kurds, who inhabit contiguous parts of four States but have no single Government ready to represent them. The modern Nation State was invented in the 17th century to serve relatively monoethnic countries: France, Holland, England or Sweden. Yet, today, even the most homogenous Nation States and Cities comprise substantial minority populations. Los Angeles is an extreme case: primary education is available to children of the City in some ninety languages. On a lesser scale, however, multiethnicity is a phenomenon of contemporary life almost everywhere.

At the inaugural conference in San Francisco, the UN could clearly not have been launched as the United States Organization, even though that name is less misleading: the name "United States" was preempted. (In any case. people find plenty of reasons to claim that the UN has been an instrument of American power.) Still, the official terminology has it right: membership in the United Nations belongs to Member States, not to Member Nations.

The closer we come to the political pinnacles of the UN Organization, as a result, the less guarantee there is that the people who have standing to speak in its councils speak for Nations, rather than that for State Governments-these too often represent monoethnic, oligarchic subgroups of a given population. (Fill in your own examples.) When spokespersons for Member States address, say, the Security Council, informed listeners know that their speeches present the opinions of subgroups in the domestic politics of that Member State, and interpret the speeches in light of that information. But, when the debates concern worldwide problems like Human Rights or Population Control, it is hard to cut a way through the thickets of domestic politics to the serious transnational issues. As a result, the hermeneutics of Councilspeak generate cynicism, of the kind that was evident in the counter activities of the NGOS at the Vienna Human Rights conference of 1993, and again, in 1994, at the Population conference in Cairo.

THE VARIETY OF NGOS

This last example brings us to the central topic of this essay. My subject is the tension in the institutions of global governance, between Nation State Governments and Non-Governmental Organizations. We will first sketch the number, scale and variety of the "nongovernmental organizations" active in different practical situations: this done, be better placed to map the particular areas in which this tension is most evident. The term "nongovernmental" is what Aristotle calls a privative term: it defines its instances by what they are not. A familiar everyday example is the term "amateur", as applies in Sport: "amateur" golfers do not play golf for a living, do not teach others to play golf, do not sell golf clubs and equipment, nor do any other things that endanger their amateur status. (Despite its etymology-the word amateur, from the Latin amat refers to one who "loves" an activity-amateurs do not lose their status if they stop enjoying the game!) In its broadest sense, the term "nongovemmental" is applied to any organization or institution that performs a public function, but is not a part of the Government of the territories in which it works.

To narrow the overall class of NGOS down a first stage: in the mid 20th century, Nation State Governments began to hive off public functions that were previously the responsibility of government departments, to newly established bodies set up in ways that insulated them from political criticism. This activity had gone a long way, before State enterprises began to be explicitly privatized in the 1970s or '80s: before that, the line between the "governmental" and the "non-governmental" had become very thin-the Arts Council in Britain, which gives public funds to orchestras, art museums etc., and the SNCF, which runs the French railways, were dependent on and answerable to the Government for overall policies and control of their budgets, so they might as well have been government departments. With this in mind, the Economist launched the name quangos: "quasi-nongovernmental organizations." The insulation of such bodies from Government was something of a pretense, and to this extent their independence was a sham. So let me begin by setting "quangos" aside. as outside the class of NGOS I shall be discussing here.

We alsc say little in this essay about a second, and more numerous class of NGOs. In many countries, including some of the poorest in Africa, farming cooperatives and other local organizations are set up without any blessing from the Government of the Member State in which they operate: these organizations facilitate, or finance, better methods in farming, mitigation, medicine, education and other cooperative activities. These NGOS are typically local, and operate on a small scale: in a single country, or a single locality. They raise funds from a variety of sources: partly, as loans from IDA, the low interest branch of the World Bank, more often from charitable organizations like Oxfam, sometimes as grants or loans from the U.S. AID, the British ODA, or similar agencies in other Governments: notably, those of Canada, the Netherlands, and the Scandinavian countries.

These local NGOS have strictly delimited goals, and are usually somewhat fragile-dependent on one, or a few, funders and activists. Their need to keep good standing with their donor agencies obliges them to guarantee the quality of the "work product" from their grants or loans; so they tend to keep their heads down, and are disinclined to develop an independent stance over matters of general policy.

Moving to a somewhat larger scale of operation, a substantial number of agencies are not confined to limited localities, but maintain more extensive-or even world wide-areas of concern. Once these organizations have developed international ambitions, they seek "observer status" at the United Nations, which can give them access to UN Headquarters, to papers that the UN Secretariat prepares for circulation to recognized NGOs, and to some direct participation in conferences in their special areas of concern. (More of this later.) The status is so helpful that people sometimes think of NGOS in ways that treat only nongovernmental organizations with UN observer status as being genuine "NGOs" at all. However much the potential role of NGOS was a factor in the preparatory discussions of the UN Charter, it is worth recalling that many influential NGOs were established, and proved their worth, at a time when cooperation between the UN and external NGOS was in a very early stage of development. In a few cases, indeed, the lifetime of particular NGOS had long antedated the UN itself: the ICRC-the International Committee of the Red Cross-is a prime example.

Having set on one side the nongovernmental organizations I am not concerned with in this essay, let me sharpen my focus, and identify the large, transnational NGOS that are my main concern. Several kinds of organization are relevant here, and have much in common. Their scope is world wide, and they pursue their topics on a global scale. They operate on a transnational basis: for administrative purposes, their headquarters may be located in one particular country, but their work is carried out by networks of local organizations, which have local autonomy and raise most of their own funds. Typically, they take no money from either industry or government, but get it through subscriptions from individuals who have their "cause" at heart. Most crucially, they seek to protect their independence of judgment, and their claim to be impartially critical, by keeping a distance from both Nation State Governments and the United Nations-dining with them (as the English saying is) "using a long spoon."

The purest instances are those transnational single-issue NGOS that concentrate, in some cases, on humanitarian issues, in some on problems of the environment, in some on abuses of human rights. The first group includes the ICRC, the Oxford Committee for Famine Relief (Oxfam), Medicines san Frontieres and the Save the Children Fund; the second includes Worldwatch, the World Wild Life Fund and-most particularly-Greenpeace; the third includes Amnesty International (the pioneer post-1945 NGO), the network of regional organizations that makes up Human Rights Watch, and such impromptu organizations as the group of Nobel Peace Laureates who joined to exert pressure on the Military Government of Burma to release the country's elected leader, Aung Sang Suu Kyi.

Another group of NGOS is grounded in shared commitments of professionals in different disciplines and countries. Physicians together, or lawyers together, find a common cause in the distinctive values of their professions. Organizations such as the World Psychiatric Association, World Medical Association. or International Physicians for the Prevention of Nuclear War, conduct a transnational defense of medical values-including the values of the public health movement-in a way that transcends the policy of all Nation State Governments. (Israeli and Palestinian physicians who meet over the injured body of a shared patient, will approach his treatment in the same frame of mind, and set aside all considerations that rest only on questions of citizenship or nationality.) The same can be said in the legal profession for, e.g.. the International Commission of Jurists and other such institutions.

Finally, a few transnational NGOS engage in charitable work from a commercial, not a professional or academic angle. In modus operandi, a business consultancy like McKinzie resembles Greenpeace or Amnesty: it has branches in two dozen countries, each of which is an independent operation with traditions and experience that allow it to address the special problems of its own country; but which pool technical ideas about working with clients, and handling other issues that go beyond their own boundaries. Meanwhile-though the NSGS of Europe grumbled at "unscrupulous currency dealers"-the Soros Foundation started the Central European University in Budapest and Prague in less time than it took the European Bank for Reconstruction and Development, its intergovernmental counterpart, to buy marble for its grandiose entrance hall. In the background, of course, older Foundations of commercial origin (Rockefeller, Ford, Carnegie, etc.) continue to operate multinationally, or sometimes transnationally.

None of these groups of organizations-humanitarian, professional or commercial-is tempted to act as agents for a National Government. If anything, their relations with Government are conducted at arm's length to preserve both the appearance and the fact of independence. As we shall see, the efficacy of their operations, and their credibility for those who benefit from them, depends on keeping a real distance in these relations, so that political disputes among States or peoples do not touch the NGOs' reputations as honest brokers or disinterested bringers of aid.

In number and variety, the NGOS have multiplied since World War II, but their historical origins are much older. Like so much of the educational or social services given by the State in modern secular societies, the work of NGOs was in earlier times undertaken by Churches and religious orders. (In Europe from 1200 on, the Medieval Christian Church was in effect a transnational institution, with a standing above, and apart from the secular rulers of the time.) As we know it now, the tradition of NGOs dates from the establishment of the ICRC in Switzerland in 1865. To this day, indeed, the ICRC succeeds, by acting with great care, in keeping the confidence of countries with very different cultural and religious traditions: peoples and governments in most parts of the world have learned to accept its impartiality and independence.

REASONS FOR THE INFLUENCE OF NGOS

So much by way of background about the general nature and standing of NGOs. Now, let me turn to the central issue for this essay, about the significance of the large, financially independent transnational NGOS in global affairs. The fact that NGOS have been increasingly influential over the last twenty years is clear to observers of current events. The decline of the USSR's political authority on the international stage was accelerated by its hostile reactions to the award of Nobel Prizes to Boris Pasternak, Alexander Solzhenitsyn and Andre Sakharov, while Amnesty's campaign for Soviet prisoners of conscience only made matters worse: Mikhail Gorbachev therefore felt bound to invite representatives from Amnesty International to visit Moscow, to discuss reforms that might help restore Russia's standing in the larger world.

More recently, humanitarian, environmental and human rights organizations have worked with the international Press and Television to draw their viewers and readers' attention to ecological catastrophes and oppressive regimes, massacres and famines, from Alaska to Rwanda, Somalia to Guatemala, Bosnia to Kashmir. In response, the World Powers, large or small, have felt bound to acknowledge disasters they might have preferred to ignore, and have reacted by despatching mobile hospitals and food supplies, election observers and armistice monitors. Suffering that is visible on the TV screens of richer countries touches the conscience of electors, and so of politicians also: what the Eye cannot help seeing, the Heart cannot help grieving about.

The fact that NGOS are influential is undeniable: what is less obvious is why their influence has increased at this time. The alliance of NGOS and the media is a potent instrument of change; but about the deeper significance of NGOs something more has to be explained. In particular, what we face at this time is not just a growth of influence for NGOs, but a shift in the balance of influence as between NGOS and Nation State Governments. The significance of NGOS becomes more apparent, as people find more and more suspect the claim of NSGS to "sovereignty". In a dozen ways, we are at a turning point in the history of State Power and Sovereignty: the spotlight is leaving the governments of totally Sovereign Nation States, and other actors are becoming visible on the global stage. In the long run-I shall argue-the Nation State Governments can no more monopolize the political conduct of global affairs than OPEC can monopolize the World market for petroleum.

The heart of the matter is this. The birth of Nation States from the 1650s on, after the Peace of Westphalia, was-in practical terms-the work of Louis XIV of France. After a brush with dissident nobles in the Fronde, he used all available force to create the unitary State that France has since remained, both as a monarchy and as a republic. In theoretical terms, European ideas about the power of the Nation State are dominated by the model in Hobbes' Leviathan. On this view, the prime function of the Sovereign is to provide security to his Subjects or Citizens: for this he is given a monopoly in the legitimate exercise of Violence in the State. The authority of the Sovereign is displayed in the use of State Violence, to preserve domestic order by the power of the Police, and to protect the State's external integrity by the power of its Armed Forces. Against the Sovereign's legitimate Force, Hobbes saw no scope for any legitimate resistance. The execution of King Charles I in 1649 marked for him the final breakdown of the State: even the secession of the Dutch Republic from the Spanish Crown in the 1570s or '80s had, in his eyes, been illegitimate.

In the three and a half centuries since the Peace of Westphalia, the political Powers of the World have constructed a diplomatic system in which every Sovereign is free to ensure the domestic order and external integrity of the State. By both formal and tacit agreement among these Sovereign authorities, all States respect each other's monopoly in the domestic use of Violence, and they will resist each other's external use of Force, only if their own compelling interests are threatened. In this sense, the Westphalian Order created a Cartel of Nation States.

The United Nations Treaties did nothing to weaken the power of this Cartlel: rather, they created a new instrument for existing Sovereign States to use in their own interest. Under the UN Treaties (as in other Treaties) States took on voluntarily accepted limits on their Sovereignty: in principle, at least, they retained their option to leave the UN, and resume unqualified authority to defend their State interests as they thought best. Since the end of the Cold War, the authority of States to protect Sovereign interests has been qualified in ways that are now familiar. A new rhetoric constructed around such novel ideas as human rights law and the international community-a community with needs and interests of its own-is winning currency in debates at the UN, as well as in other forums: the force of this rhetoric deserves careful scrutiny.

The crucial transition was the case of lraq vs. Kuwait. Initially, the attempt by one member of the UN and OPEC Cartels to seize the assets of a fellow member was found unacceptable for purely Westphalian reasons. But the penalties to which the Sovereign State of lraq was exposed, and the lengths to which the alliance opposed it went in its interpretation of the Security Council's resolutions, give evidence of a change of view. The use of those resolutions, for instance, to warrant intervention between the Baghdad authorities and their Subjects in Kurdistan to the North, and in the Delta to the South, imposed restraints on the exercise of lraqi Sovereignty that had very little to do with its seizure of Kuwait.

On the contrary, these actions rested on pre-Westphalian ideas of State Sovereignty. In short, the actions of Saddam Hussein against the Kurds and the Marsh Arabs were condemned as those of an "unjust" Sovereign: Iraqi Kurds were entitled to appeal for support and understanding in resisting those actions, as much as the Netherlanders of the 1570s were entitled to support and understanding against religious persecution by Philip of Spain's Army. On the Hobbist view, the only "injustice" a Sovereign can do to his Subjects is to fail to preserve the State's domestic peace and its external integrity: acting on this view, most Member States of the UN are quick to object to any "external" interference in their "internal" affairs-e.g., the People's Republic of China, challenged about Tibet. Yet this is just the argument the Security Council did not let Saddam use in his own cause.

On a pre-Westphalian view, however, a Sovereign's obligations went beyond those of preserving domestic peace and external security. Legitimate Violence may be a way to create and maintain an effective State; but, if a Sovereign were to retain legitimacy, his actions must meet other conditions. In general, it was not acceptable for Subjects to rebel, but the way in which Philip II persecuted the Netherlands Protestants gave them a right to "abjure" their earlier loyalty to the Spanish Crown. Loyalty was a two-way affair.

The Sovereign was expected to act in his Subjects' interests, not just vice versa: if he failed in these requirements, he invited difficulties of other kinds. The murder of Thomas Becket (say) made King Henry II of England an object of contempt to people of conscience all the way across Europe: as a result, he was not forced but shamed into submitting to the authority of the Church.

Claims about a Sovereign's "injustice" carried conviction for Aquinas but, until 1991, they had little weight in the UN. At the high point of the Modern Nation State, matters of Power were interpreted as questions about a State's ability to bring Military Force into action. (Stung by the Catholic Church's criticisms, Stalin reputedly asked, "How many divisions has the Pope?") In the early 20th century, the central issue for British diplomacy was the numbers of battleships available for service in the German, French and British navies, respectively: during the Cold War, the rival numbers of Intercontinental Ballistic Missiles (ICBMs) in the forces of the US and the USSR played a similar part in the strategic debate.

Since 1989, the capacity for Military Force is longer the only measure of political influence. Even now, Shame may only a limited ability to (say) change the minds of the Burmese junta. But limited power is not zero power: in the balance of influence, one strength of the NGOS is the role of Shame, as a counterweight to Force. So one reason why major transnational NGOS can win and retain public respect just is their manifest abstention from Violence. As I wrote some years ago, "in the eyes of decent human opinion, moral challenges are never answered by displays of force. The day that Amnesty International takes possession of a machine gun, let alone an atom bomb, its ability to gain a hearing and influence events will be at an end... Amnesty International's moral authority is that much the greater, just because it is a Lilliputian institution."

While the Superpowers boasted about nuclear arsenals, NGOS were seen as inherently nonviolent. While the policies of NSGs were slanted by their own ambitions, and the speeches in the Security Council were aimed at national advantage, NGOs seemed free of ulterior interests-grinding no axes, uncommitted to one country rather than another, speaking not for any Government but for its victims, the sufferers and the oppressed. Put idealistically, NGOS became Humanity's Conscience, and were taken seriously because their arguments were disinterested. Of course, this view involved an element of exaggeration. If pressed, UN officials who handled nongovernmental organizations would reply that NGOS can act in ways as self-interested as those of any Government. But this reply involved a counter-exaggeration, too. The basic insight still holds good: Oxfam and Amnesty are not inherently self-interested parties, and their arguments can be taken as meaning just what they say.

THE POLITICAL AND TECHNICAL FACES OF THE UN

On a less high flown level, the shifting balance of influence was in evidence at the Conferences on Environment and Development in Rio de Janeiro, Human Rights in Vienna, most recently on Population Policy in Cairo. At Cairo, a coalition of NGOS and women's groups-above all, from the developing countries that suffer most from population pressures-played a major role by preventing the representatives of NSGS from making concessions to the Vatican and other conservative male religious groups, which were trying to destroy the effectiveness of the Conference's final documents. NSG spokespeople are exposed to a clash of interests among different groups on their domestic scene: so, Benazir Bhutto presented a more conservative Islamic view than one might expect from a woman of her education. The interests for which the NGOs spoke were less ambiguous and more clearly defined; and they mounted a powerful operation to defend the central purposes of the Conference.

Here we can begin to answer one of the larger questions facing this meeting, about the relative efficacy of the UN's political and technical agencies. In ways exemplified in the Cairo proceedings, the UN's political/diplomatic activities have all the turmoil of domestic politics, but on a larger stage. They are subject to the familiar criticisms that ordinary people direct at politicians back home: that they are "corrupted by" the groups whose needs they serve, "subservient to special interests" and so uncommitted to the Public Good. The technical activities are effective, on the other hand, to the extent that their goals are defined in advance clearly enough to ensure a consensus. We may thus form an impression that the technical agencies of the UN function well, and its political institutions badly. But this impression rests on a confusion over this division of tasks. The single-mindedness of NGOS makes them natural allies of the technical agencies: in their work, they turn to the same technically equipped professionals-agricultural scientists, hydrologists or physicians-whose advice and opinions the UN agencies rely on, and whose knowledge and skills are of use in the kinds of practical situations that the NGOs also address.

In passing, let me remark on a stratagem that NGOS use to shift the field on which issues are debated. At the end of the Cold War, groups like International Physicians for the Prevention of Nuclear War and Physicians for Social Responsibility argued that nuclear weapons are a public health problem, like communicable diseases and polluted drinking water, so that nuclear disarmament has to be viewed as a public health issue. The stratagem had both strength and weakness. On the one hand, it focused attention on the catastrophes that will follow any use of nuclear weapons: the problems created in the affected countries would be too vast for the Public Health authorities to tackle effectively. Policy debates about nuclear weapons or disarmament, per contra, have for long focused not on radiation and the like, but on the balance of interests involved in nuclear deterrence: diplomatic issues that a Public Health approach cannot resolve.

Certainly, there is a virtue in replacing political and diplomatic issues by technical and professional ones, wherever this is practicable; but it cannot be done completely, or in all cases equally. On the contrary, medical information serves only to spell out, in detail, the consequences that should be a necessary component in all political and diplomatic equations: even after these have all been taken into account, there is still substantial room for NSG bargaining to go on as before.

THE REACTION OF NSGS TO THE INFLUENCE OF NGOS

Meanwhile, the very things that draw NGOS into a natural alliance with the UN's professional or technical agencies enhance the difficulties between NGOS and NSGs: these we must now turn to. They come from NSGs seeing their hands forced by the influence of NGO's and their media allies. The absolute sovereignty of Nation States is now constrained, not just by their economic interdependence, but also by the ability of selfappointed NGOs to raise a worldwide response from world opinion by their advocacy of humanitarian, environmental, medical or human rights causes.

The difficulties in question are sometimes trivial: a matter of differences of style or even injured pride. At a meeting in the Netherlands, I spoke of Greenpeace as a serious organization, and was smprised by the Japanese representative's disgust: Greenpeace and its works filled him with distaste. But it was clear that his reaction was a response, in part, to the deliberately shaming and melodramatic character of Greenpeace's public demonstrations, which are intended to put the industry or government being criticized in the wrong before the general public. Yet this is only one half of Greenpeace's mode of operation. The other half acts as a counterbalance: in the corridors of the UN, the organization tries to persuade the object of its attacks that it would do better to sign a treaty (say) or to enforce environmental controls, that they had been slow to adopt.

Behind injured feelings, however, the difficulties are real and sometimes painfully embarrassing. The intervention in Somalia by the United States and the United Nations was triggered by a humanitarian crisis, notably at Baidoa: public attention was caught by heart wrenching television images of children with swollen bellies, and other signs of disease and starvation. The first international response was a flow of medical help and food to relieve this crisis; but it soon became clear that much more was needed. The prevalence of banditry and the risk of injury and even death to aid workers, at the hands of gangs run by a dozen rival warlords, persuaded the US government and the UN to introduce military forces, hoping-vainly, as it proved-to create a framework within which a stable government could be established in Mogadishu that might regain effective authority over the rest of the country.

The story is fresh in our minds. Its opening was the most ironic of all: unarmed aid workers and television cameramen on shore near Mogadishu harbour watched and filmed Marines in full combat gear crawling ashore, as though ready to meet well dug in enemy troops, rather than American civilians. But before long the security situation became totally ambiguous: disgusted by the apparent ingratitude of people they were trying to help, politicians insisted on bringing home, out of harm's way, first the US troops, and eventually the entire UN contingent. It was (and still is) unclear if peaceful humanitarian doctors or relief workers and heavily armed government armies can operate effectively on the same ground: this is no clearer in Bosnia than in Somalia, and the dissonant policies of the United States and the European powers toward the arms embargo against Bosnia only underline the lack of a practical solution.

Yet State governments remain open to a well-intended pressure (or temptation) to interpose forces, in places where much good can seemingly be done in an otherwise desperate situation. The intervention at Goma, on the Rwanda-Zaire border, was one case where government force and humanitarian agencies cooperated to good effect in the short term, to relieve an immediate disaster; but the intervention's inconclusive political effect leaves the underlying problems as obscure as ever. For the time being, States having a capacity for disinterested helpfulness are liable to slip into political quagmires, once their help goes beyond medical supplies and food, and involves putting armed force on the ground. In President Clinton's speeches, the rhetoric of "national interests" blurs into one of "our natural humanitarian interests"; but (as in the case of Haiti) his political critics are now becoming hard nosed about the limited extent of America's truly "national" concerns.

Yet there is little doubt that the underlying tension will continue. People in the rich countries will go on demanding that their Governments react to disasters of all kinds-floods or starvation, torture or "ethnic cleansing"-and the political implications of that demand will remain as ambiguous as ever. In situations of anarchy (Somalia) or civil war (Bosnia and Rwanda) the lack of effective authority puts humanitarian workers at risk in ways no outside State can remedy, short of imposing a colonial administration. So it is no wonder that the ways in which governments react to calls for intervention in good causes are coming to sound like the alarm from the Trumpeter of Cracow-the first arrow to the throat brings it to a sudden stop.

Earlier, we remarked on the narrower, pre-Westphalian concept of Sovereignty. When a Sovereign's treatment of his Subjects deeply offended the Consciences of the other Powers, considerations of Shame could oblige him to change his policies and correct his actions, in ways that left questions about Force and Violence on one side. In the three centuries and more of the Modern era, appeals to morality and shame lost much of this effectiveness. A few rulers-King Bomba of Naples in the early 1800s-and a few major powers-the 19th century Ottoman forces in Bulgaria-acted in ways so outrageous as to attract general condemnation; but Shame was rarely sufficient to change their minds or their policies. Now, however, though we still face unresolved practical problems, our situation at least testifies to the renewed power of Shame as an influence in global affairs. Some current regimes-the Burmese junta. for instance-are still in effect shameless. Even there, however, an awareness of being international pariahs, and the experience of being besieged by a delegation of Nobel prize winners, weakens their ability to ignore outside criticism and continue imposing their power with unresuicted Force. Though something less than outright Shame, this is a move in the same direction.

TRANSNATIONAL REPRESENTATIVE INSTITUTIONS

Let me return to an idea implicit in my earlier discussion: that the tension between NGOS and NSGs today is a revival of earlier conflicts in Medieval Europe, between the Church and the secular Monarchs. NSGs today wield temporal power in the sense of Legitimate Force or Violence: the NGOs speak for longer term values, which are not (supposedly) restricted to one country or epoch. More should be said about the limits of this parallel: there are significant differences between the centralized structure of the Medieval Papacy and its modus operandi, on the one hand, and the independent and separate standing of the transnational NGOs, on the other hand. But the central point holds good: the exercise of Force by Sovereign Nation State Governments is open to criticism by transnational standards, from NGOS and others, in a way that was easier and more intelligible in Medieval than in Modern times, before the Treaty of Westphalia than after it.

To pose a topical question: "Is the effectiveness of NGOs enhanced, or lessened, by their institutional fragmentation?" The answer to that question is not clear. Would the voice of a formal NGO Assembly be louder than that of a thousand distinct NGOs? Or is the effectiveness of NGOS (paradoxically) increased by the ability of separate and independent organizations to reach consensus? Certainly, the centralized authority of the Vatican undermined rather than strengthened its credibility at the Cairo conference. Vatican representatives at that meeting acted so like Nation State Governments in, e.g., forcing a conservative position on the smaller Latin American powers, that their tactics ended by generating resentment: these were seen as inappropriate to the occasion.

This question is part of a larger institutional problem facing the whole UN: how to make the Organization more democratic. The institutions of the European Union are currently criticized for their "democratic deficit": neither the central administration in Brussels, nor the Council of Ministers, is directly representative of the peoples whose lives their decisions touch. The recent enlargement of the authority of the European Parliament go some way to correct this deficit, but much more remains to be corrected. A similar criticism applies to the institutions of the UN.

The General Assembly (e.g.) is no less a Cartel than the Security Council; and there is little chance for the citizens of any Member State to get a hearing in the agencies or bureaus of the UN-legislative or executive, judicial or technical-without cooperation from Government representatives, even where that Government treats its own citizens tyrannically. Unless that "deficit" can be remedied-it may be argued-the Governments of the Member States, however unrepresentative on the domestic level, will keep a monopoly of national representation, when the interests of the peoples over whom they rule come up for debate in the UN's institutions.

What alternative is there-a directly elected World Parliament? As matters stand, this proposal is visionary but impractical. The Governments of many Member States are unwilling to hold, on their territories, free and fair elections to which all permanent residents of the State have effective access. So there is little prospect that these States have either will or experience needed to organize elections for a World Parliament that are acceptable by transnational standards.

For want of a World Parliament, then, some people look to NGOs to make the UN more representative. Norway's Department of Development Cooperation Programmes (for instance) has commissioned a poll of NGOs aimed at two questions,

> *"How effective is NGO access to intergovernmental decision making?" and*
>
> *"How can it be made more democratic?"*

(Once again the Scandinavians took the lead in support of NGOs.) The consulting firm conducting the poll begins with a useful back-history of the problem:

> As originally conceived in the UN Charter discussions, NGOs would be recognized by the Economic and Social Council as important participants in considering issues before the Council and that's all. Subsequently, large numbers of NGOs arrived at official UN conferences and made their presence felt through specialized conferences, and UN staff planning meetings. At the... negotiations for a New International Economic Order, NGOs were given the ability to produce in-house newspapers during... meetings in order to inform Governments about the on-going proceedings. [In] the discussions of the Human Rights Commission, NGOS were "asked" to monitor the behaviour of Governments and to report back to inter-governmental bodies on the compliance of Governments to... international standards. In the World Health Organization, NGO expertise was given prominence in drafting international guidelines and standards on infant formula sometimes equal to or greater than individual Governments. The Bergen conference on sustainable development experimented with a five sided formula: Governments, business, youth, labour and environmental groups had to agree on... a statement. The European Union has now held ministerial/NGO level consultations. And the UNCED process [post-Rio] formally defined... the role of NGOS in [preparing] global conferences and their follow-up.

Several things are clear in this account. From the beginning, NGOs viewed the role grudgingly allotted to them by NSGs as insufficient. Early on, they felt the need to "make their presence felt" at meetings, by staging "counter-conferences, parallel events and demonstrations": even now they doubt if a current review of the status of NGOS by the Economic and Social Council will give their views adequate attention.

Finally they still need to follow a strategy of "counter conferences, parallel events, and demonstrations." The exemplary "counter-conference" was at the Human Rights meeting at Vienna, in Spring 1993. The Nation State Governments of the World met Upstairs in the Conference Hall, and worked their way through an agenda sanitized to avoid offending the People's Republic of China. (The Upstairs conference declined to listen to the Dalai Lama, or anybody who saw Tibet as raising issues of human rights.) Downstairs in the basement, the NGOS meanwhile listened to the Dalai Lama, took on other issues the NSGS evaded, and gave a running commentary on the meeting that the World Press by all accounts found more interesting, informative and entertaining than the Upstairs proceedings. Similar counter-events took place at the Rio Environmental meeting and the Cairo Population conference: at Cairo, the (female) Prime Minister of Norway Upstairs cooperated with the NGO Forum Downstairs, in planning initiatives that ended by being effective in the official proceedings.

Elsewhere, UN Secretariat and agencies have chosen to take NGOs on as partners: Sadako Ogata, the UN High Commissioner for Refugees, has regular meetings with humanitarian and other NGOs that work on the problems of refugees in war torn and starving regions. The documents following the Rio Conference-e.g., Agenda 21-also acknowledge the environmental NGOs, while the Commission on Sustainable Development opens up its internal planning discussions to NGOS in a way that such political agencies as the Security Council rarely do.

Still, such alliances between NGOs and UN staff do not fully overcome the UN's democratic deficit. How is it decided which NGOs shall participate in such meetings? Who chooses which NGOs sit down and talk with Sadako Ogata? At these meetings, democracy is not "one person one vote": it is syndicalism, in which representation is tied to occupation, as with the Trade Union "block vote" in the British Labour Party, or the membership of the Hong Kong Legislative Council, based on the professions. Organizationally, then, much still needs doing to create modes of collaboration among NGOS and the UN bureaux and councils, before the UN's operations can seriously claim to be democratic.

Hitherto, in any case, the major humanitarian and environmental NGOs have been unwilling to coordinate their administrative practices, let alone establish a framework of common institutions. Much of their influence (the argument goes) comes from the fact that their goals are exactly defined. There was a long and painful internal debate before Amnesty International enlarged the organization's targets to include capital punishment: similar soul searchings preceded Greenpeace's decision to extend its area of activities to the Latin American South, as well as the prosperous North and Australasia. In Britain, the Aid and Environment Group is responsible for some coordination among different NGOs, and in Europe there is similar cooperation among humanitarian NGOs. For the most part, however, this collaboration is only arranged ad hoc, in response to the needs of a particular crisis in (say) Bosnia or Rwanda, not with any expectation of creating a standing Council or permanent Assembly of NGOs.

The problem remains. From the start, the UN Organization was an "inter-national" (inter-State or inter-Governmental) organization. At its 50th anniversary, it is unwilling to broaden its representation of Citizens, at the cost of States or Governments. On the contrary, many Member States fear to offend the oligarchies that dominate their own politics. For now, the natural allies of NGOS are the UN Secretariat, or the technical and professional agencies. It is not that the goals of NGOS are intrinsically technical, but their single mindedness sharpens their attention in a quasitechnical way.

TRANSNATIONAL JUDICIAL INSTITUTIONS

The peripheral institutions of the UN have similar limitations, arising from the fact that the UN is intergovernmental not transgovernmental, international not transnational. The World Bank is a good example. Its statutes prevent it from making loans directly to agricultural cooperatives or other NGOs. All of its funds have to go via NSGs for allocation within a country, and some of them fail to reach their intended beneficiaries, being diverted to pay for Mercedes cars for the State elite. Yet, as the Grameen Bank found in Bangladesh, local agricultural cooperatives (run by women) default on their loans at a markedly lower rate than regular commercial firms, let alone Governments. This discovery has, however, been frustratingly slow to influence thinking at leading international financial agencies.

For NGOs in the field of human rights, however, the crucial global institutions are judicial; and there the weaknesses of a purely inter-governmental system are flagrant. The International Court of Justice, e.g., adjudicates only disputes between States: more exactly, disputes between States that allow it jurisdiction in the case in question. In the Nicaraguan civil war, Nicaragua tried to sue the US Government over the CIA mining of the harbour at Corinto; but the US Administration rejected the jurisdiction of the Court, so no ruling could be put into effect. This leaves no provision for actions in which individual citizens, or classes of citizens, seek to press claims against Sovereign States: specifically, claims in which NGOS like Amnesty and Human Rights Watch publicize offences by State authorities against their own citizens.

As matters stand, indeed, Sovereign Immunity-a product of the Westphalian era-stops individuals bringing suits in the domestic Courts of their own country; and the Cartel of inter-Governmental institutions stops them doing so under International Law. Even less are there tribunals in which transnational humanitarian agencies can bring "class action" suits for groups of citizens who are penalized, or discriminated against, matters of International Law, by the Government of a State. Whether as individuals, as classes, or through NGOs as guardrans Citizens have no "standing" in the tribunals responsible for adjudicating matters of International Law.

In the judicial realm, in a word, we conspicuously lack trans-national tribunals, to determine the rights of Citizens against Nation State Governments, and to hand down rulings enforceable for a Citizen, and against a State. However much NSGs may now concede their economic interdependence, few of them would think of surrendering to outside Courts any right of adjudication between the State and its Citizens. Sovereign Immunity is the last refuge of Leviathan, the last appeal of rulers who remain above the Law, so above the rights of their own Citizens-and who claim the right to do so in the name of national autonomy.

One rare exception is that created by the Treaties establishing the institutions of the European Union, e.g. the European Court of Human Rights. As before, these treaties imposed on Member States voluntarily accepted limitations; but by now there is a body of practical law, from cases in which Member Governments were held by the Court to have contravened individual rights entrenched in those Treaties. If such problems face unquestioned Citizens of European States who seek protection from the Court of Human Rights, how much harder is it for Residents who are unreasonably kept from Citizenship. If these issues of Standing were resolved, a new field of action will open up for the transnational humanitarian NGOs that now operate by the Politics of Shame: rousing public indignation, and embarrassing NSGs that find themselves held in scorn across the globe. For who would not prefer to see Nation State Governments exposed to enforceable judicial orders to right the wrongs they do their citizens and residents?

Human rights is not the only field that can profit from a transnational judicial forum or tribunal. In due course, scientific consensus may be achieved about environmental issues, and generate a world wide Code of Environmental Practice. Respect for this Code could become the subject of a global system of administrative law: opening to NGOs a chance to initiate actions before a World Environmental Court, for injunctions requiring a State to change its the laws and practices, as a threat to Nature and public health in their own or neighbouring countries.

Does this idea at present sound fanciful? If so, let me remark that the procedures for such a system are already in place and operative in the United States of America, where practices and laws that survive challenge in the system of State Courts are open to review in the Federal Courts, and can be struck down there. National Governments that resist the adoption of Federal institutions on a European scale will (needless to say) at first reject any such Federal jurisdiction; but, given the impotence of State borders in the face of a Chernobyl disaster, the obstacles to a global jurisdiction of environmental and public health issues may not for long remain insuperable.

THE NGOS: PROPHETS OR POLITICIANS

To conclude: Any account of the place of NGOs within the international system of institutions must address two fundamental issues. One of these is, at least on its face, philosophical rather than political; the other is more political than philosophical; but, in actual practice, these two issues are closely connected.

The first is the claim to "universality" often made in discussions of human rights. Historically, this idea goes back to the late 18th century philosopher, Immanuel Kant. Today, it is sometimes understood as implying that all of the rights claimed by people in the developed countries of Western Europe or North America are rights for people in any country: if it is morally objectionable for the police to torture prisoners in Holland, it is morally objectionable for them to torture prisoners in Zimbabwe, Paraguay and Malaysia as well. Universal imperatives against the deliberate infliction of cruelty do not ask where or when deliberately cruel actions are performed: at all places and times equally, avoiding these actions is part of the moral fabric of human existence.

Such claims underlie programs on which the major NGOs embark with conviction; and when the content of the moral point at issue is (say) torture. their force is not easily challenged-can torture be unpardonably evil in one country, yet defensible in another? But, recently the claim to universality has been challenged by Asian politicians-most strongly by Dr. Mahathir, Prime Minister of Malaysia. To impose worldwide respect for the rights Europeans and Americans insist on for themselves at home is, he argues, a new Cultural Imperialism: an attempt to impose Western patterns of life on countries which have their own independent systems of moral thought and practice. Rather than let organizations like Amnesty poke their noses into Malaysian affairs, Westerners had best let Asians look after their own affairs.

This reply is self serving-the head of an NSG defend Sovereign Autonomy from encroachment. But there is more to it. Western insistence on "taking rights seriously" leads to exaggerations. In California, some see it as morally objectionable for people in restaurants to impose tobacco smoke on fellow-diners; but is it just as objectionable to smoke in restaurants in Bangkok or Accra? This appeal to universality is overdone.

Immanuel Kant understood this point. He claimed only that moral maxims have a universal form. What substantive content any maxim cashes in for is a different matter: a topic for "casuistical digressions" analyzing its significance in particular situations. Between the bare statement of a rule and its specific applications, then, lie questions of its meaning for different practical situations. What counts as "honour" or "dishonour" in a given country is far more the product of local history and custom than what counts as "kindness" or "cruelty": so, there is less ambiguity over torture than (say) over matters of honour.

What can properly claim "universality" are the general themes of moral argument: their specific implications depend on the particular situations to which they are applied. One of the skills required of transnational NGOs is the discernment needed to see how general maxims match particular cases. To current critics of the claim to universality, we can reply that organizations like Amnesty International evoke world wide response: they "speak" to people in all countries alike. Subtlety and discernment are required in seeing how their general maxims fit the special problems of a new region. But many moral issues are too plain to require interpretation. Like cholera and hunger, torture or arbitrary imprisonment has the same meaning in all countries. To that extent, the vision of idealistic NGOs as disinterested Voices for Humanity-or for environmental

NGOs, as Voices for Nature-retains its philosophical charm. At this point, the second, political issue comes in, and the picture has another side. In disciplining rulers who contravened the general moral imperatives of human reason, the Medieval Church was unavoidably drawn into secular politics. The results could be unedifying. Popes and Cardinals learned to play politics like seasoned politicians, and cultivated that art to this day-as at the Population Conference. Transnational NGOs, likewise, operate unavoidably on the edge, if not the middle, of the political scene. However valid their moral claims, effective campaigns intended to put these into effect necessarily take them into the domain of public politics. In dining with NSGs, they "use a long spoon"; but they all pay a price for operating in the political arena.

With this in mind, we should return to the questionnaire to NGOs sponsored by the Norwegian Government. There, the contrast between basic moral goals and day to day political methods is much in evidence. The questions on the questionnaire's first page are very general, and remain on the level of high principles:

a. Are the 'peoples' voices heard at [the UN's] international events.

b. Are the concerns of 'Nature' heard at international events.

c. Are you heard at international events.

d. Do Governments think 'peoples' voices are heard.

e. Do Governments think 'Nature' is heard.

f. Do Governments think NGOS are heard.

By the last two pages, however, we are plainly operating on the down to earth level of practical politics, and a distinctive political has begun to show itself: At NGO international events, do you generally feel the potential dominance of a. northern NGOS/b. the larger NGOS/c. accredited NGOS/d. male-run NGOS/e. white-run NGOS/f. English language-run NGOs?.........

If you could re-structure an NGO alternate conference, the first two things that you would do are:

a. insist on gender/racial balance in NGO delegations

b. provide documentation/translation in additional languages

f. book all NGO participants into the same hotel/district

g. remove the podium and arrange chairs in a large circle...

By now, it is clear that, inter alia. the NGO movement has taken over the mantle of the radical Left. A concern for political correctness colours these questions: any procedure that fails any egalitarian demand is suspect. It is not enough that the moral goals of the NGO be achieved: they must be achieved in a perfectly equitable way.

I do not object to this coloration. The goals and methods of the Left have a long and proud historical ancestry going back, at the least, to the Sectarians of the English Commonwealth from 1649 to 1657: the Ranters and Diggers, Quakers and Levellers. I draw attention to this strand in the NGO movement here, because it helps to explain some other aspects of the NGOs' role in the practical politics of the UN. There, they also display the coloration of Left vs. Right-Equality vs. Privilege-familiar from the domestic politics of single States or countries.

Many people in NSG delegations, and some members of the UN bureaucracy, find this aspect of NGOS a stumbling block. Growing up within the comfortable etiquette of diplomacy, they react against the rough tactics of (e.g.) Greenpeace, whose public actions-notably, their attacks on Japanese whalers-they regard as deeply unpleasing: "Highly Undiplomatic: not Fair Play!"

This reaction to the NGOS is understandable, but we should avoid generalizing it. Many of the most influential NGOS-whether Amnesty Intemational, or Oxfam, or the International Commission of Jurists-are not specially radical in orientation: by origin and tradition, these organizations are Middle of the Road, if not Veering to the Right. Whatever impression we may get from the NGO questionnaire, there is no reason to expect all "non-governmental" organizations to share any uniform political coloration, any more than all members of the Roman

Catholic Church have shared political views. The deeper factors that keep NSGs and NGOs at arm's length are on a level at which spokesmen for global moral goals are inevitably distinct from rcprcoentativco of ,local political interests. So long as the major transnational NGOs protect their right to hold the activities of Nation State Governments up to public view and criticism, they create a "field" that can make it politically indispensable for NSGs to reorder their national policies, in ways that pay proper respect to the NGOs' global concerns.

In reply to this whole line of argument, some people might respond, both, that it risks drawing too sharp a distinction between democratic NGOs and nondemocratic NSGs, whose implications could be unhappy; and also, that it exaggerates the purity of the motives-i.e. the disinterestedness-of NGOs.

Both reactions call for some qualifications. As to the first: the question it puts-"Do NGOS truly represent the people whose interests they try to articulate in the World community? Do they represent, even, the views of their own field workers? In the last resort, do they represent anyone but the self-appointed activists who run them and draft their speeches?"-states a legitimate challenge. But this paper was not meant to address that challenge. Clearly, NGOs rely on us taking at face value their claim to represent poor, deprived and tortured fellow humans, or the threatened species and environments of the Globe: to put the point at its weakest, different NGOs have different records in this respect, so the whole issue of the "representativeness" of NGOs deserves fuller discussion.

Similarly, for the second response: when I said, earlier, that Amnesty and Oxfam are not "inherently self-interested parties" to the global debate, my intention was only to contrast our understanding of their speeches and statements with our understanding of speeches and statements made by the representatives of Nation State Governments. Oxfam, Amnesty and other such agencies are advocates for groups of human beings, birds, animals and so on anywhere in the globe, that have no NSG to speak for them, rather than for individuals, corporations and the like within a particular tentorial State: the contrast intended was my present one, between global concerns and local interests. (Here again, the standing of the Vatican as a "Member State" of the UN is anomalous.) On the other hand, the fields of operation of NGOs are, by now, crowded: as a result, there is an active competition for the leadership roles in any particular situation among those NGOs whose areas of concern are relevant to the case. To put the point bluntly: this competition calls into being a new realm for political activity as (e.g.) Greenpeace seeks to preempt a leading role over an environmental issue from (say) the Sien'a Club. The "internal politics" among the NGOs, too, is not the issue for this paper, though it deserves fuller discussion elsewhere.

In conclusion, let us return briefly to the role of professionalism in global affairs. Many of the areas of productive action by Non-Governmental Organizations (arguably) are ones in which the problems at issue lend themselves to professional intervention: areas in which there is enough practical experience, and intellectual consensus, for the solutions to be argued out to a stage at which reasonable agreement is within our grasp. Once issues move beyond the clash of preferences and parties, and become matters for professional analysis-as they often do in, e.g., the field of medicine or public health-the practical task is to persuade Nation State Governments to develop the political will needed to take the steps that the professionally informed community have agreed are needed to handle the problems concerned. So understood, the collaboration of NGOs with members of the UN Secretariat, in preparing the agenda and the papers for large International Conferences, takes on a new aspect.

In this respect, the record of Japanese public servants in the operations of the UN-notably, Mr. Akashi and Ms Ogata-displays a professional excellence that explains the esteem in which they are held by the Secretary-General. In the thankless and endless tasks of the High Commission for Refugees, in the difficult negotiations of the UN Transitional Authority in Cambodia and the Sisyphean demands of the Bosnian conflict-in which every constructive step forward is followed by two frustrating steps back-their record illustrates well the lessons of this essay. It has argued that a capacity for military force is longer the primary measure of political influence on the global scene. As one result, in important ways, demilitarization has strengthened, not weakened, the position of Japan in the UN.

It has also argued that, in pursuit of transnational goals, the evident good faith of non-governmental organizations makes them more influential allies of the technical and professional agencies of the United Nations, than they can ever hope to be in its more purely political Councils. Working together, UNHCR and Oxfam (say) can practice the Politics of Shame, focusing the World's attention on the tragic situations in which-thanks to them-Nation State Governments can go on leaving the sick untreated or the starving hungry, only at the price of worldwide humiliation. Given the current World Disorder and taking all things together, this is one, somewhat promising aspect of an otherwise depressing situation.

5

Services of the NGO's

RECOMMENDATIONS OF THE NGO PLATFORM

On 26-27 September 2006, about 80 European NGO representatives, active against trafficking in human beings, came together at the second La Strada International NGO Platform in Kiev, Ukraine. During these two days, the NGO representatives, among which the nine La Strada member organisations, shared their thoughts and experiences, in particular with regard to their own role in the anti-trafficking field as watchdogs and service providers.

Discussions were linked to the overall theme of the NGO platform 2006: 'anti-trafficking activity towards safe migration perspectives'. This theme was specifically chosen in support of the UN Year of Migration. The following recommendations are based on the outcome of discussions and recommendations made in the various working group sessions.

The NGOs present stressed the need for civil society and NGOs in Europe to be represented and respected as important actors in the anti-trafficking field. NGOs contribute significantly to the fight against trafficking in human beings through their advocacy and information work, their prevention programmes and, in particular, their direct assistance to trafficked persons.

Local, national and European governments should therefore take their consultation and advice into account and actively involve NGOs when developing national and European action plans, policies and infrastructure to address the issue.

Next to Action Plans, NGOs call for the effective implementation of National Referral Mechanisms (NRM). Because NGOs are still the main service providers to trafficked persons and are responsible for national as well as local information and assistance hotlines on the issue of trafficking in human beings, they should play an essential role in National Referral Mechanisms.

A National Referral Mechanism (NRM) is a cooperative framework through which state actors fulfil their obligations to protect and promote the human rights of trafficked persons, coordinating their efforts in a strategic partnership with civil society.

The NGOs that were present believe that in their lobby on NRMs towards governments, they themselves should take into account that:

- Advocacy efforts to support the implementation of a National Referral Mechanism should be based on specific and clear messages that are aimed at the responsible institutes and persons. Messages should be developed and delivered jointly together with other relevant stakeholders such as non-governmental organisations, national rapporteurs, ombudspersons and donors agencies.
- Transnational exchange of experience and cooperation should be used to inform about NGO advocacy efforts by highlighting good practice models abroad as well as by monitoring case studies in countries of destination, transit and origin.
- National action plans should be used as a tool for monitoring the implementation of various components of the National Referral Mechanism.
- The operational and policy aspects of NGO work should be linked by building advocacy arguments and messages informed by both, grassroots service provision work and international standards.
- Within the NRM, activities are monitored and evaluated in order to propose reforms. NGOs should use training

as a measure to build relations with key partners within the NRM and to change attitudes so that later different stakeholders will be more receptive to advocacy messages and recommendations for reform of the NRM.

They call upon other NGOs active in the fight against trafficking in human beings, to take the above into account as well. It is felt that a clear distinction between the role of NGOs and the role of governments should be made. Next to close cooperation with governments, NGOs see their role as monitors (watchdogs) for governmental actions, in particular to ensure that when governments implement their actions, the human rights of trafficked persons are respected. Although the term 'human rights' is very popular these days and frequently used by all actors, the proposed actions, policies and measures are often not based on the essential human rights principles or they do not protect the human rights of the affected groups. In the international anti-trafficking debate, too much focus is still put on repressive strategies to fight trafficking, instead on empowering strategies to prevent trafficking.

NGOs therefore call for the implementation of a human rights based approach in anti-trafficking activity. Governments should implement non-harmful anti-trafficking strategies and address harmful policies and actions. In addition, monitoring and evaluation mechanisms should be established to evaluate actions.

NGOs are aware that also their own actions and organisations should be monitored and evaluated to make sure that their actions are not counterproductive or even negatively affect the rights and position of trafficked persons. To avoid this, they are committed:

- To make more conscious use of human rights based principles in the practice of their organisations/structure, as well as in the decision making process.
- To continue the discussion on a human rights based approach in anti-trafficking initiatives, but also in the way this approach is applied at the NGO organisational level.

- To strengthen and encourage a participatory approach also on advocacy and lobbying level.
- To create a check list of human rights principles that NGOs can use to monitor their programmes and to evaluate how well the principles of a human rights based approach are followed.

The present NGOs call upon other NGOs active in the anti-trafficking field to commit to the above principles as well.

Next to the protection of human rights, the present NGOs also urge governments to address prevention of trafficking further and to focus more on root causes of trafficking in the countries of origin and destination, such as poverty, unequal gender relations, traditional social structures, the lack of safe and legal migration possibilities and the demand for cheap and exploited (irregular) labour.

The issue of trafficking should be looked at from a broader perspective, including other forms of labour exploitation and the human right to migrate. The trafficking debate so far has concentrated too much on trafficking for sexual exploitation and sought solutions in specific prostitution policies. The aspect of safe migration possibilities and labour rights for migrant workers-in order to prevent trafficking-has hardly been explored. The NGO platform therefore urges governments to sign and ratify the International Convention on the Protection of the Rights of All Migrant Workers and Members of Their Families. It also calls for guarantees to safe migration and migrant protection, referring to the guidelines that PICUM developed to protect migrant workers.

In order to address this issue further, NGOs active against trafficking in human beings should:

- Develop closer ties with migrant rights organisations.
- Work towards reliable data collection and 'proof' collection; the NGO Platform should be used to set up a data exchange/collection forum.
- Better use the legal system to claim human rights. If there are no anti-trafficking laws, make better use of labour and human right legislation, for example, the

claim for compensation to be granted to trafficked persons.

- Strengthen advocacy efforts, using public shame, ethical branding, fair trade and other methods to advocate for access to social systems and for obtaining a legal status for undocumented migrants.

NGOs have noticed that the trafficking debate has become highly politicised and polarised. For NGOs, the main goal is the protection of the rights of trafficked persons and affected groups as well as their empowerment. NGOs therefore protest against States and donors who want to impose their political and ideological ideas on NGOs through financial pressure and are concerned about the political, social and cultural pressures NGOs face in countries of origin and destination.

NGOs call for financial support from governments and donor agencies for their work, but believe that NGOs should at all times remain independent from and critical towards governments and donors, regarding existing actions, policies and criteria. In order to improve funding possibilities for anti-trafficking activity, anti-trafficking NGOs should:

- Jointly lobby towards donors for funding for NGOs, in particular for anti-trafficking work.
- Support and cooperate each other in fundraising efforts, but remain critical to partners they cooperate with and the project proposals that are made.
- Establish donor criteria and be critical towards donors and other sources of financing. NGOs should be cautious not to become too dependent on donors and not to automatically accept all criteria donors put on them. NGOs should use negotiations to get funding for the activities they want to implement.
- Try to reach sustainability and try to receive different forms of income.
- Fulfil certain standards, e.g. being a reliable partner for donors and other NGOs.

NGOs further call for structural actions and the minimisation of ad hoc initiatives, set up arbitrarily after public and political debates, such as the actions around the World Football Cup in Germany. The present NGOs believe these actions are less effective and might do more harm than good. Regarding hotlines, anti-trafficking NGOs believe that:

- Hotlines on trafficking issues should be independent, confidential and not temporary, as hotlines need time to develop and become effective.
- Hotlines should be promoted with a strong campaign using various forms of publicity.
- Hotlines should be part of a National Referral Mechanism.
- New problems or developments in the field of trafficking should be linked to existing hotlines.
- Hotline consultation should be linked with other new methods of consultation (e-mail, online counselling), which should be investigated and further developed.
- There is an urgent need for training hotline managers and consultants.

With regard to prevention programmes, NGOs should cooperate closely with other actors. When establishing prevention programmes NGOs should keep in mind that:

- Materials for training and prevention work should be based on reliable research and respond to trends identified through research and service provision.
- Prevention work should ideally be developed and implemented with a participatory approach. The target audience should be actively involved in the design and activities. This way prevention work is not only about information, but also about empowerment and supporting others to be proactive.
- Prevention activities should be regularly monitored and feedback should be requested from target audiences so that materials and methods can be adapted in the future to be more effective.
- Prevention programmes should also ensure motivation and further training for specialists and trainers. For

example, this can be done through participation in international meetings and through facilitated exchange of experiences and good practice.

- Different methods should be developed to reach different audiences. We should consider how best to use media and new technologies in our prevention work.

THE GLOBAL COMPACT AND HUMAN RIGHTS

The Global Compact Office would like to thank the team at Wilton Park and the UK Foreign & Commonwealth Office for putting together this promising conference. Sphere of influence and complicity-core themes at this conference-are key concepts for the Global Compact. "Sphere of influence" is actually a phrase that the Global Compact introduced to the field of corporate citizenship/CSR, and "complicity" is a concept that the Compact has helped to popularize in this context. We welcome the opportunity to discuss the concepts in detail and hope for viable suggestions for how to give them practical meaning for companies and other organizations around the world. We are delighted to be associated with, and to have contributed to the preparations for, this event. We hope to pick up some new ideas to make our own business and human rights work programme more effective.

As important background for this event, we would like to offer the following refresher on the Global Compact, our approach to human rights and the role of the Compact in the context of calls for greater accountability for business.

REFRESHER ON THE GLOBAL COMPACT

The Global Compact was introduced in 1999 because many felt that globalization was not delivering all it had promised. In particular, its benefits were dramatically unevenly distributed. Although the primary responsibility for implementing international agreements on human rights, labour standards, the environment and anti-corruption lies with governments, business was seen as having an important role to play. In fact, one of the founding premises of the GC is that without active involvement of business, there is the danger that universal principles, including those embodied in international human rights instruments, will remain unimplemented.

The Global Compact emphasizes the business case for improved social and environmental performance and business' own operations and activities not the traditional CSR concept that is based on philanthropy. We believe that the largest impact that business can have is through conducting their business in a sustainable way that respects human rights and limits their environmental impact, treats their workers well and avoids corruption.

The Compact, itself, is both a set of universal principles and a network-based multi-stakeholder initiative with a change model for how to raise the level of business' social and environment performance. The Secretary-General derived the principles from international instruments that enjoy wide consensus like the UDHR, ILO Declaration, Rio Declaration, and UN Convention Against Corruption.

Businesses initiate their participation through a commitment by their CEO endorsed by their Board expressing their support for the principles and their intention to work towards their implementation within their own operations. This is a key element of the Compact's leadership model. Effective positive change requires a leadership commitment and it is our intention that change agents inside companies will use their CEO's expression of commitment to help them to more easily make necessary changes inside the company to improve its social and environmental performance.

The Global Compact is not a seal of approval for or endorsement of the companies or other organizations participating in it. Nor is it a regulatory or compliance based model. The Global Compact Office has neither the mandate nor the resources for that. As a result, we encourage improved performance and positive change through the means available to us as an initiative inside the UN Secretariat: learning, dialogue, networks, initiatives, projects and promoting greater transparency around company social and environmental efforts. We also work with the financial incentive system within which companies operate to encourage the mainstream financial community to take into account companies' social and environmental performance in making their valuations.

Global Compact Office was established in July 2000 with less than 50 companies. Today, there are 2268 participating companies in 87 countries, dozens of civil society and labour organizations and more than 40 local networks engaged.

THE GLOBAL COMPACT'S APPROACH TO HUMAN RIGHTS

Two of the Global Compact's ten principles are devoted to human rights. However, the labour standards principles are also human rights related. The two human rights principles are positive and negative, that is, they emphasize doing good as well as not doing harm.

Human rights is a major priority area of the UN Global Compact Office as it remains one of the newest and least familiar for many of the company participants. We've been doing a fair bit of work in this area and plan to continue doing so. We feel we are making an important contribution although much more clearly remains to be done.

Our main partner in all our human rights work has been and will remain the OHCHR. They are clearly the guardians of the two human rights principles. We also work with a number of other organizations in this area, including BLIHR and the Danish Institute for Human Rights.

Located within the UN Secretariat-the Secretary-General's office to be precise-the Global Compact Office must be as pragmatic and non political as possible. We focus on the practical "How" question, namely, how to implement human rights within a business's own operations and activities, especially on what businesses can do to eliminate their potentially negative human rights impact. Two recent publications that we have produced in this area are: Raising the Bar; and Embedding HR in Business Practice. One of our major activities in this area has been fostering tool development and recommending proven tools to help with the implementation process. Rather than reinvent the wheel, we help disseminate information about existing tools with a proven track record, such as the Business & Human Rights Resource Centre's website, the Danish Institute Human Rights Compliance Assessment quick check tool, and the BLIHR matrix. We are also working on a human rights training package and, with partners, on a business guide to human rights impact assessment and, with BLIHR, on guidance for managers on how to implement human rights.

One of our most significant contributions to the area continues to be our efforts to build consensus among companies, other societal actors and even governments that human rights are an important business issue. Our leadership model is key here. The process for initiating involvement (CEO commitment with endorsement from the Board) means that many boardroom and/or senior executive discussions about human rights have taken place because of the Global Compact. Moreover, 2268 companies are on record as having expressed support for and intention to implement human rights. Importantly, these are companies in 87 different countries, helping to demonstrate the universality of human rights. Governments have also collectively and individually recognized the contribution of the Global Compact in a number of contexts, most recently in the 2005 World Summit Outcome document.

We are pleased to report that much learning is going on at the local level. We know that some Global Compact local networks have used our human rights publication as the basis for running their own learning activities on human rights. Many Global Compact local networks have also invited local chapters of human rights NGOs to come and speak with them to help them learn about human rights in a business context. In some countries where governments are not very supportive of human rights, business has been taking a keen interest and are slowly helping their governments to see that human rights are important.

We have also contributed to the business and human rights debate through helping to develop and refine its lexicon. As already mentioned, we helped popularize the concepts of "sphere of influence" and "complicity" as key terms that have helped focus and advance the business and human rights debate.

We also collect and disseminate case studies of the real dilemmas that companies are facing and provide opportunities for companies and others to come together to work on solutions. E.g. Supply chain, business in conflict zones (Enabling economies of peace), managing diversity and non-discrimination, and contributing to OHCHR's consultation process last year. As the UN, we can bring to the table audiences that others sometimes can't.

Is our approach having an impact? McKinsey & Company's impact assessment in 2004 found that the Compact has existential power and has had significant incremental impact in the sense of helping change to happen faster and more easily-which is our modest aim. Among the other findings were that half of all participating companies reported having changed their policies with respect to the principles. Many companies from OECD countries have signed on to Global Compact to learn about how to improve their human rights performance. For nearly two-thirds of the companies from developing countries, the Global Compact is the first corporate citizenship initiative in which they have engaged. Many do so to learn how to improve their social and environmental performance and thus enhance their ability to enter into supplier relationships with larger global firms.

There is no doubt that much more remains to be done. One of our most exciting upcoming challenges is that we're bringing our multi-stakeholder approach to China with a big Summit there later this year.

ROLE OF THE GLOBAL COMPACT IN CONTEXT OF CALLS FOR GREATER LEGAL ACCOUNTABILITY FOR BUSINESS

A word or two is also warranted on the role of the Global Compact in the context of calls for greater legal accountability for business. The first point to note is that the Global Compact is a voluntary initiative without a mandate or resources to monitor compliance.

Nevertheless, protecting the integrity of the UN and of the initiative is a legitimate concern. We therefore introduced a stricter logo protection policy and new integrity measures covering misuse of the GC logo and a complaint procedure for systematic and egregious abuse of the GC's overall aim and principles. The policy goes as far as UN legal office will allow given our status as voluntary initiative of UN Secretariat.

We also introduced a procedural requirement that all company participants communicate to their stakeholders on a regular basis their progress in implementing all ten principles. Companies not doing so for two years in a row are designated "inactive" on our website until they start communicating. This has already started to show results with media calling attention to "inactive" companies, prompting them to start communicating.

Most importantly of all, we cannot emphasize enough that the Global Compact's voluntary initiative is not intended to be a total solution. It is positioned as complementary to and not a substitute for other approaches, including for international law. Human rights issues are complex and a multitude of approaches is clearly needed.

CONCLUSION

The Global Compact is an important tool in the quest to advance the business and human rights agenda. Too often the business and human rights debate is presented as if there is a dichotomy between voluntary and regulatory approaches as if it is either/or. This is a false dichotomy. There is a huge demand for consensus building, tools and practical solution finding. The Global Compact is a key platform that can help in this regard and thereby contribute to better implementation of human rights.

THE INTERNET AND HUMAN RIGHTS: AN OVERVIEW

The Internet is a unique communications medium. Like no other medium before, it allows individuals to express their ideas and opinions directly to a world audience and easily to each other, while allowing access to many more ideas, opinions and information than previous media have allowed. Consequently, there is a vital connection between the Internet and human rights.

The Internet Is a Democratizing Medium, Uniquely Suited to the Promotion of Human Rights, But Threatened by Governmental Restrictions

Through the Internet, citizens from the most repressive regimes are able to find information about matters concerning their own governments and their human rights records that no newspaper may dare print, while denouncing the conditions under which they live, for the world to hear. The Internet allows an intimate look at other countries, other people and other cultures that few before were ever able to attain. This power to give and receive information, so central to any conception of democracy, can be truly achieved on the Internet, as nowhere before.

Further, through the use of encryption technology, citizens can have instantaneous communications with individuals all over the world that are much more resistant to government and private surveillance.

On the Internet, citizens are not mere consumers of content but also creators of content. This fundamental shift in power has created a possibility for every individual to be a publisher. Consequently, the content on the Internet is as diverse as human thought. Individuals and communities have been using the new-found freedom online to link, interact and work collectively in this global work space.

The effect of access to and use of this global interactive medium has been to promote and defend civil and political rights worldwide. This unprecedented power, however, can be very threatening to repressive regimes. The experiences of communities in different countries indicates that few things could be more threatening to authoritarian regimes than access and use of a medium that knows no boundaries and is very hard to control. While traditional methods of censorship-embargoing newspapers and closing down presses-do not work on the Internet, the online censoring techniques that these regimes attempt can be just as destructive.

While the Internet is technologically resistant to government control, it is not immune from such control. Indeed, some countries have been quite sophisticated in exploiting the control and surveillance potential to great effect, at least in the short run. Just because the younger generation may know how to "hack" through proxy servers to avoid censorship does not mean that the youth are safe.

These actions should be understood in the technological context--that such hacking is probably obvious to government system administrators, and may make people vulnerable to being identified and prosecuted. Meanwhile, nations around the world are seeking to exploit the surveillance potential of this new medium, including by asserting control over the design and development of communications networks to maximize their surveillance capabilities.

For these reasons, governments and regional and international bodies should enact enforceable free expression guarantees, promote widespread access to and use of strong cryptographic tools that will enable real security, and provide legal protections of privacy, including controls on government surveillance.

The Internet and Human Rights Work

The Internet is one of the best means for communicating on human rights, because it is inexpensive and global. E-mail makes point-to-point communication between human rights workers and among NGOs (non-governmental organizations) cheap and easy, and allows for better coordination of actions. Furthermore, the Internet has the potential of reaching global audiences, including those most in need of such information. The Internet is important to those working for human rights, as it can provide a secure means of communicating between and coordinating the work of human rights groups. Consequently, human rights activists were among the first to make use of the Internet to--

- Coordinate actions and make contacts. Perhaps the most important application of the Internet in human rights is as a great tool for NGOs and activists to be in touch with each other, to share information privately, and to coordinate actions.

- Expose human rights violations and let people know about them. Many human rights organizations throughout the world have instituted e-mail lists to propagate their press releases, alerts and denunciations vis a vis human rights violations. Many of these groups also use Usenet to post their information, or it is posted there by others, and many groups have instituted web pages to make information available.
- Solicit action. Many organizations now use e-mail to distribute action alerts calling for letters to be written on behalf of specific issues.
- Gather information. The amount of human rights information online is extraordinary-beginning with the University of Minnesota web site, and now with the UNHCHR (United Nations High Commissioner on Human Rights) site online, it's much easier to do human rights research.

By enabling early access to information, immediate dissemination of calls for campaigns, and the organization of wide international pressure, the Internet greatly increases the lobbying capacities of human rights groups.

It is vitally important, therefore, to promote freedom of expression and privacy as central elements of the development of the information society.

Internet Freedom in the US

Unfortunately, the US government's domestic policy has not been fully supportive of human rights on the Internet. The US Congress has twice enacted censorship legislation attempting to control content on the Internet. Under our strong constitutional protection of free speech, these laws have been ruled unconstitutional by the courts. Yet Members of Congress continue to press other restrictive measures, and proposals are pending to make Internet Service Providers (ISPs) liable for removing allegedly illegal or improper content. On the privacy side, the Communications Assistance for Law Enforcement Act of 1994 (CALEA) requires that telecommunications systems be designed to accommodate government surveillance, and that law has been perverted by the Department of Justice and the Federal Communications Commission to not merely preserve but to enhance government wiretap capabilities. Only recently has the US government begun to turn away from its efforts to control the spread of encryption, which is crucial to security and privacy on the Internet. Still, officials in the Justice Department are trying to preserve their access to decryption keys, and the surveillance debate in the US is not over. Meanwhile, the US government refuses to publicly discuss its international eavesdropping activities, amid growing domestic and international concern over the nature of surveillance in a digital world and, in particular, the US government's "Echelon" surveillance system.

Internet Access Is Important to the Promotion of Human Rights

The most often disregarded impediment to the achievement of the Internet's democratic potential is the problem of access. Accessing the Internet requires either the possession of a computer and payment to an Internet Service Provider or access to a facility where one can connect. This means that, generally, only the affluent will have access. Governments can control freedom of expression of sections of the population by hindering their access to the Internet. This may be done directly by imposing high taxes on computer products and supporting telephone monopolies that keep phone rates high and thus discourage the use of the Internet, or indirectly by failing to support community centres where people may have low-cost access to the Internet.

However, augmented Net access without civil liberties guarantees ? in technology and in law ? may not benefit individuals and may be coupled with government control and extended surveillance capability.

Freedom of Expression

The Universal Declaration, the European Convention and other international human rights agreements enshrine the rights to freedom of expression and access to information. These core documents explicitly protect freedom of expression "regardless of frontiers," a phrase especially pertinent to the global Internet:

> *"Everyone has the right to freedom of opinion and expression; this right includes freedom to hold opinions without interference and to seek, receive and impart information and ideas through any media, and regardless of frontiers." Article 19, Universal Declaration of Human Rights.*
>
> *"Everyone shall have the right to freedom of expression; this right shall include freedom to seek, receive, and impart information and ideas of all kinds, regardless of frontiers, either orally, in writing or in print, in the form of art, or through any other media of his choice." Article 19, International Covenant on Civil and Political Rights.*
>
> *"Everyone has the right to freedom of expression. This right shall include freedom to hold opinions and to receive and impart information and ideas without interference by public authority and regardless of borders." Article 10, European Convention for the Protection of Human Rights and Fundamental Freedoms.*

No matter what the means, government restrictions on speech or access to speech of others violate basic freedom of expression protections. In addition to direct government censorship of Internet communications, or privatized censorship, freedom of speech in the Internet is threatened by diverse factors.

Blocking, filtering, and labelling techniques can restrict freedom of expression and limit access to information. Government-mandated use of blocking, filtering, and label systems violates basic international human rights protections. Global rating or labelling systems squelch the free flow of information. Efforts to force all Internet speech to be labelled or rated according to a single classification system distort the fundamental cultural diversity of the Internet and will lead to domination of one set of political or moral viewpoints. Diversity and user choice are essential: To the extent that individuals choose to employ filtering tools, it is vital that they have access to a wide variety of such tools.

"Self-regulatory" controls over Internet content, which have been promoted by some as an alternative to government regulation, ought not to place private ISPs in the role of police officers for the Internet. With regards to content, what is being suggested in the name of "self-regulation" is not that ISPs should as a group regulate their own behaviour, but rather that they should regulate the speech of their customers. This is not true "self-regulation."

The role of an Internet Service Provider is crucial for access to the Internet and because of the crucial role that they play, ISPs have been targeted by law enforcement agencies in many countries to act as content censors. While ISPs ought to provide law enforcement reasonable assistance in investigating criminal activity, confusing the role of private companies and police authorities risks substantial violation of individual civil liberties.

Privacy

The Universal Declaration, the European Convention and international human rights instruments enshrine the right to privacy. These core documents explicitly protect the privacy of correspondence and communication:

> *"No one shall be subjected to arbitrary interference with his privacy, family, home or correspondence, nor to attacks upon his honour and reputation. Everyone has the right to the protection of the law against such interference or attacks." Article 12, Universal Declaration of Human Rights*

> *"No one shall be subjected to arbitrary or unlawful interference with his privacy, family, home or correspondence, nor to unlawful attacks on his honour and reputation." Article 17, International Covenant on Civil and Political Rights*

> *"Everyone has the right to respect for his private and family life, his home and his correspondence."*

Article 8, European Convention for the Protection of Human Rights and Fundamental Freedoms

Privacy is becoming increasingly important for citizens in the information society. Electronic communications can be very easily intercepted by anyone who wants to. Sending an e-mail message is thus the equivalent of sending a postcard. In the human rights arena especially, many matters discussed among NGOs are extremely confidential. Names of witnesses to human rights violations, for example, need to be kept from those who would harm them. Repressive governments commonly use their intelligence services to tap the phone communications of human rights groups and intercept their mail. It is very likely that they are also intercepting electronic mail.

How Privacy can be Protected on the Internet

Unlike phone calls and paper mail, however, electronic mail can be easily encrypted so that only those to whom it is directed can read it. This means that anyone, such as NGOs, wanting to communicate delicate information freely can do so, without having to fear the consequences of others, such as governments, accessing it. Therefore, we believe that policies concerning cryptography should be based on the fundamental right to engage in private communication. Unfortunately, national governments have already taken steps to detain and harass users and developers of cryptography. Nonetheless, strong cryptography is already in use by human rights advocates and its further widespread use should be affirmatively promoted. We oppose efforts that would lead to the development of communications infrastructures designed for surveillance.

Anonymity

Central to free expression and the protection of privacy is the right to express political beliefs without fear of retribution and to control the disclosure of personal identity. Protecting the right of anonymity is therefore an essential goal for the protection of personal freedoms in the online world.

The right of anonymity is recognized in law and accepted by custom. It has been an integral part of the growth and development of the Internet. Some governments are working to extend techniques for anonymity. But other efforts are underway to establish mandatory identification requirements and to limit the use of techniques that protect anonymity. For example, the G-8 recently considered a proposal to require caller identification for Internet users. Some local governments have also tried to adopt legislation that would prohibit access to the Internet without the disclosure of personal identity.

Governments should not require the identification of Internet users or restrict the ability to express political beliefs on the Internet anonymously. Efforts to develop new techniques to protect anonymity and identity should be encouraged. ISPs should not establish unnecessary identification requirements for customers and should, wherever practicable, preserve the right of users to access the Internet anonymously.

Summary and Policy Recommendations

When formulating policy with respect to the Internet, governments should be guided by certain core principles ?

- Prohibiting prior censorship of on-line communication.
- Requiring that laws restricting the content of on-line speech distinguish between the liability of content providers and the liability of data carriers.
- Insisting that on-line free expression not be restricted by indirect means such as excessively restrictive governmental or private controls over computer hardware or software, the telecommunications infrastructure, or other essential components of the Internet.
- Including in the global Internet development process citizens from countries and regions that are currently unstable economically, have insufficient infrastructure, or lack sophisticated technology.
  * To ensure that Internet services are designed to ensure universal access, governments should provide full disclosure of information infrastructure development plans and encourage democratic participation in all aspects of the development process.

  * They should also advocate widespread use of the Internet and strive to provide adequate training.
  * In addition, governments should urge citizens to take an active role in public affairs by providing access to government information online.
- Prohibiting discrimination on the basis of race, colour, sex, language, religion, political or other opinion, national or social origin, property, birth or other status.
- Ensuring that personal information generated on the Internet for one purpose is not used for an unrelated purpose or disclosed without the person's informed consent and enabling individuals to review personal information on the Internet and to correct inaccurate information.
- Allowing on-line users to encrypt their communications and information without restriction.
- In order to guarantee the privacy of on-line communication, governments should put in place enforceable legal protections against unauthorized scrutiny and use by private or public entities of personal information on the Internet.
  * In addition, governments should conduct investigations on the Internet pursuant only to lawful authority and subject to independent judicial review.

6

International Human Rights Law and NGO's

INTRODUCTION

The activities of non-governmental organisations are generally recognised as an important element not only in the initial establishment of a genuine democracy but also in ensuring that, once achieved, it remains healthy and flourishing. The contribution which such organisations make is often political in the broader and non-party sense but it is also manifested in their pursuit of a vast array of interests-such as culture, recreation, sport and social and humanitarian assistance, to say nothing of the rights of those at work and the simple personal fulfilment of those who belong to the bodies concerned-that underpin the vitality of civil society.

However, the essential role played by non-governmental organisations, although not open to question, is not one that is appreciated by all States at all times, not least because it does entail an unambiguous commitment to democracy. Nonetheless realising and sustaining such a commitment is an objective of paramount importance for global and regional organisations such as the United Nations, the African Union, the Council of Europe, the Organisation for Security and Cooperation in Europe and the Organisation of American States and it is thus not surprising that provisions guaranteeing and promoting the rights of non-governmental organisations have readily found a place in many of the instruments adopted by all these bodies.

The principal basis for securing the position of non-governmental organisations rests upon the guarantee of freedom of association but there are also a limited number of instruments directed specifically to such organisations and the latter are also able to rely upon other human rights guarantees that have a particular bearing on the pursuit of their activities. This chapter focuses primarily upon the nature and scope of the international guarantee afforded to freedom of association, particularly the one found in the European Convention on Human Rights, but interweaves into the discussion an account of the provisions in international instruments that are directed specifically to non-governmental organisations.

It first reviews the various instruments in which the guarantee of freedom of association is provided, then looks at the way in which the term 'association' is understood by those bodies charged with overseeing the effective implementation of this freedom and goes on to consider those aspects of it which the latter have identified as of particular significance. These aspects include the breadth of the categories of persons on whom freedom of association is conferred, the narrow range of circumstances in which an association's objectives might be considered objectionable, the nature of the rights that arise once an association has been formed, the general impermissibility of imposing penalties on persons solely on account of their membership of an association, the limited scope for regulating the activities of associations and the requirements governing how this should be conducted, the constraints applicable to any involvement by public bodies in the activities of associations and the particular considerations affecting the enjoyment of this freedom by public employees.

These different elements all make an indispensable contribution to the enjoyment of a freedom that is meant to be extensive and thereby play a vital part in the strengthening of civil society. However, as freedom of association continues in practice to be subject to restrictions that are impermissible (whether for substantive or procedural reasons, or for both of these), the chapter concludes with a brief review of some of the global and regional procedures available to challenge them.

SOURCES OF THE GUARANTEE

Global and regional human rights instruments contain a number of general guarantees of freedom of association which are addressed to persons forming bodies with all the concerns already mentioned-and many more besides-and the protection provided by the provisions concerned is reinforced in a number of other undertakings directed to associations with a particular type of membership or objective. The principal general guarantees are found in Article 20 of the Universal Declaration of Human Rights, Article 22 of the International Covenant on Civil and Political Rights, Article 10 of the African Charter on Human and Peoples' Rights, Article 16 of the American Convention on Human Rights, Article 11 of the European Convention on Human Rights and an undertaking made by States belonging to the Organisation for Security and Cooperation in Europe.

These guarantees are supplemented by provisions in the same instruments requiring that they be secured without any distinction such as race, colour, sex, language, religion, political or other opinion, national or social origin, property, birth or other status, as well as by specific guarantees against discrimination in the case of race, colour, descent, national or ethnic origin and gender that are to be found in the International Convention on the Elimination of All Forms of Racial Discrimination and the Convention on the Elimination of All Forms of Discrimination against Women.

Apart from the Universal Declaration, the African Charter and the American Convention, all of the general guarantees make specific mention of the freedom applying to the formation of trade unions. However, the references to unions in these guarantees are intended only to clarify the position rather than to limit their scope in some way. There are, however, several guarantees of freedom of association specifically directed to trade unions, notably Article 8 of the International Covenant on Economic, Social and Cultural Rights, Article 5 of the European Social Charter and the Convention Concerning Freedom of Association and Protection of the Right to Organise of the International Labour Organization, as well as an undertaking given by members of the OSCE. Furthermore there are a number of other guarantees concerned with the enjoyment of freedom of association by particular sectors in a society, namely, children, environmental campaigners, human rights defenders, judges, members of national minorities, migrant workers, refugees and stateless persons, as well as for non-governmental bodies of an international character. Moreover the guarantee-in Article 15 of the International Covenant on Economic, Social and Cultural Rights-of the right to take part in cultural life undoubtedly includes the possibility of forming associations for this purpose. In addition, although not formally a guarantee, it should be noted that the Council of Europe has also articulated some Fundamental Principles on the Legal Status of Non-governmental Organisations in Europe ('Fundamental Principles').

Some of the specific guarantees, particularly those relating to trade unions, undoubtedly require recognition of certain rights over and above those to be enjoyed by associations generally and it is with the latter that this chapter is especially concerned. Furthermore not all of the guarantees entail legal obligations but treaties such as the two International Covenants and those adopted by regional organisations are binding under international law on the States that are parties to them.

Nevertheless the other instruments not only reinforce the significance of the political commitment to secure freedom of association but can also help to elucidate how it should be implemented in particular contexts. However, given the lack of specificity in the language used in most of the guarantees, the most helpful source of guidance in determining the scope of the general freedom of association is to be derived from the case law generated under those instruments which enable individual or collective claims to be brought. Of all of those instruments, it is only in respect of the Convention Concerning Freedom of Association and Protection of the Right to Organise and the European Convention that there is at present a significant body of case law. Although the approach in both of them is broadly the same, this chapter will focus mainly on that relating to the latter instrument in order to ensure that there is no confusion between the general obligations and those of concern only with the treatment of trade unions.

Nevertheless it also needs to be kept in mind that this case law, notwithstanding the considerable benefit to be derived from it in understanding what freedom of association entails, addresses only those issues which have already been brought before the various tribunals. Although these are undoubtedly important ones, this does not mean that the full extent of the protection which States are legally obliged to afford to associations has yet been fully clarified. Indeed it remains the case that provisions such as Article 11 of the European Convention have not received the same degree of attention from international and regional tribunals as have many other rights and freedoms. The fact that this has begun to change in recent years means that the main elements of this freedom can now be readily discerned but this should not encourage a reluctance to draw upon other potentially useful sources of guidance as to how to interpret and apply the general guarantees.

Moreover it should not be overlooked that one possible explanation for the relative dearth of applications involving Article 11 of the European Convention may well be the limited controls applied in many European countries with respect to this freedom and that this is something that should be more generally emulated. It should also be recalled that interference with the activities of associations may well engage other legally binding rights and freedoms-notably, rights to a fair hearing and peaceful enjoyment of possessions and freedom of assembly, conscience, correspondence and expression-and appropriate account is taken of these in the discussion below.

CONCEPT OF ASSOCIATION

Although the role of non-governmental organisations has been, and continues to be, important for the elaboration, implementation and protection of human rights, specific reference to them is not frequently found in human rights treaties. Indeed this term is only used in two of them and then only with regard to the procedural competence to submit applications or petitions in respect of alleged violations of the substantive rights. The failure to recognise them may have implications not only for their ability to complain to some supervisory bodies but also to rely on the substantive rights afforded by some treaties. Nevertheless the ability of most non-governmental organisations to exist and to operate is generally well-secured by the extensive guarantees of freedom of association.

As with all terms found in international human rights instruments, the concept of 'association' is something that has to be accorded an autonomous meaning; national provisions cannot, therefore, be conclusive in determining whether something is or is not an association for the purpose of guarantees such as that in Article 11 of the European Convention. This not only means that it is inappropriate to attach too much significance to the language used in particular laws when trying to ascertain whether the exercise of freedom of association is involved but also that the conditions which laws may impose before something will be regarded as an association will not necessarily be regarded as acceptable from the international perspective. Certainly a very inclusive approach is taken at the international level to the sort of gatherings of persons that are protected by freedom of association guarantees. However, in order for those guarantees to become applicable, it would have to be demonstrated that the grouping concerned is something more than a body of persons who have a common objective since it has already been established that Article 11 does not seek to protect a mere gathering of people desirous of sharing each other's company and a different approach is unlikely to be taken to the interpretation of other guarantees.

Furthermore some forms of protest action such as demonstrations and public meetings, albeit gatherings of a more organised character, would still not be an exercise of freedom of association because of their essentially transient nature; they would, however, be regarded as activities coming under the protection of freedom of assembly, the second limb of that provision. What is thus required is that the gathering not only have been formed with the object of pursuing certain aims but also that it has a degree of stability as regards its existence and thus have some kind of institutional (albeit not formal) structure to which the persons comprising it can really be regarded as belonging.

In many instances associations will be bodies with a formal status-namely, legal personality-and this will also be what the founders of most of them want. Nevertheless the international guarantees are not limited to such bodies but also apply to groupings of an informal character so long as they have, or are meant to have, more than a fleeting existence. This is a necessary consequence of the general freedom of those associating to determine the basis on which they do so. The fact that some protection is available to the latter bodies will, of course, be particularly significant where a formal status has been improperly denied to persons who have formed an association but it will also be important where it is not considered necessary by those establishing certain groupings that they should also have a formal legal character. It is thus not open to a State to require that freedom of association only be exercised by the establishment of an entity with legal personality.

Apart from the unacceptability of common objectives that are unconstitutional or illegal, the only qualification on what might be the aim of a grouping in order for this to be accepted as an exercise of freedom of association is that it is either intended not to be a profitmaking body or, where trading activities are undertaken, any profits accruing are ploughed back into the pursuit of the common objectives rather than distributed to its membership. This is because this freedom is essentially a civil and political right rather than an economic one. Nevertheless this does not mean that an association cannot exist to advance the interests of its members; the specific inclusion of the formation of trade unions within the scope of the guarantee is the clearest indication that the securing of benefits for those who belong to an association is a legitimate objective and these benefits can be economic as much as moral, physical, social or spiritual. However, if the principal objective is trading or some other form of business activity then protection for the interests of those belonging to the body concerned should be sought in guarantees such as the right to property rather than freedom of association. The fact that express reference is only made in general guarantees such as Article 11 of the European Convention to only one form of association, namely, trade unions, might lead to the conclusion that these either enjoyed a privileged position or that this provisions was not intended to cover all other forms of association. However, as the European Court first made clear in United Communist Party of Turkey and Others v Turkey, the special mention of them is no more than a reminder that they are within the definition of associations; the conjunction 'including' in Article 11 'clearly shows that trade unions are but one example among others of the form in which the right to freedom of association may be exercised'. This conclusion was reinforced in the context of that case, which concerned the dissolution of a political party, by the incontestable view that political parties were 'essential to the proper functioning of democracy in the Convention system' and they could thus not be excluded from the scope of Article 11. Nevertheless it is evident that no category of association is a priori denied the protection afforded by the general guarantees.

Some entities that may be treated as associations under domestic law will not, however, generally be so regarded for the purpose of Article 11 or other freedom of association guarantees. These are the many bodies which are established by law and to which doctors, lawyers, architects and other members of professions are often required to join. The European Court has regarded these as being public law bodies designed to regulate a particular profession and, as such, they will not normally attract the protection of Article 11 or other freedom of association guarantees. A similar view has also been taken of bodies such as works councils which may be required under employment legislation to be established to secure staff participation in the management at a particular work place; this is the sole basis on which the 'members' are brought together and the compulsion in their formation is sufficient to preclude such councils from being associations.

The fact that groupings are established pursuant to a legislative requirement does not, however, necessarily mean that they will not be treated as associations for the purpose of international guarantees. Thus in Chassagnou and Others v France the Court had no hesitation in regarding as associations those bodies which had been established for the purpose of organising hunting where these were 'composed of hunters or owners of land or hunting rights, and therefore, of private individuals, all of whom, a priori, wish to pool their land for the purpose of hunting.' It did not matter that the way in which these associations operated was subject to the supervisory power of the prefect as this was not in itself sufficient for them to be integrated into the structures of the State. It was, however, significant that these bodies did not enjoy. Attempts to exclude a particular body from the scope of the freedom of association guarantee by stipulating, as in this case, that it is 'public' or 'para-administrative' will thus not be effective if that is not actually an accurate reflection of its essential character.

The compulsion to belong to bodies such as professional associations and works councils can have the potential to encroach upon this freedom-as well as others such as conscience and expression-because of the constraint that might be imposed upon the manifestation of beliefs and opinions by their members. Nevertheless such a problem does not tend to arise in practice because the bodies involved are primarily concerned with regulatory issues and do not have any monopoly over representing the interests and views of their members. It should also be noted that voluntary groupings established within these bodies-such as a bar association's human rights committee-could be regarded as an association enjoying the protection of Article 11 and other freedom of association guarantees. This is because they will be concerned with promoting the objectives of those belonging to it rather than with the regulation of their professional conduct.

THE RIGHT TO FOUND AND TO BELONG

The ability to form and join associations is something that the general guarantees all provide as being open to 'everyone' within a State's jurisdiction and the scope for imposing limitations on this capacity is quite limited. 'Everyone' certainly means legal as well as natural persons as association is not one of the rights or freedoms that are capable of being exercised only by human beings. The only exception in this regard would be public bodies since these are a part of the State which is bound to secure freedom of association rather than beneficiaries of this right.

The unqualified nature of the formulation in all instruments means that the freedom should be exercisable by children as much as by adults, without needing to rely on the specific guarantees in respect of the former in the Convention on the Rights of the Child and the African Charter on the Rights and Welfare of the Child. Nevertheless this would not preclude the adoption of protective measures to ensure that they are not exploited or exposed to moral and related dangers, so long as the total exclusion of the ability to associate did not result. Such measures, insofar as they are proportionate and meet the requirements of legal certainty, could be justified as a restriction on their freedom pursuant to provisions such as Article 11(2).

However, in judging the appropriateness of any such measures account would have to be taken of the need stipulated by the Convention on the Rights of the Child to respect 'the evolving capacities of the child' which would mean that the effect of any restrictions that might be adopted would undoubtedly have to be diminished as those affected grow older.

The inclusive nature of 'everyone' would also mean that freedom of association can, in principle, be exercised by people who are not actually citizens of the country concerned (whether they are citizens of another country or stateless persons). Article 16 of the European Convention does accept the possibility of some restrictions being imposed on the political activity of those who are not citizens and this is defined to cover freedom of association. However, in order to be acceptable, such restrictions ought to be compatible with the Convention's overall objectives of political democracy, freedom and the rule of law and they ought not to be disproportionate. It might, therefore, be possible to justify the exclusion of persons who are not citizens from membership of national political parties but it would certainly be harder to do so where the body was concerned only with local or non-party issues, particularly if those affected were established residents there.

There is also likely to be a reluctance to accept restrictions as being justified under Article 16 where they relate to persons from a country with which the one imposing them has close political and institutional links. Moreover restrictions on non-citizens forming or joining associations with no political objectives-such as those concerned with sport and culture-could hardly be defended by invoking Article 1667. There is no comparable restriction to Article 16 in the other general guarantees of freedom of association but the International Convention on the Elimination of All Forms of Racial Discrimination does exclude differential treatment between citizens and non-citizens from its definition of discrimination, those concerned with refugees and stateless persons sets the freedom enjoyed by certain foreign nationals as regards 'non-political and non-profit-making associations and trade unions' as the standard to be met and the right accorded by the International Convention on the Protection of the Rights of All Migrant Workers and Members of their Families is limited to trade unions and certain forms of associations and not all migrant workers can form (as opposed to join) them. It is thus unlikely that some restriction on the political aspect of associational activity in respect of noncitizens might not be considered compatible with the freedom accorded by the other, ostensibly unrestricted, general guarantees but it seems improbable that anything going beyond the approach suggested appropriate for Article 16 of the European Convention would be considered acceptable.

Freedom of association entails the ability both to form associations with others and to seek to join existing ones. However, the latter freedom amounts only to a restriction on the power of the State to impose unjustified restrictions on the ability of persons-as defined above-to seek membership of an association; it is improbable that the guarantee would be construed as conferring any general right on them to join one against the wishes of its members. The matter has so far not been directly addressed by the European Court but this seems to be the inevitable conclusion of existing case law restricting the circumstances in which someone can be required to belong to an association; compulsion to admit members would effectively amount to the same thing since it would be denying those who already belong to an association the freedom to choose with whom they wish to associate. Nevertheless there would be good justification for constraining the freedom of existing members of an association to determine whom to admit as new members where this was done in order to fulfil obligations to prevent discrimination on any inadmissible ground and thereby protect the rights of others, as permitted by the second paragraph of Article 1175.

A person's imprisonment is likely to be a constraint on his or her ability to take a full part in the activities of an association but this should not otherwise be an obstacle to his or her continued membership of it and involvement in its affairs; it would be very difficult to demonstrate that a restriction on freedom of association which went beyond the inevitable impracticality of attending meetings was something really needed for the purposes of confinement and that is the test by which the impact of a deprivation of liberty on other human rights must be judged. Nevertheless it is possible that some limits could be imposed on a person's exercise of freedom of association as a penalty for certain conduct, provided that a legitimate aim for them could be demonstrated and that they were sufficiently carefully drawn to avoid being challenged for a lack of proportionality. Thus one of the penalties imposed on a Belgian newspaper editor who had collaborated with the German occupying authorities during the Second World War was a prohibition for life on involvement in the administration, management or direction of a professional or non-profit making association or the leadership of a political association.

The principle of such a penalty was not specifically dealt with by the European Commission in De Becker v Belgium but it did consider other such indefinite restrictions affecting the applicant's freedom of expression could not be justified in so far as they covered non-political matters; the scope of the restriction was simply too broad. The issue never went before the European Court as the applicant applied to have the case struck off after the restrictions on his civil and political rights had been withdrawn and the law permitting such penalties had been modified so that they would apply only for fixed periods determined according to the seriousness of the offence. In these circumstances it was not surprising that the Commission did not object to the case being struck off. However, it is evident that the Court will require very cogent justification for such restrictions on the exercise of freedom of association and it is unlikely that they would be seen as acceptable where their scope did not correspond to the nature of the offence giving rise to them or they lasted for an undue length of time.

There is no indication in case law or other practice in respect of treaties guaranteeing freedom of association as to the acceptability of imposing a minimum number of founders before an association can established. However, the Council of Europe's Fundamental Principles, while stating that 'Two or more persons should be able to establish a membership-based NGO', does accept the possibility that a higher number might be required 'where legal personality is to be acquired, but this number should not be set at a level that discourages the establishment of an NGO'. This qualification took account of the fact that higher numbers were in fact required in the law of some of the States involved in the adoption of the Fundamental Principles. However, while a certain threshold might be appropriate where the entity then became eligible for certain exceptional benefits, it seems questionable whether a requirement of more than two-even where legal personality is being acquired-is a restriction that is really compatible with freedom of association, especially since incorporation in a commercial context can often be undertaken by an individual and no particular case other than control has been identified as the rationale for insisting upon it.

Although in practice most of the associations which are formed or joined are likely to be in the State where the persons concerned reside or are present, the freedom guaranteed by Article 11 would also extend to the creation and membership of associations in other countries and this could be restricted by reference only to the same considerations that govern regulation.

OBJECTIVES

Apart from the instruments concerned with trade unions or devoted to particular groups of person, no substantive limitations are expressly placed on the type of objectives that might be pursued by associations. However, while none of the guarantees are framed in absolute terms, neither the requirement to abide by law found in the African Charter nor the broad grounds of limitations found in instruments such as the International Covenant, the Convention on the Rights of the Child, the American Convention and the European Convention actually afford much indication as to what precisely will be regarded as objectionable.

This is a matter of concern for those who would associate-particularly where a formal process of approval or registration must be followed in order to establish an association as a legal entity-but it has also proved problematic for States in Europe on a number of occasions as the European Court has found restrictions imposed by them on the objectives of associations to be excessive and thus a violation of Article 11 of the European Convention. Nevertheless the jurisprudence which has emerged from the challenge to these restrictions now affords considerable guidance both as to what can legitimately be treated as unacceptable-with particular emphasis being placed on respect for the principles of legality and democracy-and as to the equally important basis on which any assessment of objectives for this purpose should be carried out.

LEGALITY

The starting point with respect to objectives is actually quite clear; an association should be able to pursue any activity which individuals alone are able to pursue since a grouping of individuals with the same objective does not thereby make that objective inherently objectionable. Indeed to accept the latter view would be to negate the very concept of freedom of association as a means for like-minded persons to come together. So it follows from this that, so long as the activities or objects are lawful, then it should be possible for an association to be formed to undertake or pursue them. Although an association cannot be formed to pursue specifically unlawful objectives, it should be borne in mind, when determining what conduct is unlawful in this context, that the permitted restrictions on internationally guaranteed rights and freedoms must also not be exceeded and thus make it impossible for an association to be established to pursue objects that are entirely legitimate. No blank cheque is thus given to States that would allow them to make unlawful anything to which they object.

Even where a particular activity is rendered unlawful without meeting the objection that this is through an improper use of State power, this status does not necessarily mean that the activity cannot still in some way shape the objectives of a would-be association. Certainly it is, in principle, perfectly proper for a body to be established to pursue a change in the law, so long as the intention is to do this only by lawful means. Recognition of this can be seen in X v United Kingdom in which it was found that the scope of certain offences concerned with homosexual relations was not such as to prevent the advocacy of reform of the criminal law. On the other hand, the fact that the applicant's object in Lavisse v France did not appear to be confined to such advocacy meant that no objection was raised to the refusal of the registration of an association to promote surrogate motherhood; the endorsement of surrogacy could be regarded as inciting the commission of the offence of abandoning children. Nevertheless the European Commission in that case regarded it as significant that this refusal-which meant that the association could not acquire legal personality-did not prevent the body from promoting a change in the law on this matter; it is thus implicit in the ruling that a refusal of registration to an association which merely sought to promote such a change would be incompatible with Article 1194. Similar objections that an association would cross the line between promoting a change in the law and promoting a breach of it were raised with respect to an association which wanted to promote the use of cannabis in Finland where such use was at the time a crime; in many respects the association concerned could be regarded as amounting to no more than a conspiracy to commit this very crime and thus could be seen as going well beyond advocacy of change.

The protection for the ability to propose changes in the established position can even extend to, and include, the very nature of the existing constitutional structure of a State. Thus in the European Court was not prepared simply to accept that objection could be taken to the applicant party's proposal for a federal system-in which Turks and Kurds would be represented on an equal footing and on a voluntary basis-because this would change the existing constitutional arrangements. Its reluctance to find such an objective inadmissible stemmed from the importance to be attached to political pluralism in applying the European Convention (and indeed other international human rights guarantees). On this basis it concluded that the fact that It is thus generally impossible to immunise matters from change through according them constitutional status.

DEMOCRATIC MEANS AND OUTCOME

However, there is an important qualification on the freedom to campaign for change in the legal and constitutional basis of the State at the end of the European Court's conclusion in the judgment just cited, namely, that the proposed change must not actually be anti-democratic. This qualification is both a corollary of the requirement that restrictions on freedoms such as that of association must be necessary in a democratic society and a reflection of the unambiguous stipulation in Article 17 of the European Convention that nothing in that instrument is to be interpreted as implying 'any right to engage in any activity or perform any act aimed at the destruction of any of the rights and freedoms' set forth in it. The qualification on the freedom to advocate change has subsequently been given some elaboration by the European Court in Refah Partisi (The Welfare Party) and Others v Turkey, demonstrating that it is in fact comprised of two elements, namely, that firstly the means used to that end must in every respect be legal and democratic; secondly the change proposed must itself be compatible with fundamental democratic principles.

Nevertheless it is a qualification that should not be taken entirely at face value. In the first place, although the insistence on the means being democratic rightly entails a process that respects political pluralism, the requirement of lawfulness must still be read subject to the need for any restrictions that ought to be observed being themselves compatible with international human rights standards; it is certainly conceivable that the means which have been rendered unlawful are in fact well-established elements of Convention rights or freedoms and this cannot be an acceptable constraint on the freedom to advocate change. Moreover the qualification in a concurring opinion by Judges Ress and Rozakis ought also to be noted, namely, that insufficient account is taken in the Court's formulation of the scale of the violation of the law. Certainly this must be correct as far as the sanction of dissolution is applied for the occurrence of such violations that are minor since otherwise the well-established principle of proportionality would not be respected. Nevertheless this does not affect the general inadmissibility of an association seeking to use unlawful means to achieve its objectives.

There should also be some concern about the way in which the second aspect of the qualification on the freedom to advocate change is applied, even though there is no basis for disputing the European Court's view that: a political party whose leaders incite recourse to violence or put forward a policy which fails to respect democracy or which is aimed at the destruction of democracy and the flouting of the rights and freedoms recognised in a democracy cannot lay claim to the Convention's protection against penalties imposed on those grounds.

The need for concern arises from the fact that it is not generally going to be self-evident that the objectives of an association are necessarily anti-democratic or violent and thus inherently objectionable. It is true that there were some early cases in which it was accepted that a State could, without further justification, object to bodies that had as their aim the promotion of fascist or communist ideology because these were organisations that were automatically to be regarded as being against the constitution and democratic values but the rulings in them now have to be approached with some care as more recent decisions demonstrate that over-simplistic conclusions can be drawn too readily about the possible threat posed by an association's stated objectives, especially where the latter use terms or concepts which are open to a pejorative construction but that is not their only possible meaning.

Thus in Vogt v Germany the European Court took into account the fact that the communist party had not actually been banned in the course of finding that the applicant's dismissal as a schoolteacher because of her membership of, and active role within, that party could not be necessary in a democratic society. It accepted that the dismissal was an act motivated by the legitimate aim of protecting constitutional democracy but the Court emphasised, that in determining the justifiability of such a step, the focus had to be on individual conduct and not abstract aims. In examining the former, it was evident not only that the applicant in this case had never confused her political and working lives-by using the classroom to promote party ideas-but also that she had asserted her belief in the German constitutional order.

Furthermore the absence of a formal ban on the party made it even harder to conclude that there was any danger being posed to that constitutional order by the employment as a teacher of someone who belonged to that party. The Court in that case was not actually concerned with whether it would have been acceptable then in Germany to have banned the party but the importance that was attached to what it did, rather than conclusions to be drawn from its general objectives, would certainly have made it very unlikely that a cogent case could have been made for the imposition of a ban; whatever suppositions there might have been about the nature of the communist party's objectives, it would at that time have been scarcely credible, given the way it actually operated, to regard it as being anti-constitutional in practice.

Similarly, while in Refah Partisi (The Welfare Party) and Others v Turkey it was generally accepted that preserving secularism was necessary for the protection of the democratic system in Turkey, it was only in the particular context of remarks showing a wish to bring into being an order based on religious rules that the advocacy of changes in the law to take account of certain religious concerns-such as with respect to the wearing of Islamic headscarves and the organisation of working hours in the public sector to accommodate prayers-would necessarily be regarded as threatening secularism and thus be objectionable.

Reaching Conclusions about Objectives

The danger of authorities being too ready to assume the worst about the objectives of an association is all too real. Certainly there have already been a significant number of cases, in a relatively short period of time, in which the European Court has found that they had been precipitous in reaching the conclusion that what certain associations were proposing to do posed a serious threat of unconstitutional or unlawful, notwithstanding that the particular restrictions involved were themselves entirely legitimate.

Thus in United Communist Party of Turkey and Others v Turkey, the Court rejected the view that either the party's choice of name or certain statements in its programme about the treatment of Kurds in themselves demonstrated a real threat to either Turkish society or the Turkish State as to make its objectives inadmissible.

The issue of the name had arisen out of the fact that it included the word 'communist' and there was a law making it an offence to carry on political activities inspired by communist ideology. However, the objection taken to this by the authorities was partly unsustainable because that law had been repealed but, even if that had not been the case, the Turkish Constitutional Court had itself concluded that the mere choice of name did not mean that the party was seeking 'to establish the domination of one social class over the others' Indeed it was evident that this particular party satisfied the requirements of democracy and so there was no basis for objecting to the party on account of its name.

Furthermore the European Court could not be persuaded that the reference to the Kurdish 'people', 'nation' and 'citizens' in its programme was necessarily intended to promote the unconstitutional objective of secession. The view of Turkey was that the distinction that was being made between the Kurdish and Turkish nations had revealed an intention of working to create minorities that would pose a threat to its territorial integrity. However, there was actually nothing in the programme describing the Kurds as a minority or claiming special treatment for them, let alone an assertion of a right to secede from the rest of the Turkish population.

Indeed it was evident from that programme that the party was looking for a solution to the Kurdish problem that would enable the Kurdish and Turkish peoples to 'live together of their free will within the borders of the Turkish Republic'. In the Court's view there was no more than a wish to have a non-violent political dialogue as to how to resolve one of the country's problems and it emphasised that: there can be no justification for hindering a political group solely because it seeks to debate in public the situation of part of the State's population and to take part in the nation's political life in order to find, according to democratic rules, solutions capable of satisfying everyone concerned... that was indeed the TBKP's objective.

The mistake in the approach of the Turkish authorities had been to focus on matters of form rather than to consider issues of real substance as regards the nature of the party's objectives. There was a similar failure in The Socialist Party and Others v Turkey, which was concerned with the fact that references to the right to self-determination of the 'Kurdish nation' and the latter's right to secede had been taken out of their context; they were not meant to encourage unlawful secession but to emphasise that a proposed federal system should not come about without the freely given consent of the Kurds, to be given by way of a referendum. Equally the European Court found it unjustified in Freedom and Democracy Party v Turkey to conclude that a party's support for 'the just and legitimate struggle of the [Kurdish] peoples for independence and freedom' meant that they wished to incite people to use violence or otherwise break the rules of democracy; the use of the term 'struggle' was rightly recognised as a commonplace term used by parties in Europe for their political demands. Furthermore, as in the previous case, references to 'self-determination' of the 'national or religious minorities' were not to be taken out of their context; there was no intention to encourage people to separation from Turkey but to emphasise the need for the consent of the Kurds to the political reforms being proposed.

It is thus evident from these cases that any evaluation of objectives, particularly where this has a bearing on conferment or retention of some legal status, must be well-informed. Furthermore such an evaluation must itself be respectful of the political pluralism underlying the European Convention and other international human rights guarantees; different views must be respected and any conclusions as to where they will lead must not be shaped by prejudice or narrow-minded perspectives. In general freedom of association will be better respected if the imposition of restrictions is guided by the deeds of the body concerned rather than the terms used in its formal statement of objectives. The focus should thus be much more on the regulation of the former instead of on exercising control at the time of formation.

LEGAL PERSONALITY AND OTHER RIGHTS

The essence of freedom of association is the pursuit of the common objectives of a group of persons (natural or legal). This may be achievable through the individual legal capacities of those persons but in practice the objectives may be best pursued through the body concerned having a distinct legal personality from those persons who seek to establish or belong to it. Such a personality will certainly entail certain basic legal capacities and possibly some others essential for the pursuit of its objectives but it certainly does not follow that associations should enjoy all the rights which might prove useful for that pursuing them. Moreover the fact that some of these additional rights are conferred on certain types of associations is not inherently objectionable so long as the principle of non-discrimination is respected.

LEGAL PERSONALITY

There are undoubtedly certain activities that will be essential for the basic operation of an association, such as the ability to enter into contracts related to the pursuit of its objectives and to make payments for the goods and services thereby obtained. The former will range from the printing of documentation through the arrangement of appropriate advertising and the renting of premises (both for offices and meetings) to the employment of staff and they may also include matters as diverse as the purchase and maintenance of vehicles, the purchase and storage of food, clothing and other humanitarian supplies and the organisation of training and educational programmes. In theory these are all activities that could be carried out on behalf of the association by those belonging to it, relying on their own legal personalities and also their private bank accounts for the purpose of making payments in respect of the contracts concerned.

However, this is often likely to be an impracticable solution for a number of reasons. Certainly members of associations may be discouraged from acting as a conduit for its transactions because of the tax liability that they might face on account of the funds flowing into their bank accounts, as well as the potential for incurring obligations to meet civil liabilities in circumstances over which they had no direct control. Furthermore many organisations are likely to be reluctant to deal with an association in this indirect way since they may be concerned about the possibility of funds going astray and the absence of clear lines of accountability, to say nothing of possible legal restrictions on them contracting through an intermediary.

Most importantly, however, such an arrangement is likely to make the day to day working of many associations subject to inappropriate delays and uncertainties and result in the pursuit of their objectives being at best extremely difficult and at worst impossible. There is, of course, no reason why an association should not choose to work in this way-indeed it may be unproblematic in the case of ones with very limited objectives, a preference for less formal structure or both-but it is unlikely that it would be suitable for most associations. It is not surprising, therefore, that the European Court readily accepted in Sidiropoulos and Others v Greece that the refusal to register the applicants' association-with the result that it was denied legal personality-was an interference with freedom of association. The fundamental importance of legal personality being granted for associations was further underlined by the Court when it went on to state that:

The most important aspect of the right to freedom of association is that citizens should be able to create *a* legal entity in order to act collectively in a field of mutual interest. Without this, that right would have no practical meaning.

It is essential, therefore, that the option of acquiring legal personality be available to those who wish to establish an association unless it can clearly be demonstrated that the lack of such personality will not impede the pursuit of its activities, with the latter being potentially of particular significance while an application for recognition is being processed. This personality should, of course, be clearly distinct from that of any or all of its members and officers and thus they should not be personally liable for its debts and other obligations. This obligation to grant legal personality to associations where this is sought relates only to ones actually being established within the country of the State concerned and does not appear to extend to recognising the personality of organisations established elsewhere, although a failure to do so could have implications for the association rights of persons in that State as well as the property and fair hearing rights of any organisation whose personality is not recognised.

However, there is also a quite distinct obligation under the European Convention on the Recognition of the Legal Personality of International Non-Governmental Organisations. Under this convention a State party is generally obliged to recognize the legal personality of an association, foundation or other private institution established under the law of another State party, but only where the body concerned has a non-profit making aim of international utility and is carrying on its activities in at least two States and its statutory office, management and control is in the territory of a State party. However, provision is made for 'restrictions, limitations or special procedures governing the exercise of the rights arising out of the legal capacity' to be recognised when these are 'required by essential public interest'.

Furthermore there is provision for excluding the application of the Convention in respect of a non-governmental organisation if the body invoking it by its object, its purpose or the activity which it actually exercises: a contravenes national security, public safety, or is detrimental to the prevention of disorder or crime, the protection of health or morals, or the protection of the rights and freedoms of others; or b jeopardises relations with another State or the maintenance of international peace and security. Nonetheless it would be very surprising if either of these possibilities could legitimately be given a broader construction than that seen in the earlier discussion of acceptable objectives for associations or in the discussion below of regulation. It should also be noted that the legitimacy of international human rights non-governmental organisations operating within individual countries is increasingly being recognised.

It remains to be seen whether an ability to establish branches should be regarded as an inherent aspect of the internal organisational capacity of an association, at least where these are not intended to have a distinct legal capacity. However, in many countries branches are automatically subject to registration requirements than can be as problematic as those governing the acquisition of legal personality by the parent association.

The requirement that legal personality should be capable of being acquired-in the event that this is the wish of an association's founders-is, of course, subject to the objectives being acceptable and it certainly does not entail an obligation to ensure that every possible legal capacity should be enjoyed.

However, in addition to the legal capacities already mentioned it may also be essential to recognise that an association can exercise ownership rights in respect of property since this is likely to be an important means of pursuing its objectives, both directly (such as the premises in which they take place) and indirectly (as a source of finance for them). Furthermore it should be able to protect those property rights, as well as any other legal interests that it may have, and this would undoubtedly necessitate the possibility of being able to bring and defend legal proceedings. The failure to accord such a right, or rather the taking away of it, was characterised as a violation of the right to property in the case of Holy Monasteries v Greece but, although it was not considered in that case that any issue arose in respect of Article 11, the latter could be significant in other circumstances; loss of control over property could, for example, frustrate the purpose of an association.

This case is, however, also a useful reminder that rights in addition to freedom of association in some international human rights treaties can sometimes also be invoked to protect associations; interference with their activities will thus not always be just a matter of being able to associate. The need to recognise that associations are able to enjoy some form of property rights does not, however, necessitate they must also have the right to acquire it in particular ways; a bar on them benefiting from legacies was not, for example, objectionable where an association had other means of acquiring income. Nonetheless non-binding instruments do point to the need for associations to be able to solicit and receive funding not only within the State party concerned but also from other countries.

It is not particularly significant what form the legal personality acquired by an association takes; many countries have a special regimes governing such personality but there would no be anything inherently objectionable in the provisions regarding corporate entities also being used for this purpose, if they did not create any difficulties regarding the pursuit of an association's objectives. It is also possible for the law to require associations for certain purposes to take on even more specific legal forms, as commonly happens in the case of religious associations and trade unions but such forms, while possibly advantageous for the purpose of regulation or the conferment of benefits, should did not create any unjustifiable impediments to the pursuit of a particular association's objectives

OTHER RIGHTS

Apart from enjoying these essential aspects of legal personality, an association is not generally entitled by virtue of freedom of association to the grant of any other rights-no matter how useful those might be-in order to pursue its objectives. The reluctance to regard other rights as inherent in freedom of association is premised on the assumption that the absence of them does not render the fact of association devoid of all practical meaning; thus it will still be possible for the collective objectives to be advanced, even if the preferred means cannot be used. Thus an association could not expect to have an automatic entitlement to be able to challenge the lawfulness of some activity in the courts simply because this has a bearing on some matter that falls within its objectives. So the concern of, for example, an environmental group about certain construction being contrary to the applicable law would not be a sufficient basis for it to be able to insist that it should be able to bring legal proceedings to challenge the authorisation for this construction to proceed.

An environmental group would only be able to bring such proceedings by reference to freedom of association where its own interests were directly affected and, in the absence of that, such a challenge would probably only be feasible if country concerned took a very generous view of standing in public law proceedings in general. It is the context of cases involving the activities of trade unions that the relatively limited expectations that an association should have following its formation can most clearly be seen but it is evident from these cases that a minimalist approach should not be taken to extremes as there are certainly some positive obligations within Article 11 as to the maintenance of a favourable environment for associations.

Certainly the Strasbourg institutions have rejected claims based on freedom of association that unions should be able to insist on collective bargaining with employers, on rights of consultation by government prior to the adoption of legislation and on representation on a national labour council. Furthermore it has also not been accepted that a right to strike should be seen as an inherent aspect of freedom of association.

However, in reaching the conclusion that such rights could not be regarded as being secured by freedom of association, considerable emphasis has always been laid on the ability of the unions concerned to pursue their interests through other means than the ones they had claimed under Article 11. Thus it has been repeatedly suggested in particular that it followed from the reference in Article 11 to the joining of trade unions 'for the protection of his interests' that a trade union should still be heard, even if this guarantee did leave a State a free choice of means as to how this was to be effected. Although the European Court has in the past always been persuaded that some such means of protecting the interests of trade union members existed when rejecting claims for particular rights, it had no hesitation in finding in Wilson and Others v United Kingdom that there was a violation of Article 11 when it saw that an employer was effectively allowed by the law to undermine or frustrate a trade union's ability to protect its members' interests.

This situation arose because employers were entitled to use financial incentives to induce employees to surrender important union rights, such as the termination of a collective bargaining arrangement; those employees who did this by signing new contracts were awarded substantial pay rises and this was clearly 'a disincentive or restraint on the use by employees of union membership to protect their interests.' It is, however, unlikely, that any treatment of union members that is less favourable than that of other employees will be regarded as amounting to a violation of Article 11 unless it is so significant that union membership becomes either pointless or seriously unattractive.

Notwithstanding the specific trade union context, the recognition that there must be some means of pursuing the collective objectives is undoubtedly also of more general significance; it is highly likely that Article 11 will have been violated if the restrictions imposed by a particular legal structure on the operation of any association (and not just a trade union) are such that it can do no more than exist. There may thus be no guarantee that particular means can be employed but the essence of an association is the pursuit of objectives rather than the simple union of those persons who hold them to be important. In this regard it is undoubtedly significant that instruments concerned with specific forms of association have recognised that they should be able to undertake certain forms of activity, notably, observation of trials and other proceedings, participation in public affairs and criticism of governmental actions, promotion of human rights ideas, provision of advice, provision of information to international organisations and seeking information.

It is, however, improbable that the ability for associations to undertake trading activities, let alone the possibility of being able to do so on some preferential basis vis-à-vis the business community generally or the granting of other kinds of privilege (such as some exemption from taxation), could normally be regarded as essential for the pursuit of objectives and thus an implied aspect of freedom of association. Nevertheless it should always be borne in mind that the international guarantees for this freedom are imposing only minimum obligations and there can be little doubt that the promotion of associations through this capacity can serve wider interests; such an empowerment of associations will not only benefit the development of civil society but is also likely to facilitate the achievement of many social objectives which would not be so readily accomplished through governmental structures. It may be, of course, that benefits are conferred on some but not other associations and it should not be overlooked that this could always be open to challenge on the basis that it is unjustified discrimination, invoking Article 14 of the European Convention to expand the protection afforded by Article 11. On the other hand there is no barrier to a State choosing to grant some advantages to some forms of association so long as any differentiation between these forms has a rational and objective basis.

PENALTIES FOR MEMBERSHIP

One positive obligation that the right to freedom of association imposes on States that ought not to be overlooked is that improper sanctions should not be imposed on persons merely because of their membership of an association. Thus there ought to be remedy for anyone dismissed because of his or her trade union activities and the same principle would also be applicable to dismissal because of the activities and objectives of any other form of association and indeed to any other forms of sanction-apart from the refusal to associate with someone-that are imposed simply because of the person concerned's membership of an association.

There is also a need to provide protection against even more aggressive forms of action taken against persons on account of their membership of an association, namely, harassment, intimidation and the use of violence, although the failure to do so could also engage responsibility for violations of other rights such as life, liberty and security and the prohibition of torture and inhuman and degrading treatment.

The only exception admissible to the prohibition on sanctions would be where membership of the association is clearly incompatible with performance of the employee's responsibilities or with other obligations. An example of such an incompatibility in the former context can be seen in Van der Heijden v The Netherlands where no objection was taken to the termination of the contract of the regional director of a foundation which promoted the interests of immigrants and provided them with advice because he was a member of the bureau of a party which advocated a policy of repatriating immigrants. In the circumstances of the case the European Commission considered not only that it was reasonable for the employer to have some discretion concerning the composition of its staff but that also, in view of the applicant's professional duties and the specific nature of his work, the employer.

This was a situation in which there was a very public contradiction between the two aspects of an individual's life; the same outcome might not be appropriate where the employee had no direct responsibilities regarding the either the direction of the foundation or the provision of advice but was, for example, only responsible for cleaning its centre and had no direct contact with those coming to it for advice. Certainly the imposition of a sanction for membership will not be considered justified where there is no direct evidence of incompatibility but it is only a matter of supposition.

Thus a violation of Article 11 was found by the European Court in Grande Oriente D'Italia di Palazzo Giustiniani v Italy when persons belonging to Masonic lodges were disqualified from appointment by a regional authority to various positions in public and private bodies; this was an inappropriate response to a generalised concern about the Masonic influence over public decision-making when there was nothing actually reprehensible in someone belonging to a lodge.

Regulation

There is, of course, a certain inevitability about the consideration given by governments to the need for some form of regulation whenever any kind of activity is undertaken and such consideration in which those establishing and running associations are involved is certainly not an exception in this regard.

Furthermore, given both the possible concern about objectives already discussed and the desirability of conferring certain advantages on at least some forms of associations, there is no a priori basis for objecting to the fact of regulation. Nevertheless the very fact that the European Convention and other international human rights treaties recognise freedom of association as a right which must be respected necessarily entails some limits on the degree of regulation to which the establishment and operation of associations can be subjected. Indeed the presumption must actually be against the need for regulation and, although there are some interests which can legitimately be invoked to restrict this freedom, the burden of proving that certain limitations are required is undoubtedly on those who would impose them.

The very essence of freedom of association is the ability of those belonging to a body to decide how it should be run;

this necessitates both a minimalist approach to regulation and very close scrutiny of attempts to interfere with the choices which associations and their members make about the organisation of their affairs.

Formation

In many instances the first problem confronted by an association is its very coming into existence and, in particular, the degree of control exercised over this process by State institutions. Although it has been indicated that there is an obligation on States to provide for the possibility of an association acquiring legal personality, a State is not generally entitled to insist on this being acquired by those who wish to form association; if a group of individuals prefer a relatively informal status then it would be difficult to justify compulsion for them to establish something with a more formal character. However, no objection could be raised with respect to a requirement that an association have a formal status where either that is seen as essential for the pursuit of pursuing certain activities (such as a trade union or a religious organisation) or that is a prerequisite to acquiring certain benefits (such as tax privileges) as the essential obligation under the right to freedom of association in this connection is to be able to exercise certain legal capacities rather than to be a particular type of legal person.

Nevertheless, even in such cases, there will still be a need to ensure that the degree of regulation is not unduly oppressive.

Although in some countries the acquisition of legal personality can be the automatic consequence of forming an association and thus not be subject to any further formalities, it is in principle compatible with freedom of association to insist that an entity go through some form of recognition or registration process before such legal personality is achieved. Such a process can, as has already seen from the discussion of objectives, involve an assessment of whether the objectives and proposed activities of particular associations are either contrary to the constitution or are in some other respect unlawful. Where this is found to be the case-bearing in mind the limited extent to which it is possible to make such a judgement at this stage-it will be admissible for recognition or registration to be refused.

This is certainly not a matter in which all room for judgement can be excluded but, apart from those cases where there had been some genuine misjudgement in the approach to drawing conclusions about activities or objectives, it is evident that in some countries the process is in reality being used as a means of exercising an entirely unfettered discretion with regard to the conferring of a formal status on a grouping of individuals and such an abuse of the regulatory power is clearly incompatible with provisions such as Article 11 of the European Convention. In order to minimise the risk of this occurring and to facilitate the exercise of judicial control over an allegedly improper refusal of recognition or registration, the grounds for taking such a decision-which should be for one of the legitimate aims identified in the limitation clauses on guarantees of freedom of association-must be stated with an appropriate degree of precision and be such as to permit objective assessment of their observance. As a consequence it is not only improbable that broadly framed criteria will be regarded as acceptable but it is also most likely that they will encourage improper refusals of recognition or registration.

Other than in those situations in which the objectives and activities of an association are properly found to be contrary to the constitution or the law, there are likely to be only a limited number of circumstances in which a refusal of recognition or registration might be justified. They would certainly include such a refusal in cases where the proposed name of the association belonged to that of another body or could be confused with it or was in some other way damaging to it or could in some way be genuinely regarded as misleading to the public. However, no matter how well-intentioned, the process of approval should not generally be used to impose constraints on the ability of associations to draw up their own rules, to administer their own affairs or to make links with other bodies as these are essential elements of freedom of association.

Any interference with that freedom would be admissible only if it was capable of being justified under the limitation clause, such as the imposition of requirements that are necessary to preclude unjustified discrimination or to protect the legitimate interests of members.

However, well-formulated criteria will never be an absolute guarantee against the refusal of recognition or registration for reasons not permitted under guarantees of freedom of association and that is why there is a need not only to give those making these decisions appropriate training but also to ensure that there is effective judicial scrutiny of any such refusal, as regards both the interpretation of the law and its application to the particular facts of the case.

Furthermore, in order to facilitate such scrutiny there should always be a reasoned decision where recognition or registration has been refused and this must, of course, be adequate. In addition, given the potential significance of such decisions for associations and those forming them, the possibility of bringing a legal challenge to a refusal must be something that can be speedily pursued. If these conditions are not met then it is likely that there will be not only a violation of the right to freedom of association but also, in many instances, violations of the rights to a fair hearing and to an effective remedy.

However, it is also important that the actual process of dealing with an application for recognition or registration-where this is required-takes place in a reasonably speedy manner so that delay does not become a means of frustrating the pursuit of an association's objectives. A useful point of comparison in judging what is reasonable might be the time taken to register corporations or businesses.

These also have objectives which need to be checked and in most countries these can still be registered in a matter of days rather than of months. There is, therefore, no clear need for a significantly longer period to be needed for the process of recognising or registering an association and it is undoubtedly the sort of yardstick that the European Court and other international tribunals would taken into account when dealing with any complaints about undue delay in reaching a decision.

PROTECTING MEMBERS' RIGHTS

There is a legitimate interest in a State undertaking some regulation of associations in order to secure the rights of others and this would justify, and indeed require, legal provisions designed to protect members from any abuse of an association's dominant position. This might entail establishing a means of redress to prevent members from being expelled contrary to the association's rules or from being subjected to certain disadvantages that could be regarded as amounting to considerable hardship, or even to prevent the adoption of rules that could be construed as wholly unreasonable or arbitrary. In such cases appropriate protection would generally be satisfactorily afforded by some legal basis for the member concerned to challenge the matter in the courts; there would rarely be any need for a State entity actually to intervene on his or her behalf.

As freedom of association is primarily the right of the individuals belonging to the entity, there will also be some obligation to ensure that they are not being unduly coerced into joining. This recognition of a negative dimension to freedom of association has led in the trade union context to any requirements that individuals forego their objections to membership in order that they retain their job or can continue to pursue their livelihood being found unacceptable.

However, it is a concern that is equally applicable outside the trade union context. Thus the European Court has upheld a complaint by small landholders being required to belong to a hunting association and allow hunting on their land despite their being opposed to hunting. It does not matter whether the constraints imposed on someone belong to an association are directly imposed by the law or are merely facilitated by it.

However, they are less likely to be seen as objectionable where they do not involve deeply-seated objections to membership being overridden or entails no more than the exercise of legitimate forms of trade union activity. Moreover the mere fact that there may be tax or other advantages in joining an association will not in itself make the incentive impermissible.

Furthermore, as has already been seen, there has not so far been any objection to a requirement that individuals join a professional association. However, although the individual interest in freedom of choice is undoubtedly offset to some extent by the public interest in regulation, it has been a feature of all the cases concerned with such associations that there was no restriction on the members setting up their own organisation in addition to the one which they were obliged to join; in other words they were still in a position to voice their opinions in their own way.

Any compulsion to belong to professional associations is thus likely to be viewed much less favourably if these associations were the only means through which their members could express an opinion in the relevant sphere and if the structure of them was such that the coerced members did not even have a genuine opportunity to influence the policy-making process.

CONTROLS OVER MANAGEMENT

Concern about regulation should also extend to the uses to which a State might try to put a particular association. It is certainly not uncommon to find what might be thought to be State objectives being secured with the assistance of private bodies, whether commercial entities or private associations with an objective common to that of the State and whether by means of some kind of partnership, contractual arrangement or other form of delegation. There can be no objection to this and indeed, as has already been noted, this is one of the very reasons for encouraging civil society to develop; the non-governmental sector can often provide greater flexibility in responding to some problems and the fact that it is often much more closely linked to those in need of assistance can make it much better equipped to judge where efforts can most usefully be applied.

However, while it would be foolish not to draw upon such a useful resource, attention will always need to be paid lest this results in attempts by the State to take over particular associations and effectively make them agencies working under its control. In these circumstances the entity concerned will have lost the freedom to organise its own affairs and, insofar as this is not voluntary, there will be a violation of the right to freedom of association. An instance of this happening can be seen in the attempt to use a taxi association as a way of administering the provision of taxi services in Iceland. The regulation of such services was undoubtedly in the public interest and might well be a sufficient basis for requiring membership of a public law body but the co-option of what was a private association in this case meant that the latter was no longer in a position to run its own affairs, which is one of the principal elements of freedom of association.

For the same reason it would be very difficult to justify attempts (whether at the registration stage or subsequently) to prescribe in detail how an association should organise its affairs-whether it ought to have this or that management structure-and there should certainly not be attempts to interfere with the choice of its representatives. Furthermore, although public accountability will be a relevant consideration where an association is working with public authorities and/or enjoys some public benefits, this should certainly not permit unimpeded access to the way in which particular choices are being made by an association and in the first instance is likely to extend only to the provision of relevant information. Thus it would be entirely legitimate for an association's decision-making to be taken in closed meetings but there could be a requirement that a proper record be kept of the proceedings.

Nevertheless the State will have responsibility for ensuring that both its interests and the rights of others are protected; this would justify requirements for financial reporting and independent auditing of accounts. It would also justify an obligation that those responsible for decision-making in the association should be clearly identified; there may be instances when this gives rise to legal liabilities and private bodies or the State will need to know against whom proceedings should be brought. However, there is no need for this to be subject to oppressive regulation and while it could be a matter of notifying the authority responsible for recognition or registration, there are undoubtedly other ways in which this objective could be achieved in various ways; for example, a record at the association's bank of those authorised to take decisions on its behalf would undoubtedly be as effective.

In contrast to a State having a legitimate need to know the executive officers of an association, there is no obvious justification for requiring disclosure to it of the names of members; individuals have a right to respect for private life under provisions such as Article 8 of the European Convention and indeed disclosure might also be a discouragement to joining and, therefore, an unacceptable inhibition on freedom of association.

Policing

There may, of course, be instances where associations do engage in improper activities and this may require some intervention by the State. However, it ought to proceed on the same assumption that applies to individuals, namely, that what someone is doing is lawful in the absence of contrary evidence. There ought not, therefore, to be any power to search the association's premises and seize documents and other material there without there being objective grounds for taking such measures. Furthermore the authorisation for them ought to be given by a judge and the terms of an warrant ought to be precise; there must be clear identification of what the search is in connection with and no permission can be given for a general trawl in the hope of finding something interesting. A judge also ought to be prepared to refuse authorisation for a search where no evidence justifying one is provided. This is all wellestablished in the case law under Article 8 of the European Convention and it applies whether or not the object of the source is an individual or an association. It should also be noted that monitoring of an association's activities or members through surveillance techniques such as the interception of communications must also be capable of justification in accordance with the requirements of Article 8; in the absence of this there would be legitimate grounds for complaint about non-observance of this or other comparable provisions.

Where, however, there is good justification for taking action against an association, whether because it has not observed some of the requirements concerning recognition or registration or because it has engaged in other conduct which is impermissible, the appropriate powers can then be exercised by the State. However, in such cases a sense of proportion is still required; technical failings should not have serious consequences for either the association or the individuals concerned. Thus consideration should first be given to whether the matter can be adequately handled through the issue of some form of directions, whereby only subsequent non-compliance will give rise to sanctions, rather than the immediate institution of criminal proceedings. The latter does, of course, have the inherent safeguard of judicial supervision and it is important that any administrative measures are also subject to this condition. The mere fact that the administration asserts that an impropriety has occurred does not mean that this is correct; the assertion may be based on a mistaken interpretation of the law or there may have been some misunderstanding or incomplete information which led to it being made.

In either event it is imperative that the association be in a position to challenge the position adopted by the State before an independent judge with full jurisdiction over these matters. If this is not possible then there will undoubtedly be violations of the rights to a fair hearing and an effective remedy. Furthermore where the validity of any requirement that an association should desist from a particular activity is in dispute, it should be possible to apply to have this suspended until the outcome of the relevant proceedings; there would have to be very grave circumstances for this to be denied and it would be essential that any such refusal should itself subject to prompt judicial challenge. Without the latter safeguard an allegedly 'urgent' suspension of an association's activities could be used as a pretext for stopping its pursuit of entirely legitimate ones.

Dissolution

In most instances the appropriate sanction against an association for not observing the legal requirements applicable to it will merely be the requirement to rectify its affairs, some form of civil liability and/or the imposition of an administrative or criminal penalty on it and on any individuals directly responsible. The application of such penalties should, of course, always observe the principle of proportionality as otherwise they are likely to be an indirect inhibition on freedom of association.

However, there may be circumstances where the conduct of the association would warrant its enforced dissolution. These are likely to be very rare indeed and would probably cover only situations in which the association undertook anti-constitutional activities, failed to desist from other illegal conduct after appropriate warnings and opportunities to rectify such failings or had such prolonged inactivity that it was necessary to intervene to ensure that its funds were properly applied.

The need for an extremely well-founded basis for such a drastic action as dissolution has been repeatedly emphasised by the European Court. Thus in United Communist Party of Turkey and Others v Turkey, which concerned the dissolution of this political party by the constitutional court after the former had sought a ruling from the latter, with a view to taking part in an election, as to the compatibility of its objects with the constitution, the Court made it clear that the protection afforded by Article 11 was not limited to the mere formation of an association but lasted for its entire life and that, while there was a need for rigorous supervision of all restrictions on freedom of association, especially where political parties are concerned such scrutiny is all the more necessary where an entire political party is dissolved and [as also occurred in this case] its leaders banned from carrying on any similar activity in the future. It may be that the scrutiny will not be quite as strict in cases where the association being dissolved is not a political party-although it is unlikely that there would be a significant difference in the approach in respect of such a party and an association whose objectives might be seen as political in a non-party sense-but the fundamental requirements are the same for all associations; these are that a measure such as dissolution must not only be proportionate to the legitimate aim being pursued-dissolution must remain an exceptional step-but the reasons for it also have to be clearly "relevant and sufficient".

In the United Communist Party of Turkey case it was particularly significant that the party had been dissolved even before it had been able to start its activities and that the dissolution was therefore ordered solely on the basis of the party's constitution and programme. The two grounds derived from these by the constitutional court were that, contrary to a provision in the criminal code making it an offence to carry on political activities inspired by communist ideology, the party had included the word 'communist' in its name and that it sought to promote separatism and the division of the Turkish nation. In the European Court's view a political party's choice of name could not in principle justify such a drastic measure as dissolution, without there also being other relevant and sufficient circumstances. However, these were clearly lacking; the formalistic approach of the Turkish constitutional court-which proceeded on the assumption that the use of the name automatically triggered the application of the provision in the code-was undermined by the fact that by the time of the dissolution this offence had been repealed and the constitutional court had itself found that the party, notwithstanding its name, was not seeking:

> to establish the domination of one social class over the others, and that, on the contrary, it satisfied the requirements of democracy, including political pluralism, universal suffrage and freedom to take part in politics.

In these circumstances the choice of name could not support a conclusion that this party had opted for a policy that represented a real threat to either Turkish society or the Turkish State and so this was insufficient to justify its dissolution. Although the second ground invoked by the constitutional court, namely, an inadmissible objective, would undoubtedly be capable of justifying such a drastic measure as dissolution, it is still necessary to demonstrate that this exists and, as has already been seen, the Court's examination of the party's constitution and programme-which took into account the difficulties associated with the fight against terrorism in Turkey-failed to disclose anything that could be regarded as objectionable in what was being proposed.

It did concede that the party's programme might conceal objectives and intentions but it added that these could be verified only by comparing that programme with its actions and the positions that it defended and that this was impossible given the peremptory dissolution of the party after its formation. Given the latter consideration, such drastic action was understandably seen as a disproportionate measure to protect the constitutional order and thus a violation of Article 11. Indeed dissolution at such a stage is always going to very difficult to justify since, as in the case of a refusal of recognition or registration because of what an association's objectives or activities are thought might entail, there will so little basis to substantiate the need for such action.

The absence of any concrete action by the body being dissolved was also important in Socialist Party and Others v Turkey. In this case the party-which, unlike the party previously considered, had been in operation for some time-had been dissolved because of various public statements which the constitutional court considered to constitute evidence that was binding on it even though the person making them had ceased to be its chairman. As has already been seen, the European Court found nothing in those statements that could be considered a call for the use of violence, an uprising or any other form of rejection of democratic principles; it noted on the contrary that he had in fact stressed the need for democratic change, even if strong language had been used in the statements. Furthermore the latter had to be read in their context, so that references to self-determination and secession had to be understood in terms of the need for any federal system that might be adopted in Turkey being based on the freely given consent of the Kurds.

There was thus nothing anti-democratic in the statements and, in the absence of anything that would belie the sincerity of the speaker, action was effectively being taken against the party for conduct that was no more than a legitimate exercise of freedom of expression. As a result its dissolution, notwithstanding the legitimate aim of the protecting national security, could only be regarded as disproportionate and thus unnecessary in a democratic society. However, it can still be possible to substantiate a case for dissolution, as is evident from the ruling in Refah Partisi (The Welfare Party) and Others v Turkey.

In the European Court's view there was a sufficient basis in the remarks and policy statements of the party's leaders to conclude that its objective was anti-secular and thus anti-democratic, in that they had advocated setting up a plurality of legal systems, the introduction of discrimination between individuals on the ground of their religious beliefs and the operation of different religious rules for each religious community, in which sharia would be the applicable law for the Muslim majority of the country and/or the ordinary law. Furthermore they had given the impression that it did not exclude the possibility of recourse to force in certain circumstances in order to oppose certain political programmes, or to gain power and retain it. In these circumstances, it considered that a State might.

It was important, however, that the danger posed by such political aims was not something that was merely theoretical or illusory but was achievable since such drastic action as dissolution could only be justified where there is a genuine and immediate threat to public order. Such a threat was considered to exist in the present case because the party had significant influence-through holding more than a third of the seats in the national assembly and through its increasing success in local elections-and because of the success that other political movements based on religious fundamentalism had in the past in seizing political power and then setting up the societal model which they advocated. Furthermore the action was not seen as disproportionate in its effect since, apart from the dissolution, only five of the party's leaders temporarily forfeited their parliamentary office and their role as leaders of a political party. Nevertheless the very thorough examination of the various remarks and policy statements demonstrates that dissolution remains an extremely difficult measure to justify and that it is not something that should be lightly undertaken. Where dissolution does appear to be justified, it is a measure that must be subject to effective judicial supervision in order to remain valid; without this there would be no effective remedy against a possible interference with freedom of association and thus there would be a violation of provisions such as Article 13 of the European Convention.

Furthermore it would be only in the most exceptional case that the effect of a dissolution decision would not be suspended until the outcome of any challenge to its validity; one of the factors in leading to the conclusion that dissolution was disproportionate in those cases where a violation of Article 11 was found was the 'immediate' effect of the measure and its drastic character would undoubtedly be mitigated if the possibility of suspending it existed.

In the all the cases of dissolution just considered, one of the automatic consequences of it was the transfer of the assets of the associations concerned to the State. This may well be an appropriate approach where anti-constitutional activity is involved but it will also be a factor which could contribute to the possibility of the measure being seen as disproportionate. Certainly such a transfer would probably not be justifiable where the dissolution is based on other considerations, such as the prolonged inactivity of the association. In such a case there is no reason why this should lead to a windfall for the State; appropriate respect for the objectives of those giving property to the association would be to ensure it was transferred on to a body with similar objectives. In addition to the violation of Article 11 in respect of the association and its members, a failure to do this would probably violate the rights of the donors to control the use of their property under Article 1 of the First Protocol.

Public Employees

The last phrase of Article 11 of the European Convention speaks directly to the scope of the freedom of association that can be enjoyed by certain persons in that the guarantee is expressed not 'to prevent the imposition of lawful restrictions on the exercise of these rights by members of the armed forces, of the police or of the administration of the State.' Whereas it will be relatively clear who falls within the first two categories, the reach of the third may be more problematic because of the varying approaches taken by States with regard to the organisation of the public sector.

Nevertheless it is a category which the European Court has indicated should be 'interpreted narrowly' and it is unlikely that the fact that someone is paid out of public funds or is formally categorised as a public servant will be decisive. The Court has left open the question of whether it applies to teachers, notwithstanding the domestic designation of them as public servants and in a different set of proceedings other public servants were only brought within the limitation because the purpose of the institution in which they worked resembled that of the armed forces and the police. Furthermore in Grande Oriente D'Italia di Palazzo Giustiniani v Italy the Court was not prepared to regard appointees by a regional authority to membership of various public and private bodies as coming within the scope of the limitation since their link with that authority was seen as even less close that of the teacher in the Vogt case with her employer. It is thus possible that the term 'administration of the State' will ultimately come to be regarded as applying only to higher-ranking officials, with restrictions being held appropriate because of the level and nature of their responsibilities but nonetheless it is still likely to cover a wide range of people.

In imposing limitations on the freedom of association on those who do fall within the scope of this clause, it is clear that these must always have a basis in law, be for one of the purposes identified in the second paragraph of Article 11 and observe the principle of proportionality, even if they may be more extensive than the restrictions that would be considered acceptable in respect of anyone else. Thus in Vogt v Germany the dismissal of a language teacher because of her membership and active involvement in the communist party was found to be a disproportionate measure to protect constitutional democracy when the party had itself not been banned and the applicant had not only asserted her belief in the constitutional order but had also never promoted the party ideology in the classroom.

On the other hand in Ahmed and Others v United Kingdom-where the limitation clause was not actually invoked-the European Court upheld restrictions which prevented certain local authority employees from being active in an organisational and administrative capacity in political parties or from being office-holders in such parties as justified in order to maintain a longstanding tradition of political neutrality on the part of those advising and guiding elected members of the authority. In so doing the Court attached particular significance to the relatively precise functional definition of those covered by the restrictions and the fact that they did not preclude either membership of a political party or involvement in all the activities of such a party.

In Rekvényi v Hungary the European Court accepted that a complete prohibition on members of the police even belonging to a political party, as well as engaging in various forms of political activity, could be justified on account of 'the desires to ensure that 'the crucial role of the police in society is not compromised through the corrosion of the political neutrality of its officers'.

In this regard it saw as particularly significant that Hungary was in transition from a totalitarian regime which had greatly relied on the direct commitment of the police to the ruling party-the aim was that 'the public should no longer regard the police as a supporter of the totalitarian regime but rather as a guardian of democratic institutions'-but, as the Ahmed case indicated, political neutrality is of importance for all democratic societies and it is unlikely that a similar restriction could be justified merely because the recent political history of the society concerned was not similar to that of Hungary. However, in upholding this restriction, the Court emphasised that considerable scope was still left to police officers to engage in political parties so that it could not be regarded as disproportionate in its effect on either freedom of association or expression.

GLOBAL AND REGIONAL PROTECTION OF THE GUARANTEE

It has already been noted that the right of individual petition under the European Convention extends to non-governmental organisations. This means that those associations (and not just their members) whose rights under Article 11-as well as under its other relevant provisions-are apparently being infringed can have recourse to the European Court in Strasbourg in the event that there is no effective remedy available to them within the country where this is happening.

It will be of no consequence in this regard that the association either has not yet acquired legal personality or has lost it through dissolution, not least since these may be the matters which are being challenged. This provides an assurance that the European standards with respect to freedom of association are observed in practice and not just in theory.

However, in the case of the International Covenant it would appear that only members of associations who are natural persons can complain under its First Optional Protocol about interferences with freedom of association and its allied rights since legal persons-whether members or the association-are not regarded as 'individuals' for the purpose of Article 1 of the latter instrument, notwithstanding that this restriction does not apply to the substantive rights guaranteed.

Nevertheless this still provides a means of seeking a remedy for those situations in which the international guarantee of freedom of association is not properly respected by the members of the associated affected. The avenue of proceedings on behalf of members by natural persons is also the only possibility of redress under the African Charter and the American Convention as the substantive guarantees are restricted to such persons.

CONCLUSION

There is still little specific provision for non-governmental organisations in international human rights instruments that are legally binding but their entitlement to exist is certainly now well-founded on the extensive guarantees that many of them afford to freedom of association.

Furthermore such guarantees ensure the legitimacy for their pursuit of an extremely wide range of objectives, with the only limits to this being set by the need to maintain democracy, human rights and the rule of law.

However, although the right to pursue these objectives is especially assisted by the right to enjoy legal personality wherever this is considered desirable, the scope of the particular capacities that should come with this personality continues to be in the process of elaboration. Nonetheless the guiding principle in such elaboration is undoubtedly one of ensuring the essential effectiveness of non-governmental organisations and indeed there is increasing recognition of the need for States to establish legal and financial environments that will facilitate their work.

The latter has particular implications for the regulatory structure and approach governing the existence and operation of non-governmental organisations. Thus, while the permissibility of regulation cannot be questioned, it ought not to be unduly cumbersome or bureaucratic and should certainly never embody an inherently hostile or oppressive attitude to the existence or activities of these bodies. Rather regulation should always be founded upon a full appreciation that non-governmental organisations are an essential constituent of any society committed to democracy, human rights and the rule of law.

The positive attitude required of governmental entities in respect of non-governmental organisations should also extend to their members, including those in the public service, with restrictions only being imposed where there is a fundamental incompatibility between membership and some other role or obligation that is itself admissible. Although there is often still a substantial discrepancy between the rights accorded to non-governmental organisations and their observance in practice, greater respect for the former will undoubtedly make a significant contribution to both the realisation of all human right and the safeguarding of a democratic society.

7

Factors and Hindrances in Working

This chapter assesses factors that influence the adoption of a human rights-based approach (RBA) by northern development NGOs. In order to provide a basis for assessment, thirty development NGOs that have the highest incomes were selected. Twenty characteristics of these NGOs were tested statistically to identify factors that have relationships with the behaviour of RBA adoption. The first section of this chapter provides definitions of the terms used in the study. The second section discusses the process of data collection and the measurement of the six independent variables. The third section then provides descriptive statistical data of the samples, followed by discussions of the results of the regression analysis and correlation tests. The chapter concludes with an interpretation of the results.

WORKING DEFINITIONS

A common perception of NGOs is that they are organizations working on development or on poverty issues, such as health, education, and income generating projects. In practice, NGOs work on a variety of issues, and play different roles, such as advocating for policy change and linking global processes with people on the local level (Fisher 1998). These organizations face challenges including improving services to communities, catalyzing change processes, and creating partnerships among different agencies (Lewis 2001).

This study will use the definition of NGOs Lindenberg and Bryant (2001) suggest, describing NGOs as organizations that:

(a) Provide useful (in some specific legal sense) goods or services, thereby serving a specified public purpose;

(b) Are not allowed to distribute profits to persons in their individual capacities;

(c) Are voluntary in the sense that they are created, maintained, and terminated on the basis of voluntary decisions and initiatives by members or a board of directors; and

(d) Exhibit values-based rationality, often with ideological components" (Lindenberg and Bryant 2001, 5-6).

Development NGOs here refer to NGOs that work on poverty reduction and economic growth issues (Linderberg and Bryant 2001). Relief NGOs are those that focus on responding to natural disasters and man-made disasters (relief work is increasingly called humanitarian work) (Lindenberg and Bryant 2001, 112).

Finally, humanitarian NGOs are those that work on relief and reconstruction with people whose human rights have been violated" (Lindenberg and Bryant 2001, 112)

In this research, besides development NGOs, relief and humanitarian NGOs are included for two reasons. First, relief and development work is interconnected. Second, it is also possible for relief and humanitarian NGOs to be human rights-based approach organizations, using human rights principles and tools in their emergency and relief work (ActionAid 2000b).

In fact, it is argued that the dichotomy between humanitarian and development came to an end in the 1990s when it was discovered that both use an RBA (Slim 2000).

The Top 30 NGOs

Financial size was used for ranking NGOs for the purposes of the study, as annual incomes can partly indicate the influence of NGOs. In addition to doing relief, humanitarian, and development work, other conditions for selecting the top 30 NGOs in terms of financial resources in this study included: (1) the NGOs must work in the field of relief and development work as defined above; (2) the NGOs must be founded and based mostly in northern countries, including North America and Western Europe; (3) the NGOs must work to create change for or provide services to the poor or the disadvantaged in at least five developing countries in Asia, Africa, and Latin America.

THE MEASUREMENT OF THE VARIABLES

Dependent and Independent Variables

The dependent variable of this analysis is the adoption of a human rights-based approach to development by northern development NGOs. The independent variables are six factors that may influence the RBA adoption. Independent variables such as working methods and issue areas precede RBA adoption for all NGOs that adopted RBAs.

The Measurement of the Dependent Variable

In measuring the adoption of an RBA, two criteria are used to classify the adopters and non-adopters of a human rights-based approach. An adopter must meet both criteria. Otherwise it is classified as a non-adopter.

1. They must state explicitly that one of their goals or working methods is to respect, protect, and fulfil all or parts of human rights, enshrined in the UDHR or in other international human rights standards. This could be an explicit statement in their mission statement, development policies, strategies, or programs.
2. They must:
    a. Adopt human rights goals or principles in their vision statement, or mission statements, or goals, or working methods; OR
    b. Frame key or most arguments around, or on the grounds of, human rights in their campaign, advocacy and other important activities; OR
    c. Apply a human rights framework and tools in most parts of their program processes; OR
    d. Promote or defend human rights with reference to the principle of obligations of duty bearers and entitlement of rights holders.

The Measurement of the Independent Variables

This section will test to see if six characteristics of development NGOs have any relationships with the adoption of a HRBA. The six independent variables are the following.

First, "percentage of acceptance of government funding" is measured in terms of percentage of all incomes. It includes grants and other forms of incomes both conditional and unconditional. When testing, acceptance of government funds is put together in the following three groups: (a) over 41%; (b) between 16-40%; (c) 15% and below.

Second, the "number of member NGOs in the family or confederation" refers to the most recent number of member NGOs that have official status of being NGO members, and not sections that are pending or waiting to be accepted.

Third, "country associated" refers to (a) the country in which the NGO was founded, meaning where the first NGO in the family was founded, which could now be a branch, and not necessarily the headquarters; (b) country of the head office, referring to the headquarters, or the international secretariat, or alliance office. In case there is more than one head office, the most central office will be used.

Fourth, religious association is measured on a nominal scale: Does this organization have a religious association, or does it not? NGOs that have religious association are ones that have official associations with religion, or a branch of a religion, or an NGO that uses religious teaching doctrines as part of their relief and development work.

Fifth, four working methods are being tested: working on advocacy, working on empowerment, working on campaigns, and working with the UN. Work on advocacy is measured on a nominal scale: Does this organization work on advocacy, or does it not? NGOs that work on advocacy are ones that lobby and/or advocate for changes in governments' laws, policies, and practices-alone or as part of its relief, humanitarian, or development work. Work on empowerment is measured on a nominal scale: Does this organization work on empowerment, or does it not? NGOs that work on empowerment are ones that develop and implement programs aimed at empowering local NGOs, grassroots organizations, community leaders, or groups of the poor in urban or rural areas.

This can be done as part of other work, or as projects by themselves, but it must be done substantially. Work on campaigns is measured on a nominal scale: Does this organization work on campaigns, or does it not? Campaigns are a set of activities bound together in order to achieve certain goals. They generally involve mobilizing support from certain groups of people. NGOs that work on campaigns are ones that use public campaigns to achieve their stated goals. Finally, work with the UN is measured in a nominal scale: Does this organization work with the UN, or does it not? NGOs that work with the UN are ones that have a substantial level of engagement with UN agencies as partners or as subcontractors in work relating to relief, humanitarian, and development work, such as, UNICEF, UNDP, and UNAIDS.

Finally, five issue areas are being tested: working on IFIs, working on HIV/AIDS, working on women, working on children, and working on trade, debt, and aid. Work on IFIs is measured on a nominal scale: Does this organization work on IFIs, or does it not? NGOs that work on IFIs are ones that carry out programs or projects opposing policies or development projects of the World Bank or the International Monetary Fund (IMF), or regional development banks such as the Asian Development Bank. Work on HIV/AIDS is measured on a nominal scale: Does this organization work on HIV/AIDS or does it not? NGOs that work on HIV/AIDS are ones that run programs aimed at improving certain aspects of HIV/AIDS, such as awareness raising, prevention projects, aspects of various cures, access issues, or campaigning for a lower cost of HIV/AIDS medicines.

Work on women's issues is measured on a nominal scale: Does this organization work on women's issues, or does it not? NGOs that work on women are ones that implement programs on aspects of women's work, and not only on women's' rights, such as the reproductive health of women, and income generation projects for women. Work on children's issues is measured on a nominal scale: Does this organization work on children's issues, or does it not? NGOs that work on children's issues are ones that carry out programs or projects on behalf of children, such as children and education, children suffering from HIV/AIDS, street children, child labourers, and child prostitution. Finally, work on trade, debt, or aid is measured on a nominal scale: Does this organization work on trade, debt, or aid, or does it not? NGOs that work on trade, debt, or aid are ones that have developed and implemented programs on one of these three issues. The organization might be conducting research, carrying out campaigns, or taking action on issues around trade, debt, and aid, such as their impact on the poor (especially from the south), debt relief of poor countries, the use of international aid and human rights practice of governments.

DESCRIPTIVE STATISTICS OF THE TOP 30 NGOS

The descriptive statistics can be summarized as:

NGOs that adopt an RBA

Out of the top 30 NGOs, seven of them have adopted an RBA approach, accounting for 21% of the sample. These seven NGOs are: International Planned Parenthood Federation, CARE International, Oxfam International, Save the Children, Doctors of the World, Doctors without Borders, and ActionAid. Most of them state explicitly that they work for the realization of human rights as enshrined in the UDHR and other international human rights standards, or that they use a human rights-based approach in achieving their goals.

Characteristics of the Top 30 NGOs

The first characteristic is the acceptance of government funding. NGOs do receive money from governments in various forms. The top 30 NGOs receive an average of 23.58% from government funds, ranging from 0% to 88.71%. When dividing the NGOs into three groups, it was found that 53.85% of NGOs have government money make up less than 15% of the annual budgets. Interestingly, none of NGOs in this group have adopted an RBA. Within this group, there are eight organizations receiving government funds totalling less than 5% of their total annual income. Half of these are considered to have religious affiliations, and none of these eight organizations have adopted an RBA. For the second group, government money makes up between 15.01 and 40% of their annual income. This group has the highest portion of RBA adoption (57.14%). And, five NGOs in the top 30 receive more than 41% of their annual budgets from government funds.

Table: Percentage of Revenue from Governments

Number of NGOs		Percent	Number of RBA NGOs	Percent
41% and over	5	19.23	2	40
Between 15.01-40 %	7	26.92	4	57.14
15% and below	14	53.85	0	0

The second characteristic is the size of NGO families. Fifty percent of the NGOs in the top 30 have their families and membership systems. The other half are individual NGOs. Among the group that has a family, an average family member is 38, with the highest number of NGO members at 181. Of all thirty NGOs, 23.33% have more than fifteen NGO members and 26.67% have between six and 15 members.

The third characteristic is country associated. Most of the NGOs in the top 30 were founded in the US (66.67%). Other countries where the top 30 NGOs were founded are the UK (16.67%), France (3%), Ireland (3.33%), and Switzerland (3.33%). Similarly, countries where the central offices are located are mostly in the US (60%). Others are in the UK (16.67%), Switzerland (3.33%), France (3.33%), Ireland (3.33%), South Africa (3.33%), and Belgium (3.33%). Interestingly, none of the NGOs that adopt RBAs has their headquarters in the US.

Fourth, in regards to associations, NGOs in the top 30 have a high percentage of religious associations (40%). None of the religious associated NGOs have adopted an RBA. Although some work on issues relating to labour, none of the top NGOs have direct associations with labour unions.

Fifth, in terms of working methods, a fair number of NGOs in the top thirty (about 30%) use advocacy as one of their working methods. Over sixty percent of these NGOs have adopted an RBA. A rather surprisingly higher percentage of these NGOs-53.33%--use empowerment as a development tool. Of these NGOs, about a third has adopted an RBA. Similar to advocacy is the use of campaigns as a tool for change. Of the top 30 NGOs, 26.67% use campaign tools, and three quarters of them have adopted an RBA. Only a third of the top 30 NGOs work with the UN, and a third of these have adopted an RBA.

Table: Countries where NGOs are found and Countries of Central office

Country NGO found		Country of Central Office		
Number	Percentage	Number		Percentag
France	3	10	1	3.33
UK	5	16.67	5	16.67
USA	20	66.67	18	60
Switzerland	1	3.33	2	6.67
Ireland	1	3.33	1	3.33
South Africa	0	0	1	3.33
Belgium	0	0	1	3.33

The last characteristic is issue areas. Only two NGOs (6.7%) work on IFIs, both have adopted an RBA. More popular is HIV/AIDS with as many as 70% of the top 30 NGOs working on this issue.

Table: Associations, Working Methods, and Working Themes of the Top 30 NGOs

Number of NGOs	Percent		Number of RBA NGOs	Percent
Religious association	12	40	0	0
Work on advocacy	9	30	6	66.67
Work on empowerment	16	53.3	5	31.25
Work on campaigns	8	26.7	6	75
Work with the UN	11	36.7	4	36.36
Work on IFIs	2	6.7	2	100
Work on HIV/AIDS	21	70	7	33.33
Work on women	16	53.3	6	37.50
Work on children	20	66.7	4	20
Work on trade, debt, or aid	7	23.3	4	57.14

About a third of these have adopted an RBA. Women and children receive attention from more than half of NGOs in the top 30 with 53.3% and 66.7% respectively. Moreover, 37.5% of NGOs working on women's issues and 20% of NGOs working on children's issues have adopted RBAs respectively. Finally, 23.3% of the top 30 NGOs work on trade, debt, or aid and half of them have adopted an RBA.

THE RESULTS OF LOGISTIC REGRESSION AND TEST OF CORRELATION

Logistic Analysis

From the logistic analysis, it was found that seven risk factors have relationships with the adoption of RBAs. Among these factors, two of them have negative relationships and are negative risk factors-thereby reducing the chance of having RBA NGOs: (1) country NGO where the NGO is founded (USA); and (2) religious association. The other five factors have positive relationships and are positive factors-increasing the chances of having RBA NGOs:

(1) government funding (16-40%);

(2) NGO members (16-40%);

(3) work on advocacy;

(4) work on campaigns; and

(5) work on trade, debt, and aid.

Table: Logistic Analysis of Risk Factors that have Relationship with the Adoption of RBAs

	Factors that have relationships with and are risk factors of the adoption of an RBA	Significance level	Odd Ratio (OR)
1.	Government fund (16-40%)	0.026	8.889
2.	NGO member (6-15 members)	0.050	6.333
3.	Country where NGO was founded-USA	0.025	0.111
4.	Religious association	0.006	0.304
5.	Work on advocacy	0.003	40.000
6.	Work on campaigns	0.002	63.000
7.	Work on trade, debt, and aid	0.026	8.889

First, while countries in which the centre offices are located, and other countries where NGOs were founded do not show a relationship with the adoption of an RBA, the country where NGOs founded USA has a negative relationship with the adoption of an RBA adoption at the significance level of 0.05 (P-value at 0.025). The OR suggests that the chance of finding an NGO founded in the USA that has adopted an RBA is 0.111 times less that the chance of finding an NGO founded outside the USA that has adopted an RBA.

Second, religious association has a negative relationship with the adoption of an RBA at the significance level of 0.01 (P-value at 0.006). The OR suggests that the chance of finding a religious associated NGO that adopts an RBA is 0.304 times less than the chance of finding a non-religious associated NGO that adopts an RBA.

Third, advocacy has a positive relationship with the adoption of an RBA at the significance level of 0.01. The OR means that the chance to find an NGO that uses advocacy and has adopted an RBA is 40 times higher than the chance of finding a non-advocacy NGO that has adopted an RBA.

Fourth, campaigning as a working method has a positive relationship with the adoption of an RBA at the significance level at 0.01 (P-value at 0.002). The OR suggests that the chance of finding an NGO that does advocacy work and adopts an RBA is 63 times higher than finding an NGO that does not do advocacy work and adopts an RBA.

Finally, trade, debt, and aid as development issues have positive relationships with the adoption of an RBA at the significance level of 0.05 (P-value at 0.026). The OR tells us that the chance of having an NGO that works on trade, debt, or aid and adopts an RBA is approximately nine times higher than having an NGO that does not work on either trade, debt, and aid and adopts an RBA.

Test of Correlation

Besides the seven risk factors above, eight other factors are found to have relationships with the adoption of RBAs.30 The first is the percentage of government funding (15% and below). Receiving government funding at 15% and below is a factor that has a negative relationship with the adoption of an RBA at the 0.01 significance level (two tailed). Interestingly, while this factor has a negative relationship with RBA adoption, receiving government funding at 16-40% of an organization's annual revenue is a positive risk factor at the significance level of 0.05. However, receiving government funding over 41% of annual revenue does not have a relationship with RBA adoption.

Table: Correlation Test of Factors that have a Relationship with the Adoption of RBAs

	Factor that has relationship with the adoption of an RBA	Significance level of Pearson Correlation (two-tailed)	Type of Relation-ship
1.	Country of central office-UK	0.05	Positive
2.	Country of central office-USA	0.001	Negative
3.	Country of central office-Belgium	0.005	Positive
4.	Percentage of government funding (15% and below)	0.005	Negative
5.	Number of NGO members (0-5 members)	0.005	Negative
6.	Work on IFIs	0.005	Positive
7.	Work on HIV/AIDS	0.05	Positive

The second factor is the number of NGO members (0-5 members). To be in a family that has up to five NGO members has a negative relationship with the adoption of RBAs. Again, while this factor has a negative relationship in terms of RBA adoption, to be in a family that has six to fifteen NGO members is a positive risk factor at the significance level of 0.05. To be in a family that has more than 16 members, however, does not have a relationship with the adoption of an RBA. Third, UK as a country where the central office is located is founded to have a positive relationship with the adoption of an RBA at the significance level of 0.05. Fourth, USA as a country where the central office is located is found to have a negative relationship with the adoption of an RBA at the significance level of 0.01. Fifth, Belgium as a country where the central office is located is founded to have a negative relationship with the adoption of an RBA at the significance level of 0.01. However, to have a central office in other countries, including Switzerland, France, Ireland, and South Africa, does not have a relationship with the adoption of an RBA. Sixth, while working with the UN does not have a relationship with the adoption of an RBA, working on IFIs does. Its relationship is positive and is significant at the 0.01 level. Seventh, working on HIV/AIDS has a positive relationship with the adoption of an RBA at the significance level of 0.05.

Other factors with no relationship with RBA adoption are the number of member NGOs (16 and above), the country where the NGOs was founded (except for the case of the US), the country of the central office, labour union association, work on empowerment, work with the UN, work on women, and work on children.

PUTTING THE NUMBERS IN PERSPECTIVE

Percentage of Government Funding

Common sense suggests that the more money an NGO receives from governments, the less they are likely to adopt an RBA-assuming that an RBA leads to increasing risk of tensions between the governments and NGOs. This study shows two things to prove that common sense may only be one third of the picture. First, the chance of finding an NGO that adopts an RBA when it receives a medium portion (16-40%) of government funding is 8.889 times higher than the chance of finding an NGO that adopt an RBA when it receives a higher percentage of government money (over 41%) or a lower percentage (below 15%) of its annual income. Second, that an NGO that receives less than 15% in government money of its annual income has a negative relationship with the adoption of an RBA.

The partially true part of the common sense explanation is the situation where an NGO receives government money, comprising more than 41% of its annual incomes, and not when it is 16-40%, or below 15%. It is possible that at this point (over 41%); NGOs have high percentage incomes from governments so that an adoption of RBA may generate a strong sense of insecurity, resulting in the deterrence of adopting an RBA. It should be noted, however, that this study does not find statistical evidence to support these claims. Again, the NGOs in this study are northern NGOs, receiving northern government money, to work mostly in southern countries. This is far different from the situation in which NGOs receive money from repressive governments to work against them.

There are two reasons why receiving government money between 16-40% is a positive risk factor for RBA adoption. First, NGOs in this group are in the position to enjoy financial security from not having too high of a portion of their income from government funds. This enables them to take manageable risks as a result of challenging the state, which may be the results of RBA adoption. Second, that they do receive money from governments encourages them to work and seek cooperation and partnership with governments, which is an important step in working in a human rights-based approach.

Instead of having the group that least depends on government funding adopting RBAs at a higher rate, this group receiving less than 15% of their incomes from the government has a negative relationship with RBA adoption. There are two reasons for this. First, these NGOs receive good financial support from individual donors and private institutions, and do not rely on, or have to compete for, government grants. The lack of competition leads many NGOs in this group to keep to traditional development work, mostly relief and service delivery work. As statistics shows, NGOs in this group have a negative relationship with using advocacy as a working tool (Pearson Correlation significance (PC sig.) (two-tailed) at the 0.01 level). They tend not to use empowerment in their work (negative relationship with using empowerment at PC sig. at the 0.01 level); and tend not to use campaigning (negative relationship with campaigning at PC sig. at the 0.05 level). Second, NGO in these groups have important characteristics of non-adopters of RBA. For instance, more than half of these NGOs are religious associated (which reduces the chance of being an RBA by 3.28 times), 85.71% of them were founded in the US (which reduces the chance of being an RBA by 9.009 times), and 85.71% of them are US-headquarters-based NGOs. So, instead of finding the most RBA NGOs in this group receiving less money from governments, we discover some financially independent, conservative US-based NGOs.

Number of NGOs Family

Statistical tests give us two viewpoints. First, the chance of finding NGO families that have 6-15 members and adopting an RBA is 6.3 times higher than finding NGO families that have members higher or lower than the range. Second, NGO families that have less than five members have a negative relationship with the adoption of RBAs.

To put these findings in perspective, we can infer that the size of NGO families are influential factors in RBA adoption. If the family is very large, with over 16 members, it may be difficult to reach agreement among its members, if the family wishes to adopt an RBA. This, of course, does not matter, if the family does not wish to adopt an RBA. An NGO family with 6-15 members, if it wishes to adopt an RBA, has the size of membership that is not so high as to make it difficult to reach agreement, and not so low that it lacks the dynamics and productive interactions among its members. The group of NGO families with less than five NGO members, which has a negative relationship, is mostly comprised of US-founded (85.71%) and US-based (86.67%) NGOs, which have a low rate of RBA adoption. This group has a positive association with the factor that they were founded in the US at the 0.05 significance level (which reduces the chance of adopting an RBA by nine times). It also has a positive association with the factor that they have their headquarters in the US at the 0.01 significance level (which has a negative relationship with the adoption of RBAs). Finally, it has a negative association with the campaigning working method at the 0.05 significance level (which is the most positive risk factor of the adoption of RBAs, OR at 63 times).

Country Where the NGO was Founded

This statistical test proves that the USA as an NGO's founding country is a significant risk factor in terms of the adoption of an RBA. It increases the risk of not adopting an RBA by nine times-the highest negative risk founded in this study. If an NGO is founded in the USA, the chance that they will adopt an RBA is 0.111 less than the chance of a non-USA-founded NGO that adopts an RBA. In other words, if a NGO is not founded in the US, it is approximately nine times more likely to adopt an RBA, compared with a US-founded NGO.

This analysis confirms Jochnick and Garzon (2002)'s observation that NGOs in the US are less likely to adopt an RBA. This can be the result of at least three factors. First, the US government is one of the major donors of many NGOs. These NGOs may not want to increase tensions with a major donor, which may shake their financial security-one of the most important assets of NGOs in a competitive environment. USAID, for example, can deter NGOs from adopting an RBA (Jochnick and Garzon 2002). Second, the US does not have a political culture that encourages the promotion and protection of economic, social, and cultural rights (ESCR) or an RBA. It refuses to adopt the key international instruments on ESCR, the International Covenant on Economic, Social, and Cultural Rights (ICESCR), arguing that it is only aspirational, and not "real" human rights.

There are less active discussions and debates among academics and practitioners on RBAs and ESCR in the US. Third, it may be the case the US-founded NGOs follow what is called the "Anglo-American development tradition," which uses the language of equal opportunities, or moral imperative to give back to the poor through charity (Lindenberg and Bryant 2001), rather than the language of human dignity as human rights, requiring state obligations, which is more popular in Europe. The former is obviously less friendly to an RBA than the latter.

Country of Central Office

The statistical tests show us that the specific countries in which central offices are located have both significant positive and negative relationships with the adoption of an RBA. The positive relationships are with the UK and Belgium, and the negative relationship is with the US. Countries where the central offices do not have relationship with RBA adoption are Switzerland, France, Ireland, and South Africa.

The reason why NGOs who have their central offices in the UK are more likely to adopt an RBA can be explained by two factors. First, in general, UK-based NGOs have enjoyed the support of human rights from the Department for International Development (DFID) of the UK government, as the organization itself is an adopter of an RBA. It is a key donor and partner of many UK-based NGOs, helping set the tone for RBA adoption. Some even argue that UK-based NGOs adopt RBAs because donors like DFID are more willing to support them (Harris-Curtis 2003). Second, the NGO community in the UK has been both progressive and active in debating human rights issues. Third, the UK is home of early advocate organizations for RBAs, including Rights and Humanity, Oxfam GB, Save the Children UK, and ActionAid. Finally, in a study on recent NGO trends in the UK, it was found that there have been increasing funds for NGOs to do human rights-based work (Wallace 2003).

Belgium is often chosen to be a clearinghouse of Europe. It has long served as headquarters of both international organizations and NGOs. The NGO community has worked in the atmosphere of the European language of upholding individual human rights. The European Commission and the EU have generally been supportive of the human rights agenda. These factors have resulted in an environment that is friendly for development NGOs to adopt human rights language, values, and tools.

For the US, the three factors discussed earlier (the US government as a key donor, weak political culture for ESCR, and the Anglo-American development tradition) have made the US an environment that is not encouraging for NGOs to adopt an RBA. The negative relationship between headquartering in the US and RBA adoption may also be the result of RBA NGOs choosing not to have their headquarters in the US, and instead, maintaining small offices to carry out advocacy work, targeting international organizations and the US government in Washington DC and New York.

Religious Association

Religious association is a risk factor for adoption of an RBA; it increases the risk of not adopting an RBA by 3.28 times. The chances of finding a religion-associated NGO that adopts an RBA is 0.304 times less than the chance of finding a non-religion-associated NGO that adopts an RBA. In other words, a non-religious NGO is 3.28 time more likely to adopt an RBA, compared with a religious NGO.

This finding contradicts those of Harris-Curtis (2003) who claims that religious associated NGOs, such as Norwegian Christian Aid, adopt an RBA because it finds that human rights principles are part of the bible. If this is true, it may be limited to the examples that Harris-Curtis uses, or to the Scandinavian churches, and not to others. This study shows that as high as 40% of NGOs in the top 30 are religious associated, but none of them have adopted an RBA, resulting in a risk factor 3.28.

A more plausible reason is that religious NGOs have their own teachings on which they base their relief, humanitarian, and development perspectives and practices. As the RBA movement gains popularity among progressive development groups and the UN, religious NGOs may reassess the compatibility of human rights and their teachings. Most will likely find that though there are differences, these perspectives do not contradict one another, and may help fulfil each other's goals. These results form a general impression of religious NGOs as non-adopters and quiet supporters. This may lead them to say, for instance, that the RBA movement is a good thing, we support it, but we still do things our way.

Work on Advocacy

Advocacy is a positive risk factor. An NGO that uses advocacy as a working method has a 40 times greater chance of adopting an RBA than an NGO that does not use advocacy. This working method is generally used among human rights organizations. After they witness and document human rights violations, they advocate for change in policy and practice based on their documents, including lobbying and pressuring powerful and influential actors such as superpowers and international organizations. Similarly, in RBA development work, there are certain factions in development that believe that coordination for relief work is not sufficient, pressing the need for advocacy for changes in development policy, measures, and practices that exacerbate poverty. It may be the case that NGOs that work on advocacy are better acquainted with and more appreciative of the importance of development policies.

Work on Campaign

Campaigning is the strongest influential factor for the adoption of an RBA in this study. The chance for an NGO that campaigns to adopt an RBA is 63 times higher than that of an NGO that does not campaign. Campaigns are one of the key tools of human rights organizations increasingly gaining popularity among development NGOs.

Human rights NGOs use these tools by designing a set of activities to achieve certain goals within a period of time, particularly by choosing issues and target groups, timing, messages, and actions after the documentation of human rights violations. In contrast to relief and reconstruction, campaigns generally work through the mobilization of people to create awareness and/or to take actions and pressure for changes in government policies, measures, and practices.

As such, a campaigning organization tends to have three characteristics. First, it works as an agent for change, rather than as a direct implementer of change-which when adopting an RBA acts to monitor and advocate for changes in development policies, rather than acting as an implementer of development policies.

Second, a campaigning organization focuses on specific actors, particularly the state and other responsible bodies, and often calls on them to act and be accountable, which is an important link to RBAs which work through holding the state responsible to its human rights obligations.

Third, a campaigning organization often creates change through mobilizing people. Human rights provide legal and "moral high ground" for the mobilization that a campaigning organization needs. These three factors make development NGOs that campaign more familiar with and connected to the role, the focus, and implications of RBA, and therefore more likely to adopt an RBA than those that do not campaign.

Work on IFIs

NGOs working on IFIs have a positive relationship with RBA adoption. This is due to at least four factors. First, some of the World Bank's large scale development projects and the IMF's economic policies violate ESCRs, bringing human rights dimensions into development NGOs. Second, the Bank and the IMF are largely accountable to their Boards who are mostly representatives of developed countries, and do not have a tradition of being responsive to calls from outsiders. Human rights provide legitimacy, which strengthen the call of NGOs for the institutions to also be accountable to the poor in developing countries. Third, these calls of NGOs are usually packaged in campaigns and advocacy series, making development NGOs familiar with human rights tools. Finally, human rights provide platforms for universal solidarity, linking grassroots organizations that try to get their messages across internationally with international development NGOs.

Work on HIV/AIDS

NGO's work on HIV/AIDS has a positive relationship with the adoption of an RBA. This is due to five factors. First, HIV/AIDS as a development issue has been developed and linked to international human rights framework more progressively than many other development themes. One example is the development of international guidelines by the UNAIDS and OHCHR (2002). Second, one of the key issues of HIV/AIDS is that it is involved with the element of discrimination, which lies in the heart of human rights and human rights-based approach to development. Third, human rights provide legitimacy, moral, and legal grounds for some HIV/AIDS-related campaigns, such as campaigns on the cost and access to HIV/AIDS drugs. Fourth, HIV/AIDS is one of the areas that an RBA can clearly help strengthen development NGOs, particularly on issues of access to healthcare, education, and work, which are much stronger when the issues are framed in a human rights framework (Plipat 2004a). Fifth, traditional human rights areas help broaden and highlight HIV/AIDS issues in less familiar territories of development work, such as HIV/AIDS in prisons and HIV/AIDS and drug users (Plipat 2004b).

Work on Trade, Debt, and Aid (TDA)

NGOs' work on TDA has a positive relationship with the adoption of an RBA. In fact, the chance of having an NGO that works on TDA and adopts an RBA is 8.9 times higher than the chance of having an NGO that does not work on TDA and adopts an RBA. The reasons being are that, firstly, trade, debt, and aid are all macro and structural development issues. Development NGOs do need a moral high ground, international legal framework, and international standards, which human rights can offer, to drive their agenda on trade, debt, and aid forward. Second, to address these macro-structural causes of poverty with international organizations and developed countries, development NGOs need solidarity space, which human rights can provides. Third, a human rights approach is based on the notion of human dignity. It brings up and highlights individual faces to development debates at the macro and structural level, giving meaning and a humanistic side to the economic-dominated nature of trade, debt, and aid issues.

OTHER FACTORS AFFECTING RBA ADOPTION

This research starts with six possible factors that may influence the adoption of an RBA. It finds that all six factors have relationships with RBA adoption. There are other factors that this research has not assessed, areas for future research. Among these, two factors stood out during the course of the study and interviews: NGO leadership, and the funding factor.

First, NGO leadership is likely to be an important cause of RBA adoption. Some NGOs leaders are supporters of human rights agendas and could lead their organizations to start a human rights learning process, and eventually become RBA organizations. Save the Children Sweden and Oxfam America are some of the examples of organizations that have increasingly engaged in RBAs due to their leadership. Conversely, although an organization is in an RBA-supportive environment, without interested and committed leadership, the organization tends not to become a rights-based organization. Save the Children US (SC US) is a good example of this latter case. While staff from SC US attended trainings organized by SC Alliance like other SC members, a rights-based approach has never made it to the organizational agenda of SC US. There is room to be more political in the US context, but its leadership does not make use of it. It is reluctant to do advocacy work or speak on behalf of human rights victims. It did not engage in lobbying the US government to ratify the CRC, its organization's fundamental instrument. A senior officer of Save the Children Sweden sums it well, "Without strong and committed leadership, a rights-based approach would be an impossibility of Save the Children"

Second, donors have rather strong roles in shaping the policy and development strategies of development NGOs directly and indirectly. This includes the case of the human rights-based approach to development strategies. Some have discussed how institution donors, such as bilateral development agencies and foundations, can be influential in RBA adoption (Harris-Curtis 2003). The debate here focuses on the influence of individual donors in RBA adoption by development NGOs.

ActionAid is a good case to illustrate the influence of such donors. The organization is paying a cost of RBA adoption by developing new sponsors and new relationships with existing sponsors, as well as reviewing funding sources and internal investment policies. This includes developing AA's own understanding of what types of rights-based work sponsors are willing to support (ActionAid 2000a).

The organization has for a long time enjoyed donors' support in its Child Sponsorship Program, one its top funding sources. Through supporting individual children and family, donors can see the changes they contribute to children and their families; for instance, how many children can go to school and how many meals the children and their families will have. When the organization approaches the same donors with a new framework that won't be emphasizing relief and service delivery work, but instead will fight for human rights, one can imagine the donors' response "go ahead, do what you want, but I am not supporting you." To secure funding, the organization has to take steps to help donors understand how a human rights-based approach could help those families in the long run. While drawing donors to move towards the organization, ActionAid also draws itself to donors in order not to allow too wide a distance between the organization and donors. That is, in practice it has to do both service delivery and rights-based work, instead of jumping to only the latter. In essence, the desire to retain their donors' supports does put some restraints on the organization who might otherwise completely engage itself with a rights-based approach.

CONCLUSION

This chapter analyzes factors that affect the adoption of an RBA by relief, humanitarian, and development NGOs. The sample is comprised of the top 30 NGOs in terms of total annual income. Income was used for this selection process as it can be considered a surrogate for the individual NGO's level of influence or power. Six factors are measured to test their relationship with the adoption of an RBA. These factors are:

(1) the percentage of annual revenue from governments;

(2) number of NGO members (in the NGO family);

(3) country associated;

(4) group associated;

(5) working methods; and

(6) issue areas.

A logistic regression shows us that all six factors have relationships with the adoption of an RBA. These include two negative risk factors: USA-as the country where NGOs were founded; and religious association. These two factors increase the risk of not adopting an RBA to 9 and 3.28 times higher than NGOs that do not have such factors. The other five factors that have positive relationships with the adoption of RBAs are:

(1) government funding (16-40%);

(2) NGO member (6-15%);

(3) work on advocacy;

(4) work on campaigns; and

(5) work on trade, debt, and aid.

The chance of finding an RBA NGO that has such factors is 8.889, 6.333, 40, 63, and 9 times, respectively, higher than that of an RBA NGO that does not have such factors.

The test of correlations also shows significant negative and positive relationship between the adoption of an RBA and seven factors. The factors that have negative relationships with the adoption of an RBA are the US as the country where the NGO's central office is located, percentage of government funding (less than 15%), and the NGO family's size of less than five members. The factors that have positive relationships with the adoption of RBAs are: the UK and Belgium as the countries where the NGO's central offices are located, working on IFIs and working on HIV/AIDS.

Having found the six factors affecting RBA adoption, we will turn to the first step of this adoption process-the interpretation. The next chapter examines how development NGOs construe the meaning of RBAs to fit their organizational background and expertise, which, ironically, is the first dimension of the policy process that results in a weakening RBA.

8

RBA's and NGO's

Interpretation is the first step in RBA adoption by development NGOs. It is generally assumed that there is only one RBA, especially in international meetings and conferences. This is due to a dominating interpretation of the ESCR school of RBA thinking. This chapter assesses how NGOs actually interpret the concept of RBA and how the interpretations lead to different development policy and strategies, organizational process, and implementation.

Stephens Marks (2001) identifies five ways development writers and practitioners interpret the human rights framework for development: the holistic approach, the capabilities approach, the right to development approach, the responsibilities approach, and the human rights education approach. Marks (2003) later updated his work and added two more approaches: the human rights-based approach and the social justice approach. He calls these interpretations "approaches," referring to a "conceptual framework or way of dealing with complex issues or set of issues" (Marks 2003, 2). In Marks' work, RBA is classified as one of seven interpretations of human rights framework for development.

The RBA that Marks refers to is that of the Human Rights Council of Australia (HRCA), which he correctly points out as having based its entire development policy and program on international human rights laws, the only agreed upon international framework for development cooperation. Marks did not elaborate further what practical implications each of the seven interpretations could have. The implications suggested at the end of his paper-ostensibly for seven types of interpretation-were already laid out in the RBA manual of the HRCA (Frankovits and Earle 1998). Generally, different interpretations should lead to different actions. But in Marks's case, all seven approaches lead to the same set of RBA actions. This poses a question of whether the other six approaches are interpretations of an RBA, or different emphasis of RBAs, or both. This chapter analyzes approaches that lead to different strategies and actions. It discusses the interpretation of an RBA by development agencies, identifies key components of the interpretation, and points ou᛫ strengths and weakness of different interpretations. It argues that although there seems to be areas where development agencies can agree on what is meant by a human rights-based approach to development-as has appeared to be the case at international meetings-in reality, NGOs interpret RBA differently. This chapter further argues that these differences are not mere surfacing or emphasizing, but they are significant differences, leading to a variety of foci, priorities, and strategies taken to achieve their goals. Finally, it is argued that this difference is the result of NGOs' interpretation in ways that fit their organizational background and expertise. Such interpretation is the first of a three-step process that weaken the radical concept of RBAs.

The chapter starts with four models of interpretation of RBA by development agencies, including bilateral development agencies and international development financial institutions. These four models are as follows: first, the Apolitical Assistance group sees development work and their roles as apolitical, while human rights are political and therefore exist in different spheres.

This group does not integrate human rights into their development programs, but claim that their work contributes to human rights. Second, the Democratic Governance group views democratization as the backbone of development. Human rights for this group mean civil and political rights. They do not integrate human rights into development program, but adopt some principles, such as participation. Third, the Caesar Salad group emphasizes sustainable development. They mix campaign development concepts together, including participation and accountability. They state that human rights are encompassing both civil and political rights; as well as economic, social and cultural rights, but mean largely the former. This group integrates some human rights norms into their development programs. Finally, the RBA group believes that human rights and development have the same goals. They seek to integrate human rights standards and principles into development programs.

The chapter then focuses on three cases of Northern development NGOs: ActionAid UK, Oxfam GB, and Save the Children Sweden (SC Sweden). The second section introduces the three NGOs and their entries into RBA. The third section analyzes three models of RBAs, identifying key features of the three interpretations.

The fourth section assesses the three models at work by analyzing the framework for turning policy into programming. The fifth section examines the three models' policies towards development partners, particularly NGOs and governments. Finally, the closing section sums up strengths, weaknesses, and challenges of the conceptual framework of the three models and how their interpretations weaken the concept of RBAs.

THE FOUR MODELS OF INTERPRETATION OF HUMAN RIGHTS TO DEVELOPMENT

Rather than using emphases of interpretations, this section assesses the interpretation of a human rights framework and development by using four indicators: (a) development goals; (b) development processes; (c) development programming; and (d) the use of international human rights instruments.

Development goals are the ultimate achievement that development agencies strive to reach. The development goals of development agencies are one of the most important conceptualizations of the relationships of development and human rights, and a product of interpretation of human rights-based development. This criterion asks: how relevant and interconnecting are development and human rights goals?

Development processes are generally procedures and tools that development agencies use to achieve development goals. Four development processes that the human rights tradition offers to development agencies, while a need-based approach tends not to, are participation, empowerment, accountability, and non-discrimination. The inclusion of these four development processes will be used to differentiate the interpretation of the relationships of human rights and development. This criterion asks: to what extent do development agencies apply the human rights principles in their development processes?

Development programming is how development agencies use its tools and processes and applies them to practical programs and projects. Basic programming elements include situation analysis, identification of target, program design and planning, program implementation, and evaluation. This criterion asks: to what extent are human rights principles used in practice, particularly at each stage of a program cycle?

The Use of UN Human Rights Instruments is the fourth criterion, used to differentiate between various development agencies' approaches. It includes the reference to, the interaction with, and the use of UN human rights bodies, international and regional human rights treaties and standards, and other international human rights mechanisms. This criterion asks: to what extent are international and regional human rights standards and mechanisms used by development agencies in formulating policy and implementing their development work?

Type 1: Apolitical Assistance: Development agencies of this type see human rights as political and see themselves as apolitical development professionals. They endorse the international human rights standards and norms, but do not see them as development goals, or as significant tools that can be used to achieve the goals. Therefore they do not seek to integrate human rights principles or frameworks into their development programs. In fact, they rarely refer to international human rights norms and standards and do not use international human rights bodies or instruments in their development work.

These agencies see their work as traditional development assistance. Democratic and good governing is seen as an important component in achieving economic and political stability, which in turn will promote sustainable development. To establish democratic and good governance, they emphasize the functionality of democratic structures, particularly a national legal framework, electoral systems, judicial institution, and at times, anti-corruption mechanisms and public administration reform. These organizations are concerned with gender issues, both in the processes of development assistance and in the societal and political sphere in general. Civil and political rights are sometimes promoted to enhance the check-and-balance and stability of the political system. Examples within this group are the World Bank, Asian Development Bank (ADB), and AUSAID.

The World Bank does not adopt a rights-based approach and enjoys developing its own tools along the line of a human rights-based approach, such as, Community-Driven Development (CDD) and Social Accountability. These tools are more sellable to its influential economists. The Bank's goal is the same as ActionAid and other progressive development NGOs-to fight poverty. But the Bank's poverty, despite some expansion of the concept, still relies on a large part on traditional macro economic indicators, such as, GDP. Human rights are seen as civil and political rights. They are seen to be having different goals than development, whose primary goal is to reduce the number of people living under a given poverty line. As part of the UN system, the Bank acknowledges international human rights norms and standards, but rarely mentions them. The organization does not use international human rights bodies or mechanisms as it works. In fact, the World Bank for political reasons tries not to use the term "human rights" in its work, although it increasingly uses similar terms, such as health rights.

Type 2: Democratic Governance: The organizations in this category believe that human rights and development goals are different. This group considers that human rights and the development movement have been developed from different traditions. Although human rights mechanisms and principles have much to offer and contribute to development goals, they differ in essence from development. That is, while contributing, human rights are not central to development. Similar to the first group, they believe that sustainable development can be achieved only when the state and society are democratized, the only domain where human rights can contribute to development goals. They use the language of democracy and governance-structurally, but they emphasize more the role of participation than the first group, particularly during assistance delivery.

Development programs emphasize democratic institution building, legal reform, electoral procedures and sometimes, on the rule of law, public education, and civil society strengthening. They use a needs-based development framework and programming to identify groups that most need development assistance. Effective delivery is a key achievement. Human rights mean civil and political rights. The group recognizes international human rights norms and standards, but rarely refers to or uses them. Like the first group, the relationships between development agencies and the people are that of givers or aid providers and receivers or beneficiaries. Examples of this group are USAID, CIDA and JICA. USAID is a good example of the Democratic and Governance model. USAID's work is categorized into sectors, such as, agricultural, environment, democracy and governance. Human rights are a small part of the four areas under democracy and governance. Human rights mean civil and political rights, whereas ESCR are rarely mentioned. As a component in contributing to democratic society, human rights work is narrowly interpreted as supporting legal reform, improving the administration of justice, and increasing citizens' access to justice.

Type 3: The Caesar Salad is the type that accepts and blends in most interesting concepts and tools into its work, sometimes regardless of the compatibility of conceptual frameworks or the implementability by the staff. This group considers that human rights and development goals have a lot in common. In general, they both aim to improve the quality of people's lives. Human rights tools have been used in development processes, including participation, accountability, and rule of law. They shift the emphasis from technical and sectoral development assistance, as the first two groups do, to poverty eradication. Participation is widely applied in development cooperation, as opposed to development assistance, with which effective service delivery is emphasized. Capacity building and partnership with local organizations and the poor play greater roles promoting sustainable development.

However, contrary to the fourth group, this group has limited use of international human rights mechanisms. Human rights have not yet become its organizational values and norms or the driving force of the organization. In addition, they are rather reluctant to address the issues of unequal power relations between the poor and other stakeholders, particularly the state, resulting in a limited advocacy element of their work. Often, both civil and political rights and economic, social and cultural rights are referred to, but greater emphasis is given to the former. Examples of this group are UNDP, SIDA, and EU. UNDP is a good example of the Caesar Salad type. The organization adopts most "trendy" ideas and approaches coming into the development enterprise, at the risk of having minimal strategic plans for operationalizing such ideas. It mainstreams them into the organization, resulting in superficial visits of development concepts that are not necessarily translated into action. The adoption of the SHD/PCD (sustainable human development and people-centered development) in the mid 1990s is a classic example. Despite some attempts, the organization left a gap between theory and practice, or ideal and reality (Nicholls 2000). In 2000, the organization jumped into an RBA approach, linking human rights with its previous concept of human development (UNDP 2000)--an attempt that is again seen as an interesting concept without clear practicality (Uvin 2002).

Type 4: RBA: Development agencies in this group, despite the differences in traditions and contexts under which each emerged, consider human rights and development goals to be almost the same. Most human right tools and principles are used in the development processes, including participation, accountability, non-discrimination, and the rule of law. Development programming emphasizes human rights analysis, addressing root causes of development problems, identification of rights-abused groups, and empowerment. Some have engaged in public campaigns, policy advocacy, and human rights education as a means to strengthen accountability and meeting their development goals. Both civil and political rights, and economic, social, and cultural rights are seen as indivisible and interdependent of one another. Examples of this group are Oxfam, the Department for International Development of the United Kingdom (DFID), ActionAid, and some Save the Children. DFID is an example of the RBA group. The organization emphasizes the development of pro-poor policy and empowerment of the poor. Its development programs aim toward strengthening the accountability of government. Human rights principles are widely used in different stages of development processes, including participation, equality and non-discrimination, and accountability.

It is important to note that development agencies are moving from one category into another. Some features of development agencies can fall into more than one category, both in policy and practice. For instance, some conceptual frameworks of SIDA can be categorized in both type 3 and 4. The boundary of the four groups is not always clear. Some development agencies have characteristics, belonging to more than one group. The four categories, however, are a useful framework showing how development agencies construe the meaning and relevance of human rights and development. More importantly, by setting up the four criteria, this framework helps differentiate the levels of integration and engagement of human rights of development agencies in a context where most claim to be RBA organizations. The next section will take a closer look at three organizations of type 4 and assess further how the same type of development agencies can vary in terms of interpretation, development policy and programming.

THE BACKGROUND AND TURN TOWARDS AN RBA OF ACTIONAID UK, OXFAM GB, AND SAVE THE CHILDREN SWEDEN

ActionAid UK, Oxfam GB, and Save the Children Sweden (SC Sweden) are all in the RBA type. At the end of the 1990s, the three organizations shared the same threats and opportunities of changing political, social, and economical environments, such as economic globalization, worsening poverty conditions, racism-based conflicts, and growing use of communication technologies. But these three NGOs started to integrate human rights into their organizations differently. The starting points of the adoption varied as to each organization's history, previous work, and working methods. This section examines their background and how each turned into adopting a human rights framework in their work.

ActionAid UK

ActionAid is a development NGO working in 30 countries throughout the world. Founded in 1972 with a sponsorship program, ActionAid began its work with 88 UK supporters, sponsoring 88 children in Kenya and India. The organization's focus during the 1970s and 1980s had been on delivering specific services to individuals and providing children with education. ActionAid then expanded its work to help families and communities to support themselves covering the development areas of education, health care, access to food and water, and income generation. Now ActionAid is the third largest NGO in the UK in terms of operational budget.

The change from need-based and service delivery to a human rights-based approach started slowly in the late 1980s and intensified in the late 1990s. The key drives of the change were both from within and outside the organization. Internally, during periodic reviews of development outcomes in a set up of strategic plans, frequently asked was the question of whether the basic service delivery approach was effective. Consensus was gradually built on the notion that the service delivery approach of previous work did not eradicate poverty because it failed to address or tackle the root causes of poverty, which the organization believed to be from unequal distribution of power and resources. As a consequence, reflected in many documents of the organizations, it is stated that to better tackle root causes of poverty, a rights-based approach needs to be adopted (ActionAid 2000a). Externally, the movement toward a rights-based approach, which originated in Europe, has gained currency and influenced the organization. Amartaya Sen's concept of the entitlement of the people as a way to sustainable development has influenced the organization, as well as the work of other NGOs, especially that of Oxfam. All these factors contributed to ActionAid taking an RBA. Since then, the organization has started a learning process on how to transform human rights concepts into development work.

However, RBA is not the only approach the organization has adopted in the past decade. In the early 1990s, ActionAid adopted a "people centered and sustainable development approach". At the time the organization had taken on the new approach without internal agreement as to the meaning of the new approach. When combined with the complexity of the approach, the limited influence at an international level, the limited capability in policy advocacy and reaching the poorest of the poor, and resistance from trustees, the organization faced several difficulties in implementing the new approach- while at the same time making significant strides in adopting the new approach.

By the end of 1990s, the people centered and sustainable development approach was less discussed, paving the way for RBA discussions. This time the organization elaborates, in one of ActionAid's early writings on RBA, that they decided to adopt an RBA because it:

(1) Provides a sound legal and moral basis for addressing the complex ethical questions that ActionAid faces;

(2) Strengthens the links between programming and advocacy work and the macro and micro linkages;

(3) Helps clarify the roles and responsibilities of the different actors, particularly the state;

(4) Places central power in the hands of those whose rights have been denied and violated, to hold the state and non-state actors accountable;

(5) Offers a comprehensive and coherent analytical framework for more effective planning, implementation, and evaluation of emergency programs;

(6) Provides objective criteria for cooperation and coordination;

(7) Promotes self-reliance and dignity of people suffering denial and violation of rights, instead of reducing them to passive recipients of services (without excluding the possibility of emergency response when necessary), and

(8) Focuses on the systematic denial and violation of rights and this encourages the development of long-term and sustainable solutions (Morago-Nocholas 2000; and ActionAid 2000a).

ActionAid's point of entry to an RBA is around food rights, one of the strongest themes of the organization. In 2002, ActionAid campaigned on food rights, advocating for poverty reduction to be at the centre of trade agreements, particularly in WTO rule making. Its campaign focused on the impacts of Trade Related Intellectual Property Rights (TRIPs) and the Agreement on Agricultural (AoA) on food security and poor farmers (ActionAid 1999b; 2001a; 2001b).

It is important to note that throughout ActionAid's history, it has experienced working on the ground at the grassroots level and developed the skills of working with poor communities. This has become an important strength of the organization that very few international NGOs have. This grassroots experience has influenced the organization's interpretation of an RBA when it comes to formulating development policies and strategies, which will be discussed in the next section.

Oxfam GB

Oxfam GB was founded in the United Kingdom in 1942 in response to the famine in Greece under German occupation during the World War II. In 1943, when other committees dissolved, the Oxford Famine Relief Committee remained at its work and registered as a charity whose objective was the "relief of suffering in consequences of the war". Six years later, the mandate was enlarged to include "wars or other causes in any part of the world". The organization continued to focus on disaster relief throughout the 1960s, during which period the organization formally adopted the name "Oxfam," which had became a well-known abbreviated telegraph address of the Oxford Committee. The 1960s also marked a time of significant growth of Oxfam's shops where 22,000 volunteers helped fundraise in more than 830 shops.

In the 1970s the organization expanded to development project work. Oxfam GB hired 11 expatriates and was working in 800 communities in 19 countries by 1971. A Public Affairs Unit was set up in the 1970s to provide research and analysis of poverty. This research work has helped provide a basis for advocacy and campaign work of the organization beginning in the 1980s. Oxfam GB started to do lobbying work around issues of food aid, pesticides, and debt of the Third World, and campaign on international trade from the 1980s.

By the 1990s, Oxfam had become an international campaigning organization as well as a relief and development organization. During the decade, Oxfam organized and ran a number of international campaigns on various issues, including debt relief, the cost of basic medicine for the poor, universal education, fair trade, and child soldiers. Oxfam's work on fair trade, initiated in the 1970s, was intensified after the 1999 Seattle riot, which generated support for Oxfam work and its new 2002 "Make Trade Fair" campaign.

Oxfam GB also built up its lobbying capacity in the 1990s. It set up an international advocacy office in Washington DC to lobby international bodies, including the World Bank, the IMF, and the UN in 1995. Now Oxfam has gained experience in campaign work and received respect as a leading organization in the field. It is also often seen as a "campaigning" development NGO with a strong research and analysis capability. Oxfam GB's entry point to RBA started in the early 1990s when it started a campaign called "basic rights", covering its own list of ten human rights, including the right to health and the right to education. The campaigning ended in the mid-1990s, leaving Oxfam with valuable experience working explicitly on human rights, which paved the way for Oxfam to adopt an RBA more explicitly after its strategic review in 1997-1998.

This strategy review started the early 1990s as part of a process to position the organization better within a changing world. The organization took a comprehensive approach with a large consultation with partners in reviewing its strategy. During 1997-1998, it set up a committee to commission an independent report, based on interviews with 194 stakeholders in fourteen countries. The report recommended strategies concerning a wide range of issues, such as prioritizing partnering, especially in the south, building strong links on the ground, and strengthening advocacy work (Lindenberg and Bryant 2001).

The foundation of Oxfam's RBA, which was the product of a strategy review, was the development and adoption of the five Aims and their "Strategic Change Objectives" (SCOs), which correspond to five sets of human rights. This helped the "generalist" development agency link its different themes together with an international human rights framework.

THE THREE MODELS: CONCEPTUAL FRAMEWORKS

ActionAid UK

When a human rights-based approach came into ActionAid at the end of 1990s, it did not totally replace the previous approach-the people-centered and sustainable development (PC/SD), but instead the new RBA concept is mixed with the PC/SD, and vice versa. There are components that the two approaches have in common, but there are also key components, differentiating them from each other, such as the RBA holds that people are entitled to human rights, while PC/SD does not. Despite differences between the two approaches, ActionAid finds ways to put them together. For instance, "People are the centre of a rights-based discourse. People are the ones who need to benefit from this approach (RBA)." The interaction of the new and existing thinking, together with organizational history, strengths, and culture, brings in a new type of RBA, which in this case, is the Popular RBA.

The Popular RBA's analysis of poverty is that it is caused by unequal power relationships, resulting in unjust distribution of resources. It believes that poverty will continue, unless the root causes of poverty are tackled. It holds that poverty is a denial of basic rights, such as education, food, healthcare, water, livelihood, information, and participation (ActionAid 1999). ActionAid's development analysis has touched upon North-South relationships in the context of global poverty. It has produced policy papers analyzing the impacts of globalization, trade, and international financial institutions (IFIs) on the poor and the marginalized. The organization is of a view that to eradicate poverty, the globalization process must be shaped in a way that does not exacerbate the situation of the poor in the South as is the case at present.

ActionAid's development goals are not the same as human rights goals, or the enjoyment of all human rights enshrined in international human rights standards. Its development goals are based on a new poverty framework-one that is much broader, and is based on the entitlement concept-but smaller in scope compared to that of human rights. It states that its mission is to work with the poor and marginalized people to eradicate poverty by overcoming the injustice and inequality that cause it. The organization states the popular "fighting poverty" theme, but what is unique is its interpretation that empowerment of the poor and the marginalized is key to the solution. Its "local up" method arises from its belief that through the creativity and energy of the poor, they can overcome abject poverty. ActionAid's conceptual framework is largely influenced by its experience working in rural areas with grassroots organizations and poor communities in the south.

Its use of international human rights standards is limited. ActionAid holds that poverty is a denial of human rights and acknowledges some human rights tools, such as participation and empowerment. However, it has yet to further develop its human rights framework. ActionAid does not use international human rights norms as its strategy nor as the basis for its programs. Its development framework has little to do with the UN human rights bodies. In fact, the organization strategy for 1999-2003 treats human rights as a sectoral program of work, rather than a framework of all the work of the organization (ActionAid 1999).

The limited use of the UN human rights framework poses big challenges for ActionAid. As empowerment of grassroots groups becomes the key to the organization's strategy, ActionAid must have human rights education as one of its key tools-if not a goal in itself-and help the poor learn about their rights so that they can claim them. However, there is limited knowledge of human rights and little skill in designing and delivering human rights education sessions. It also should be noted that ActionAid's human rights education is important to the poor or the "victim categories," and not all groups.

In sum, ActionAid's conceptual framework in relation to RBA can be described as a "Popular" RBA. Its RBA stems from a thorough analysis of poverty and powerlessness, starting from the local situation and linking it to the global context. Its development goals are defined in a new expanded poverty framework, with reference to entitlement. Most importantly, ActionAid's "local up" development process leads to its utmost strategy of empowerment of the poor and the marginalized-support people so that they can claim their human rights. Instead of advocating for change at the international level, the Popular RBA starts at the grassroots level upward. The Popular RBA use international human rights in a limited fashion. Its RBA is rooted in the belief that the poor can make the changes, but they are deprived of their human rights necessarily to live their dignified lives. The Popular RBA works to support people to claim their human rights and bring development back to the people.

"Globalization can only help to end poverty, if equity is given the same priority as economic growth." In other words, "globalization without equity isn't globalization" (Oxfam 2004a, 1). Oxfam's view of development problems is centered around equity, which also serves as a key guiding principle of Oxfam's strategy (Oxfam International 2001, 2004).

"The Oxfam's focus is on the realizations of economic and social rights within the wider human rights continuum. Equity is key in the realization of these rights. Equity is about making the rules fair for poor people and ensuring that justice prevails." (Oxfam 2001, 2)

The analysis of "global rules" and "equity for the poor" development framework is one of the most important contributions that Oxfam offers to the development enterprise. More importantly, the analysis enables the Oxfam family to take crucial steps forward, from the basic form to social justice work, based on compassion and generous giving to much more complex campaigns and actions. Oxfam's analysis on global rules and equity brings economic dimension to its "social justice" framework. The organization now gradually adds the term "economic" to "social justice," and use the term "economic and social justice" interchangeably with "economic and social rights," although it means more of the former.

This "global rules" analysis highlights inequalities, both between rich and poor countries, and within a country. It notes that poverty-"a state of powerlessness in which people are unable to exercise their basic human rights or control virtually any aspect of their lives"-is usually rooted in human action or inaction. These actions and inactions, for Oxfam, mean more at the structural level, including the global market, and institutional, and economic mechanisms.

Oxfam's development framework is rather a macro and structural view, highlighting the impacts of the world inequalities to the poor in the global south. That is, it starts from a global perspective then analyzes the impacts on the poor at the local level. The organization seeks to address the structural causes of poverty-largely at the international level, and to a lesser degree at the regional and national levels-through campaigns and development work. Examples of what is produced out of this conceptual framework are the debt relief campaign and the "Make Trade Fair" campaign.

The "Make Trade Fair" campaign, for example, is designed to communicate to the western public, showing them how the global supply chain can worsen the livelihoods of the poor in the developing country, and linking this global picture with places its audience is acquainted to, stores such as Tesco and Wal-Mart.

A recent Oxfam report demonstrates how, in the modern global trade structure, western-based companies can be "squeezed down the supply chain" and undermine the labour standards they claim to be promoting, leaving women workers in developing countries vulnerable, as rights are denied and traded away (Oxfam International 2004a).

For Oxfam GB, development goals are not the same as human rights goals. Its development goals are to fight poverty and global injustice, which is a part of the realization of all human rights. Like ActionAid, Oxfam's RBA conceptual framework is of a new poverty framework, and is not rooted in, or based on, a human rights framework itself. Its framework reflects a conception of social justice at the global level, driven by compassion for the poor and the disadvantaged and the desire for a fairer world, rather than by agreed upon standards of human rights.

Despite the advantages of using a human rights framework-which covers many dimensions of human dignity--Oxfam chooses to work in a derived social justice framework, which relies on arbitrary perception and subjective measures of human suffering and powerlessness. Putting human rights as its mission places the organization on a higher moral ground, helps mobilize people in its global campaigns-a human rights means toward a social justice end-and creates coherence between its global campaigns and country-based development programs.

Although Oxfam does not use the international human rights standards directly in its work, it does take a step further in incorporating a human rights framework in its work by rearranging its thematic work into five groups.

All groups are tied to certain international human rights standards, although the language used is not quite a human rights one. Oxfam has hardly utilized the UN human rights bodies, but it refers to a human rights framework selectively and strategically in its campaigns. It downplays the role of human rights education in its work. For Oxfam GB, human rights education is not a key to achieving an RBA to development; rather the keys are the campaign and development programs that are linked to the five sets of human rights it has clustered together.

In sum, Oxfam's tactical use of human rights aims primarily to legitimize the causes it works on and to mobilize popular supports in its campaigns and development work that have strong advocacy components. Its system of beliefs is of social justice, and not human rights. The latter comes into play at the strategic objective and tactical level to achieve social justice goals of equity in the world. For these reasons, Oxfam GB's RBA will be called an "Equity RBA."

The Three Models of RBAs: Policy, Strategy and Programming

This section assesses the interpretation of RBAs of ActionAid UK, Oxfam GB, and SC Sweden by examining their development policies and strategies. It shows whether organizations use human rights as tools to achieve development goals, as opposed to treating human rights of people as goals in themselves.

The former uses some human rights principles and adds them to its development strategies, such as participation, empowerment, and advocacy. The latter holds that governments are principal duty-bearers to human rights. They usually use human rights instruments, mechanisms, and other means to hold the government accountable and to realize people's human rights.

ActionAid's experience working with grassroots groups and poor community leads the organization to interpret RBA, focusing on what it means to its grassroots work. The answer is to empower the poor so that they can claim their rights. This helps the organization pay more attention to the root causes of poverty, which it believes to be due to unequal power relationships.

ActionAid therefore uses empowering the poor and marginalized as its key forces of change. This fits well with the issues it works on-particularly food rights and the right to a livelihood-as these themes allow them to work closely with the poor communities they aim to empower.

ActionAid UK has a common strategy shared by all its members. The strategic paper, "Fighting Poverty Together," identifies key directions from 1999-2003. The paper identifies four strategies, focusing heavily on strengthening the poor and the marginalized with a goal to mitigate barriers to poverty reduction at the international level.

Although this strategic paper gives high value to human rights and a human rights-based approach, it tends to treat a rights-based approach as an "add-on" tool to development work, rather than as a fundamental change on the policy and strategic level. The four goals and strategic objectives do not show significant integration of human rights and development. Some strategic objectives still reflect a vision of human rights as a sectoral program of development work, such as "promote basic rights" as one of the two strategic objectives of Goal 1: poor and marginalized people will increasingly realize their potential (ActionAid 1999).

ActionAid identifies its strengths and matches up its comparative advantage with the direction of its work, as follows:

(1) Listen to poor and marginalized people, achieve trust, and take a long term and holistic approach to supporting their struggles;

(2) Skills in participatory methods and approaches can be used to make the voices of poor and marginalized people heard and help make duty bearers accountable to them;

(3) Promote poor people's access to information and work to make all institutions affecting them more transparent and accountable;

(4) Form and strengthen networks;

(5) As an international organization, tackle factors that deny rights; develop policy alternatives that link micro and macro perspectives, and give the poor direct access to international and regional institutions and forums (ActionAid 2000).

The organization, however, does not intend to discontinue its service delivery through which it developed its expertise over the past decades. Under the new RBA framework, service delivery is regarded as helping the poor and marginalized attain immediate, practical improvements in their condition, while at the same time developing the new programs that nurture resistance, organization, and activism over the longer term. ActionAid UK's strategies lead to development programs that contain many capacity building and empowering elements. The organization works with communities to help them form and control the development processes and "reverse the tradition of denying them the right to define their own reality and act on their own behalf" (ActionAid 2000, 13). The organization also places a heavy emphasis on advocating for policy change, especially at the local level.

This matches the organization's capacity, as ActionAid UK tends to have a limited advocacy capacity on the international level, but much stronger experience working and advocating at the provincial and local levels.

At the national and local level, ActionAid's RBA contains much of the south's style of activism, or collective action as a means to change power relations. It believes that leader or individual action is not enough for people's rights. There needs to be a process of organizing people as a group in order to gain a right (ActionAid 2000).

ActionAid has tried quite a few development approaches and ideas in the past decades, including sustainable human development in the early 1990s and RBA in the late 1990s. For the RBA, it does not use an international human rights framework as the basis for its work, nor does it reformulate its strategies in a human rights perspective. ActionAid UK's RBA uses key human rights tools and principles-participation, empowerment, and accountability-and adapts them to its existing work, which is a key feature of the "add-on" approach.

Oxfam's interpretation of RBA is affected by its organizational background and expertise in advocacy and campaigns targeting international development actors and issues. The Equity RBA is built based on its organizational strength, rather than on international human rights standards. Its key force of change is the advocacy for changes through global campaigns.

This key force fits well with the thematic areas that Oxfam GB has chosen to work on-economic rights-for it allows the organization to use its capacity in policy research and advocacy at the global level to address and challenge the policies and practices of global economic players. Oxfam GB has successfully worked with other Oxfam members in working out a development strategy, stated in human rights terms. The paper identifies five sets of human rights that the Oxfam family will strive to achieve during 2001-2004:

1. The right to sustainable livelihoods (economic and environmental equity, and sustainable livelihoods for future generations)
2. The right to basic social services (equitable access to basic healthcare and education)
3. The right to life and security (equitable provision of protection, relief, and rehabilitation)
4. The right to be heard (equitable participation in political, economical, and social policy-making and decisions)
5. The right to an identity (equity in gender and diversity).

The present three-year strategic plan (2004-2006) retains the five sets of human rights with minor changes and emphases. For instance, it aims to shift its advocacy and campaign work from the UK to other influential countries and to the South. A new emphasis is on integration of campaigns into other areas of work, particularly the Make Trade Fair campaign.

As a major RBA product, the five aims, articulated in human rights terms, have resulted in more focused work. That is, they allow Oxfam to be more rigorous than before. For instance, in the Philippines, Oxfam's work used to be somewhat scattered, resulting in less impact. After Oxfam GB adopted the five aims, the country team has to show, for example with the right to livelihoods, how the policies, practices, and values are going to change at the local and/or global level.

Priority change is another important result of the five aims. Oxfam GB did not quite have priorities before the adoption f the five aims. On the country level in East Asia, for example, it ran short-term campaigns that came and went. Priorities in any one region or country program were determined by the need as assessed by the country team staff or by its expertise in certain areas. It lacked a centralized means of prioritizing.

These five aims serve as a tool for staff to set priorities and their associated budgets.

In terms of programming, Oxfam GB divides its work into three types of intervention: humanitarian, development and campaign work. The three areas of work are based in one or more of the five aims. Despite sharing a basis of a human rights framework, each area has been developed and integrated into a human rights-based approach at different levels.

Humanitarian work has been the area of highest program expenditure and is expected to remain at 40% of total program expenditure in the 2006/07 budget. Oxfam has invested a lot of effort in improving the quality of humanitarian work and has become a leading organization in the field.

The organization felt that it should keep humanitarian work as a key priority. The work falls under one of the aims (Aim 3). In humanitarian work, Oxfam gives the principle of the right to life as precedence of other rights as set out in the Red Cross and NGO code of conduct, to which Oxfam is a signatory. There has been little progress in applying an RBA into this area, as compared with the other two areas.

Campaigning is a cross cutting area. It is a major force in advocacy and activism at the global and country levels. Globally, it receives about 10% of the global budget. One of Oxfam's key campaign strategies is to change public opinions using newly invested media work as the organization has recruited new staff with journalistic backgrounds.

Campaigning has been integrated into country programs-this is called Programming (with a capital "P"), because Oxfam GB believes that all programs should have campaigning elements. The East Asia program, for example, has the livelihood program, which looks at labour rights. Some of this work is not primarily campaigning, but comes in the support of local organizations to improve the lives of labourers. However, it does aim to incorporate a campaign within it.

In campaigning work, Oxfam has applied human rights principles most inconsistently. The education campaign, for instance, does not make reference to, or is not based on international human rights framework of the right to education, which is more comprehensive and well-developed than many other development themes.

Previously, the campaign focused on financing of basic education and girls' education, before shifting to use the Millennium Development Goal framework. The campaign limitedly reflects priorities of the right to education, such as universal primary education and non-discrimination, or highlights the interdependence of human rights, such as health and nutrition at schools.

As part of campaigning and advocacy efforts, Oxfam has invested heavily in building capacity of advocacy efforts. It lobbies international economic institutions, such as, the World Bank, the IMF, and the WTO, as well as influential northern countries, such as, the US and the UK. There is, however, limited work on pressuring southern countries or on partnering with southern organizations in its campaigns, although it is moving towards involving government and civil society from the south.

Human rights-based principles have mostly been applied to development work, which is mostly country-based and must contribute to one of the five aims. Development priority setting has been derived out from the analysis of the external situation, which is not always in human rights terms. Along with senior management, the Regional Strategic Teams (RSTs) are key to regional strategic development. The country programs are then designed based on the regional strategies.

There has been some integration among the three areas of work-particularly humanitarian and development work-though full integration has yet to be reached. Campaigning work, which is planned and designed mostly from the Headquarters, has been weakly linked to the other two areas. The Oxfam strategic plan (2004-2006) asserts that a campaign is most effective when it has direct links with other programs, resulting in a call for continuous learning of how to link the three areas of work in the strategic plan (Oxfam International 2004). Activism is closely linked with campaigns and country work. However, most activism remains in the north with little involvement of southern organizations. Most advocacy work in the south is carried out by development programs at country levels, through capacity building of local civil society organizations, so that they can advocate for policy change in their countries.

Oxfam GB has deprioritized some program areas after the adoption of an RBA. The East Asia regional director notes that the East Asia program has deprioritized health work because there are other agencies operating with more health expertise. Besides, Oxfam GB has mostly done health work in its emergency program, and not so much in other contexts. So, the organization has now deprioritized the program and keeps it only in emergency work where it is well established.

SC Sweden's interpretation of RBA is effected by its previous work on children and the use of children's rights instruments in its work. The classical RBA is based on active advocacy and participation in the implementation of the CRC.

It plays NGO's roles as suggested in the UN reporting mechanisms, that is, to monitor and report the progress of implementation of the CRC. Other work is built upon this solid ground. SC Sweden sets its strategies and priorities based on the CRC.

It analyzes children rights' situation, using the CRC, as well as the "Concluding Observations" of the CRC Committee, to determine the most disadvantaged groups of children, and prioritizes work with them. With the CRC as the foundation document of the organization, SC Sweden's priorities have shifted from delivering community services to child protection, and more recently to child participation, with an emphasis on human rights awareness.

Issues, such as the physical environment of children, particularly youth (15-18 years old), have received a higher priority as it fits better within a child protection framework, while landmines and child soldiers have received less priority, at least in terms of resources.

SC Sweden's RBA programming aims at drawing on different traditions of actions, moving towards justice, equality, and freedom. Three traditions that should be integrated are: first, human rights; second, development, charity, and relief; and third, social and political activism.

Human rights offer a set of internationally agreed upon legal and moral standards, which cover civil, political, economic, social, and cultural rights of all human beings in all times and places. They define the obligations of governments, institutions, and individuals in terms of respect, protection, and fulfillment. Development, charity, and relief deal with the distribution of resources and access to services, including health, education, social welfare, poverty alleviation, and income generation.

Social and political activism helps mobilize people to demand a redistribution of power, such as the redistribution of wealth between the rich and poor nations through debt relief or changes in trade rules; women demanding equal pay for equal work; and landless peasants demanding a redistribution of farmland (Thesis 2002).

SC Sweden has developed a long list of program areas as a programming framework for regional and country offices to choose from and prioritize as they think appropriate to local situations. Under each program area, organization policies, objectives, strategies, and implementation methods are clearly identified, thus forming quite a comprehensive strategy paper. While Oxfam classifies its work into three categories (humanitarian, development, and campaign), SC Sweden has developed a better link of four working methods: research and analysis; direct support; knowledge dissemination and capacity building; advocacy and awareness-raising (SC Sweden 2001b).

In addition to the "program area" framework, SC Sweden has worked with other SC members to develop an important programming tool, known as "Child Rights Programming (CRP)." Compared to the program area guides, the CRP handbook is much less detailed, more complex and abstract, and thus unlikely to be a practical programming handbook.

But the CRP is the most crucial component of the organization in framing its entire work in a human rights perspective. It gives the meaning of CRP as "using the Principles of Child Rights to Plan, Manage, Implement and Monitor Programmes with the Overall goal of strengthening the rights of the child as defined in International Law" (ISCA 2002, 23).

SC Sweden also emphasizes advocacy work as one of its four integral working methods. Internationally, SC Sweden has advocated and lobbied several UN bodies and European countries, as well as the European Union.

It has been successful in getting child rights high on the agenda and has strengthened the commitment of its targeted institutions and countries. On the country level, where SC Sweden operates, its advocacy work has been done mostly through city-based civil society organizations (CSOs), with which SC Sweden has traditionally worked.

Due to limited experience in advocating or lobbying southern governments, SC Sweden chooses the approach of advocacy-capacity building of local CSOs, instead of directly lobbying itself. This has become a major part of SC Sweden's empowerment model.

Advocacy work is often integrated with activism. Before the adoption of an RBA, SC Sweden did not pay much attention to activism. Although activism had never been a strength of SC Sweden, recently it has developed as a new area of work toward which the organization is moving. Activism for SC Sweden is a mixture of traditional northern style activities (mostly used by human rights organizations), such as, public campaigning and advocacy with media work, and of traditional southern-style campaigning for the poor, the marginalized, victims, and potential victims, to demand of their governments certain rights (Theis 2003).

Human rights education (HRE) is a feature of the classical RBA. It has been one of the areas in which SC Sweden has prioritized and invested heavily (Theis 2003). SC Sweden believes that human rights education will contribute to long-term changes in attitude, knowledge, and behaviour towards children's rights.

It sees that many governments lack the capacity to fulfil their obligations while civil society has a limited awareness and knowledge of human rights and human rights mechanisms. The organization therefore designs programs to create this capacity. Trainings on various issues have been designed and conducted for different key target groups, including government officials and NGOs.

PARTNERSHIPS AND RELATIONSHIPS WITH STAKEHOLDERS

An important area of the RBA interpretation is partnerships and relationships with stakeholders, particularly with governments and partner NGOs and CSOs. Observers suggest that after adopting an RBA, an organization's relationship and strategies on relationships are likely to change. This section examines the interpretation of these three organization concerning what these changes are and the reasons behind these changes.

Relationship with Partner NGOs

It is generally agreed that RBA generates closer partnership. An RBA leads to four changes in relations to partnership.

First, an RBA bring greater partnership due to human rights solidarity underpinning the principle of universality and interdependent of human rights (Frankovits and Earle 2000).

Second, an RBA should be shared and promoted to partners (Frankovits and Earle 2000).

Third, an RBA brings changes in choice of partnership (Geidenmark 2000; Uvin 2004).

Finally, an RBA NGOs should support local human rights NGOs (Uvin 2004). The arguments on partnerships are examined here at two levels. First, in this chapter, there is an assessment of the extent that the three cases of NGOs state they would prepare for the expected change.

SC Sweden believes that by adopting an RBA it is likely to work closer with partners. Human rights goals are so broad that no single NGO has the capacity to do all the work. Moreover, RBA calls for stronger partners-building to help promote the rights of the child (ISCA 2002). Internal factors also encourage the organization towards a closer partnership with others. These factors include a limited capacity, particularly in the number of staff. In addition, the organization than has more money to divert to other local and grassroots organizations.

ActionAid agrees and acknowledges that although governments and inter-governmental bodies are primarily responsible for defining and enforcing rights, it is through the process of governance that rights are achieved or denied. Governance necessarily involves relations with markets, civil society, family and community, as well as states.

Therefore, an RBA will require ActionAid to build relationships with a wide variety of actors, beyond those with whom it has traditionally worked, including groups with which governments may not agree.

Both SC Sweden and ActionAid UK note that RBA make them work more with activism and human rights organizations (Theis 2004; ActionAid 2000).

ActionAid goes further in interpreting that its partners should also be, or willing to be, RBA organizations and that ActionAid should help them to be so (ActionAid 2000). The organization has a plan to work with fellow partners for a specific period of time in which its partners could significantly shift their work into a rights-based approach, prior to reviewing whether to continue their partnership (ActionAid 2000).

While an RBA introduces new partners for NGOs, it can also cause problems for them. A policy staff of ActionAid notes that partnerships bring with them large changes for the organization.

It has proved to be one of the most difficult problems to solve as the organization not only needs to develop common understanding of an RBA with its staff, but also with those who work with the organization. OxfamGB states clearly that working with partners is one of its four working approaches. "The Oxfams at all times work through local and accountable organizations and/or towards strengthening or facilitating the establishment of such organization or structures...and where and when local capacity is insufficient or inappropriate the Oxfams will help people directly... while working simultaneously on strengthen local capacity" (Oxfam International 2001, 2).

For Oxfam, the empowerment of local organizations is vital to secure its economic and social justice goals. It notes that in 2000 Oxfam worked with over 3,000 local partners throughout the world. (Oxfam International 2001, 2)

Relationship with Governments

A key issue that draws almost opposite interpretations of an RBA is whether the approach suggests for a change from a cooperation mode, as it was in the past, to a more confrontational mode in order to address power relations-which is widely believed to be the root cause of poverty.

ActionAid takes the lead in the interpretation favoring the confrontation mode. The organization asserts that before adopting an RBA, it had long worked in cooperation with other stakeholders, trying to avoid taking sides or opposing government policy or measures, "as it is daunting and potentially risky to challenge the supreme power in the country" (ActionAid 2000, 15). A rights-based approach changes this tradition, as the approach is inherently political, aiming to change power relations.

ActionAid further articulates its interpretation, claiming that within its RBA, confrontation can be used not only when it is necessary, but also when it is appropriate. Its assumption is first, that poverty is caused by a denial of rights and failure to protect and fulfil the obligations of the authorities. Second, to eradicate poverty, one needs to change the power relationship between the poor and the authorities.

Finally, the authority is unlikely to give up its power and instead is likely to support the status quo. A regional workshop for staff of country offices states clearly that: "Leaders, and organizations, engaging in rights-based work must be ready for confrontation and must realize that conflict is not bad. Changing the status quo calls for conflicts, as there will always be forces resisting change. Since this is a process of changing power relations, it has to be realized that power relations will not change unless challenged."

This, however, does not mean that confrontational approach will be applied to all dimensions of its work. ActionAid's decision to either cooperate or resist is calculated and informed primarily by its analysis of power relations and overall strategy. Its position is simply that it will cooperate with those who stand with the poor and the marginalized, and "challenge and resist" those who stand against the poor and marginalized (ActionAid 2000, iii).

ActionAid's position towards a confrontational approach is influenced by its experience working closely with social movements of the global south, which have traditionally confronted governments. SC Sweden's and Oxfam GB's interpretation is somewhat softer. Both agree that without challenging power relations, RBA will have much less meaning, but the ways to challenge it does not necessarily or only mean confronting governments.

Oxfam GB accepts that being political is unavoidable in adopting an RBA. But while ActionAid challenges the power at the local and grassroots level, Oxfam challenges the power at the international level through mainly its global campaigns, and to a lesser degree, through its development and advocacy programs at the national level.

SC Sweden's interpretation is more balanced. It accepts that the adoption of an RBA means becoming more political, as the approach attempts to address power relations. But the organization recognizes that governments are key to protection and fulfillment of children rights and that it should find ways to establish a constructive and productive working relationship. It sees that both cooperation and confrontation have their own advantages in advancing children's rights.

SC Sweden notes, in general, good cooperation with governments speeds up the steps taken towards the realization of children's rights, and there are times when confrontation might be needed to change the direction of the government's practices on children's rights. An organization will have to always use the best method in a given circumstance and be ready to change in a new situation.

CONCLUSION

This chapter finds that the concept of RBA, which has high potential to bring radical and powerful implications to the development enterprise, is weakened, as NGOs interpret the concept to fit their organization backgrounds and expertise. ActionAid's RBA interpretation focuses on empowerment of the poor, as the organization has expertise in working with grassroots and poor communities.

Oxfam's RBA interpretation focus on advocacy at the international level, as the organization has developed its expertise in campaigning on international issues targeting international development actors. SC Sweden's RBA interpretation focuses on strengthening protection of children rights at the national level, as the organization has expertise working on children at the national level.

Although the interpretations that are based on organizational expertise help advance some aspects of RBA, they hold back a full interpretation of what an RBA can mean to the poor, and in this process, they weaken the radical concept of RBAs.

This chapter begins with an argument that RBA is only one type of interpretation of the relationship of human rights and development. Development agencies increasingly claim that they, too, are rights-based organizations, or they too, contribute to human rights. This chapter tests their human rights-related development framework against four indicators: development goals, development processes, development programming, and use of human rights instruments.

As a result, four types of conceptual frameworks of the interconnection of human rights and development have been identified. An RBA is one of the four interpretative frameworks.

First, the "Apolitical Assistance" type sees that human rights and development goals and processes are different. They are in separated spheres and have little to do with each other, although parts of civil and political rights can contribute to development. This first type rarely uses international human rights instruments.

Second, the "Democratic Governance" sees that human right and development have different goals. Some human rights tools are used in development programs, emphasizing democratic institution building. Like the first type, though Democratic Governance does not use or refer to international human rights instruments.

The third type is the Caesar's Salad. Development agencies of this type hold that human rights and development have shared goals. Some human rights principles are applied in development programs, although the use of international human rights instruments is still limited. This group tends to add new concepts to its previous ones and tries to mix them together.

The last type, the "RBA" believes that human rights and development goals are in fact almost the same goals. This group applies a variety of human rights principles and tools in its development work. It makes reference to international human rights standards and uses some instruments.

Within the same RBA type, three variants of interpretation are identified: the Popular, the Equity, and the Classical RBAs. A further analysis of three examples of Northern development NGOs (ActionAid UK, Oxfam GB, and SC Sweden) finds that the three organizations interpret RBAs differently in important ways, resulting in a variety of policies, strategies, and programming. ActionAid's interpretation leads to the "Popular RBA," featuring a local-to-global analysis, strong empowerment of the poor and the marginalized, the "add-on" human rights principles in programming, "local-up" advocacy, and a limited use of international human rights instruments. The Popular RBA addresses power relations from the local up by strengthening and campaigning at the grassroots level.

These three variants are the results of the interpretation of RBA concepts to fit organizational background and expertise the NGOs had before the adoption of RBA. The interpretation that is aimed to fit organizational pre-position weakens the concept of RBA as some of the concepts get left out, such as equality and non-discrimination and the reference to international human rights standards. ActionAid has worked and had expertise working with grassroots groups before it created a "Popular RBA" emphasizing empowering grassroots groups. Oxfam GB has been a campaigning organization before it built up an "Equity RBA," focusing on advocacy through global campaigns.

Oxfam GB's interpretation forms the "Equity RBA", featuring a selective use of human rights norms and instruments to legitimize and mobilize people and resources in challenging power relations at the global level with its global campaigns. This RBA sees human rights-based approach as a tool to reach its economic and social justice goals, rather than having human rights as goals in itself. In direct contrast to ActionAid, Oxfam has a global-to-local analytical framework. Oxfam's RBA also features its five Aims, based on international human rights norms and linking together three types of intervention. Campaigning is a key advocacy tool for the Equity RBA, especially at the global level, where Oxfam GB has been more effective compared with the local level.

Save the Children Sweden introduces the "Classical RBA", featuring a comprehensive use of international human rights norms and instruments. It states its goals within a human rights framework, compared to a poverty framework, like the Popular and Equity RBAs. It deploys a variety of human rights and development tools in strengthening the protection and promotion of children's rights within the framework of its eleven program areas. Advocacy work is a key tool both on the international and national levels, although grassroots work has been limited.

The Popular, the Equity, and the Classical RBAs distinguish themselves in conceptual frameworks, policies and strategies, and the use of international human rights standards. The three models of RBA also show us that NGOs do not adopt all aspects of RBAs, rather they choose some of the concepts, standards, and principles that can best fit, sharpen, and improve the work, in which they already have expertise, working methods, and mandates. This weakens the concept of RBA from being fully interpreted and realized.

Partnership and relationship with stakeholders is a key area where interpretation of an RBA leads to different outcomes. The Popular, Equity, and Classical RBAs all agree that RBA adoption creates greater needs for partnerships, and with more variety of partners, including human rights groups. A more controversial interpretation is whether an RBA means more cooperation or confrontation with governments. When faced with a clear-cut challenge to take sides, ActionAid takes a strong stand on the side of the poor and chooses to confront governments when appropriate. The Equity RBA acknowledges unequal power relationships. With more experience working on political issues, Oxfam aims to address the power relations issue and confront governments and international institutions at the global level through its global campaigns. The Classical RBA is of a view that the merit of cooperation and confrontation is not absolute, but relative. It finds that constructive cooperation can accelerate the progress towards the realization of children's rights, while confrontation can be appropriate to address certain policies and practices that undermine human rights.

Having examined the problems involved in the interpretation of the RBA, we turn in the next chapter to the impact of organizational dynamics of the operationalization of the concept in development NGOs. This next chapter assesses how organizational process weakens and holds back the radical concept of RBA from being fully realized.

9

Approaches to Organizational Change

As the Popular, the Equity and the Classical RBA have been put into practice, ActionAid UK, Oxfam GB, and SC Sweden have changed parts of their organizations to better translate their RBA conceptual frameworks into programs. Theoretically, in order to implement an RBA, significant organizational changes are necessary (Nelson and Dorsey 2003).

It's been found that NGOs do change several dimensions of their organizations in order to incorporate an RBA into practice. These changes include mission statement revisions, changes to organizational structures, the creation of change processes, the interaction patterns with other NGO family members, and new staff learning and training policies. Yet, these organizational changes are the second of the factors that weaken the strong and powerful concept of RBA, in that these organizational changes of development NGOs are largely aimed at tweaking the operational status quo, rather than reinventing the organization's operations. Some key features of the RBA get picked up and translated into management tools, such as access to resources and services, while others, such as the primacy of the issues of accountability and accountability, get lost. Other factors that inhibit NGOs from delivering the full potential of the RBA are the organization's limited knowledge of human rights and the human rights approach.

This chapter will discuss the organizational changes of ActionAid UK, Oxfam GB, and SC Sweden as neither planned nor chaotic change, but "managed anarchy," a mixture of the two. Second, the organizational changes of the three NGOs are not transformative, but are transitional changes, and fall short of the level of change required for a full embracing of an RBA. Third, organizational changes in the context of the adoption of RBA, with the exception of SC Sweden, can be characterized as fine tuning, aimed at "doing things better" rather than "doing things differently". Fourth, the three NGOs have developed and implemented three different processes of organizational changes; what might be called "the experimental," "the blueprint" and the "step-by-step" approaches respectively. These change processes are non-linear. Fifth, NGO staffs are not trained in RBA interpretation and the depth of change required for an RBA implementation; subsequently there can be NGO staff resistance. Sixth, NGOs' family factors can affect the individual NGOs political capacity to adopt an RBA. Finally, training workshops as presently constructed are insufficient in addressing the lack of knowledge and skills in human rights and RBA.

This chapter will assess six areas of organizational change: the vision and mission; the process of organizational change; the human factor including incentives and resistance to change; the NGO family factor; and training and other learning policies.

CHANGES AT THE TOP

Changes in vision and mission statements are important indicators of an organization's direction and momentum in that these statements tell us not only the reason for an organization's existence, but also tell us their beliefs, worldviews, values, and development framework.

In management terms, clear vision and mission statements are essential for effectiveness because they link an NGO's purpose, policies, strategic choices, and modes of actions. Organizationally, changes in vision and mission statements are changes "at the top of a hierarchy of organizational features, which need to be in place if lower levels of organization activity are to be done well. Without these 'foundations,' serious inconsistencies between policies and real-life practices can and do arise" (Fowler 1997, 35).

After adopting RBAs, what the three NGOs have in common in terms of organizational change was that they reviewed and amended their vision and mission statements. However, as members of alliances, the three NGOs could not simply change their vision and mission statements.

They also had to advocate for change through the international or alliance offices so that other members would revise their missions and goals and maintain unity within the NGO family. This was an additional task for the three NGOs, but all of them succeeded in getting their alliance/international offices to adopt RBA vision and mission statements. What the three NGO families also share was that the processes of change within their families have been led by the three organizations. The difference among the three cases was the degree of human rights components in their visions and missions.

SC Sweden and SC UK are the leading forces of change in the Save the Children family, the International Save the Children Alliance (ISCA), home of thirty-two SC members. A key meeting, pushed by the two organizations, resulted in the vision of "a world in which all children's rights are fulfilled," and the new mission adopted was "to fight for children's rights and to deliver immediate and lasting improvements to children's lives worldwide."

Both vision and mission statements clearly refer to reasons for existence in human rights terms, which set the context and direction for further work on goal setting and strategy formation. This can be seen as a significant change and a success of the Classical RBA, given the fact that some of its powerful alliance members, such as Save the Children USA, did not support an RBA.

ActionAid UK changed its vision and mission statement by adding human rights components, such as stipulating the right to life of dignity in its poverty eradication goal. Its vision statement now is to help create "a world without poverty in which every person can exercise their right to a life of dignity." Its mission statement, "to work with poor and marginalized people to eradicate poverty by overcoming the injustice and inequality that cause it" (ActionAid 1999, 7), attempts to link human rights to a poverty reduction framework. The final product makes ActionAid's human rights stand more explicit. The mission statement follows the spirit of the vision, specifying its key target groups and spelling out key concepts that it will work on: poverty, caused by injustice and inequality. The brave action of identifying causes of poverty in the mission statement reflects the organization's efforts to move beyond healing the symptoms of poverty to addressing root causes of poverty, as in the doctrine of the Popular RBA interpretation. As such, ActionAid's mission statement sets the tone for the integration of human rights integration into their poverty framework, setting a tone throughout the entire organization.

After Oxfam International was founded in 1995, the mission statement of 1996 read: "Oxfam International is an international group of independent non-governmental organizations dedicated to fighting poverty and related injustice around the world. The Oxfams work together internationally to achieve greater impact by their collective efforts.

Oxfam does not state its mission in human rights terms. Its focus on poverty and suffering does not mention human rights explicitly. In fact, without the term "injustice" in its longer version of the mission statement, Oxfam's mission statement is very similar to that of the World Bank! However, when it comes to strategies and goals, Oxfam GB highlights its RBA and stresses that RBA is one of the four approaches that its twelve members have in common. This reflects a feature of the Equity RBA brand of Oxfam GB; it does not tie its purpose to human rights. Rather, human rights enter at the strategic and tactical level.

PROCESS OF ORGANIZATIONAL CHANGE

After redefining their vision and mission statements, the three NGOs initiated their organizational changes by articulating development policies and strategies as discussed in Chapter 5. This section takes a look at how the three organizations have managed their organizational changes focusing on the key element of change and how the change processes were designed and implemented.

The process of organizational change of the three NGOs started from quite different timeframes. ActionAid's change is the most recent, starting in the late 1990s after the problematic adoption of the sustainable development and people-centered approach. Oxfam GB and SC Sweden's changes have been on a multi-year track with acceleration at the end of the 1990s. Oxfam's organizational changes date back from the early 1990s when it conducted a major strategy review in response to the changing global environment. The more recent change was a product of the 1997-1998 strategy review, which led Oxfam to be more explicit on its RBA. SCSweden's organizational transformation came in the context of an RBA adoption, which started back in the early 1990s.

The "Experimental" Change Process of ActionAid UK

In the late 1990s, ActionAid's organizational change in terms of adopting an RBA took place against the backdrop of the de-popularizing of the sustainable, people-centered development (SD/PC) approach, which had initially triggered a major reform in the early 1990s. Similar to the time of the adoption of the SD/PC approach, ActionAid did not impose pre-set definitions or guidelines on its field staff in a top-down fashion.

While Oxfam has developed its five aims and their strategic change objectives (SCOs) based on human rights norms and SC Sweden has developed its twelve program areas as a programming framework, ActionAid has the "Fighting Poverty Together" strategy (1999-2003). The strategy uses human rights language in a limited fashion and does not fully reflect the Popular RBA. This is partly due to timing, as ActionAid accelerated in its engagement with its RBA after the strategy was launched in 1999. In fact, the first (known) staff to have an RBA and human rights background was hired in late 2000 to develop an introductory sectoral-based paper and manual on RBA and emergency work.

The changes at ActionAid really started in 2000. On the organizational structure level, the key organizational changes were: first, a revamping of regional offices. Before the adoption of an RBA, some regional offices had very limited resources, with staff often consisting of a regional director and one administrative staff. As was seen, for instance, with the Asia regional offices in Thailand and India, this small capacity naturally diminished the office's effectiveness. After the adoption of the RBA, new experts were recruited and put in positions where they could be close enough to country offices and yet free enough to work on policy development with the headquarters. There emerged a new role of regional offices, focusing on linking the headquarters and country offices and keeping the information flowing from the country offices to the headquarters and vice versa.

Second, the adoption of an RBA has brought the policy and the programming departments closer together. The two departments used to work separately. The RBA's call for closer links between policy and practice-one of the most difficult tasks-has drawn the departments together. This process largely involves getting policy advocacy work integrated into development program work. This change, however, takes place only in some offices. ActionAid UK in Nepal, for instance, has experienced this structural change, which helps bring together groups, focusing on civil and political rights and those focusing on economic, social, and cultural rights. However, ActionAid India still maintains the structure in which all of its fourteen offices are managed by program officers, all of whom, however, are new, with strong human rights backgrounds.

Third, to better work to support the poor to claim their rights as the Popular RBA suggests, ActionAid has started a kind of local emphasis at the national level. The organization is attempting to change the national offices from being branches of ActionAid to local organizations with their own governance systems. ActionAid now aims to register national offices with governments, build up the national capacity, and set up national Boards to articulate the priorities of the countries and oversee the policy, strategies, and program implementation. (Theis 2004)

Fourth, despite the new demand for the policy team to link up with the programming team, the long struggle of the policy department continues as it searches for a way to meaningfully add human rights components to development programming. Its role on the ground is still unclear; often leading to work on technical assistance, general support, and conducting fragmented projects.

The change process of ActionAid is experimental. The process is both laid back and chaotic. The headquarters is rather slow in coming to agreement on developing policy and program guidelines, leaving regional and national offices plenty of autonomy to experiment with new directions and project work. The result has been that ActionAid's organizational and programming changes are inconsistent and dependent on the interests and commitment to an RBA of the regional and national staff. Without a shared strategic and program framework, ActionAid's organizational changes are often un-directed, and sometimes, unorganized.

The organization, however, is working to learn from the experiments at its periphery so that these experiences can be integrated into the core of the organization. The strength of this experimental organizational change process is that it allows local staff to experiment with ideas that address specific local issues. This is an important method to build capacity of local and national offices and help them become key development players. Although this process takes more time, compared with a central-planned approach, it is more likely to lead to an international RBA strategic framework that has strong local relevance, through a process that is, in itself, as a Popular RBA suggests, one of empowerment.

The "Blueprint" Change Process of Oxfam GB

Contrary to the bottom-up change of ActionAid, Oxfam GB's change processes can be explained as a "blueprint," starting with allowing the germinal ideas, or yolk, to coalesce at the centre, and then push out to the regions and countries. Oxfam GB started with the development of five aims that their regions, departments, campaigns, and programs would gather around. This change process has been centrally driven, developed, and controlled from the headquarters in Oxford. At the same time, however, Oxfam GB has been moving towards decentralization, allowing authority and flexibility to its field staff in developing programs within the framework of the five organizational goals.

Finally, whereas previously it did not have any regional offices, in the past ten years, Oxfam GB has moved to a regionalized structure. Now it has pushed authority from the centre of Oxfam GB out to the regions. Regional directors, who used to work in Oxford, have been working in the regions since 1999. This organizational change process has helped strengthen communications links to country offices and the headquarters. It supports countries, organization messages, and accountability. Oxfam GB now has strong regional offices, responsible to regional programs and playing the role of adviser to country offices in choosing and planning projects.

Oxfam GB has a rather top-down approach in mainstreaming its RBA and in facilitating its learning process. This central-led approach helps create strong uniformity and it moves regional and country programs into one direction. While other organization have taken slower approaches in making changes, experimenting with various methods and resulting in little impact, Oxfam's centrally-driven plan is more effective in reshaping the organization to deliver its Equity RBA. This is made possible by strong leadership, including commitment from the Board and senior management. However, this top-down approach produces some risks, such as the potential for less creativity at the programming level, structural inflexibility and less opportunity for local staff ownership and commitment.

The "Step-by-step" Change Process of Save the Children Sweden

SC Sweden initiated the adoption of an RBA approach with strong leadership from the top whose key decision to adopt the Convention of the Rights of the Child (CRC) became the organization's foundation, since the treaty came into force in 1989. But in the last half-decade, the leadership's efforts to push the RBA forward have weakened. Mainstreaming the classical RBA during the second half of the 1990s was largely carried out by mid-management, who relied on cooperation with other programming staff. These staff members worked to set up meetings with the top management to promote understanding of an RBA and to gain support in different forms from the management. As of 2001, no meeting on RBA had been set up with the team who took the lead in organizational learning and Board of SC Sweden. However, the Board has been informed of the approach and some of the Board members attended seminars on RBAs that SC Sweden organized for its staff and partners. The weak push from the top leadership, the lack of the authority of mid-management to centrally plan for the RBA mainstreaming, and the reliance on selling the idea and cooperation, has resulted in a "soft-sell" and "step-by-step" approach. This step-by-step approach is driven mostly by mid-level program and policy officers and advisors who are committed to an RBA.

Throughout the 1990s SC Sweden continuously shaped its Classical RBA through redefining working methods and program areas to better serve the realization of the CRC. These program areas, similar to Oxfam's five aims, form the framework on which all the work must be based. Program areas though are more articulated in terms of policies, strategies, and methods for implementation. In other words, Oxfam GB's five aims are broader strategic goals, while SC Sweden's program area framework is narrower and provides more detailed strategic plans.

Unlike ActionAid UK and Oxfam GB, SC Sweden did not restructure its regional offices. These regional offices continue to have high authority, serving as the arms of the headquarters in ensuring the delivery of programs. They also collaborate on specific global issues such as corporal punishment and the UN study on violence against children. Most regional directors and key staff are sent from Stockholm-many of them Swedish nationals-to give Stockholm a more opportunity for scrutiny since the central office gives somewhat high autonomy to country offices. Country offices are a key driver of SC Sweden's classical RBA. They also have high autonomy in setting priorities, identifying strategies, designing programs, and choosing partners-all within the set program areas.

Rather than a top-down approach, the decentralized Stockholm office plays a supporting role, particularly in technical assistance, such as the development of RBA programming manual and trainings. The headquarters has limited capacity to play the role of fostering global collaboration, as staff at the headquarters has limited experience and specialization in the regions. Moreover, SC Sweden has the culture of moving staff around to new areas with the result that staff ends up having little expertise. SC Sweden compensates by hiring consultants at the country level.

SC Sweden has enjoyed a slow but sure approach in reorganizing its organization to deliver its Classical RBA. The organization, however, has gone further than ActionAid UK and Oxfam GB in changing its roles and developing new working methods. This step-by-step changing process has turn SC Sweden into a child rights organization with few characteristics of a community development NGO that it used to be. Currently, the step-by-step approach calls for more practical skills. Now that there has been more investment in CRP and children participation, there is a clear need for setting up standards for all sorts of management, such as participation and evaluation.

THE HUMAN FACTOR

Staff is key to organizational change, and very much so within the context of the adoption of an RBA, as it is staff members who actually deliver the RBA concept in practice. A number of NGOs have highlighted possible difficulties in managing NGOs' staff, especially through the process of getting them to change the approach with which they are accustomed. The CARE leadership, for instance, notes that one of the things it learned was the difficulties in helping staff to take a more analytical approach to their work (Lindenberg and Bryant 2001).

Moreover, introducing new approaches can also lead to resistance from staff. This resistance can be either hard or soft resistance. Hard resistance is resistance to change to an RBA organization at a fundamental level, such as the preference of need-based relief work over rights-based, long-term change. This type of resistance can seriously hamper organizational transformation. Soft resistance refers to staff resistance to particular aspects of RBA or particular areas of work even which they agree and support the fundamental concept of an RBA. For example, staff may support RBA principles but disagree that the organization should set up an advocacy office dedicated to lobbying work.

This next chapter section reviews staff's reaction to the adoption of the Popular, the Equity and the Classical RBAs, and discusses how the three organizations have handled the effects of the human factor in their organizations, including incentives for changing the approach to an RBA. It also assesses the effects of the RBA interpretation framework and organizational change process on staff.

ActionAid's Staff and its Popular RBA

ActionAid's staff had the strongest reactions to the adoption of an RBA, compared with the other two organizations. Before the adoption of an RBA, most programming staff came from a background in development, and almost none from a human rights background. After the adoption, there have been staff members who felt uncomfortable with the new RBA, resulting in a series of resignations of staff with development background and a wave of new recruitment of those with a human rights background. This has become a phenomenon that has indirectly helped the organization to restructure its personnel. For example, ActionAid India lost 90% of its staff in four years (1999-2002), when the headquarters increasingly pushed for the RBA. The organization has brought in an almost entirely new program staff with a human rights background in a short period of time. The same 90% figure applies for ActionAid Pakistan. ActionAid Nepal has replaced 40% of its staff through the same process and has hired a new manager with experience from Amnesty International, the largest human rights organization on the planet.

For ActionAid UK, its new staff is key to the success of the process of mainstreaming its RBA. Its Popular RBA framework requires substantial knowledge of human rights and RBA tools, such as advocacy and lobbying work. The framework generates the needs for substantial human rights skills and knowledge on some human rights tools, especially those that are applicable in grassroots work, such as human rights education for the poor-and not for human rights professionals.

The new skills and knowledge required by the Popular framework therefore lead to a recruitment policy that new staff should have a human rights background. A side effect is that there develops clear divisions between staff coming from the two different backgrounds. However, the adoption of these recruitment practices is not universal, and is dependant depending on the commitment of the leadership in each country. For example, ActionAid in Vietnam does not have such a division between its staffs. In fact, there has been no staff change at all resulting from the RBA in Vietnam. In addition to recruiting new staff with a human rights background, ActionAid also hires RBA experts to accelerate policy development at its headquarters.

ActionAid's experimental change process generated some hardcore resistance, leading to a series of resignations and high turnover rate in some countries. Although this gave the opportunity for ActionAid UK to restructure its staff, there was considerable resistance from some of the remaining staff. A key issue of the existing resistance, especially of those in the field, is that they feel that relief work is necessary. They are closer to suffering people and are keen to take immediate steps to relieve the suffering rather than talking about a rights-based approach. An ActionAid staff in Burundi, for instance, noted in a workshop, "a drowning person needs a rope, not a sermon" (ActionAid 2000b, 1).

The organization has responded in a compromising manner, reflecting its "add-on" approach. It explains to staff that the relationship of the new rights-based approach and tradition relief work is not "this or that", but a "this and that." That is, for an organization with a solid background and experience in rural relief and service delivery like ActionAid UK, RBA is likely to be added to strengthening its existing work. For instance, the emergency department has developed a rights-based framework for relief work. A challenge for ActionAid UK in this casè is how to mediate between and among the competing demands of an RBA and relief needs.

Oxfam GB's Staff and its Equity RBA

Oxfam GB's method has been to link all of its work around its five aims and apply human rights standards to its work selectively. Most of Oxfam GB's program staff has not gone against the new approach; rather, they are willing to work for the achievement of the new set of goals.

Oxfam GB's RBA Equity framework selectively uses human rights goals and tools and integrates them into their overall goals and program management tools. The foundation of the framework is poverty-reduction, and not human rights, leading to little in the way of a requirement for new skills and knowledge of human rights and human rights tools. As a result, Oxfam GB does not try to recruit program staff with a human rights background. Nor does it indirectly create pressure on program staff to know more about human rights. As a result, there has been no division between staff with human rights and development backgrounds. Unlike ActionAid, most of Oxfam GB's program staff members with development backgrounds do not leave the organization and still make up the majority of the programming team. However, Oxfam GB does put more emphasis on new staff to have some advocacy, campaign, and communications skills. Most of the programming staff with a development background has by this time learned on their own to speak the language of human rights.

For Ox fam GB, despite the most top-down change process, its "blueprint" approach has received little resistance. This is largely due to the good integration of human rights goals into the five aims and SCOs and the development of planning and evaluation tools, which help program staff manage their programs with little required knowledge of human rights. The Equity RBA framework, based on a poverty framework rather than a human rights framework, lessens the feeling of alienation due to unfamiliar vocabulary of a human rights framework. By adopting an RBA, many Oxfam GB's staff feel that the relevance and effectiveness of their existing programs have been improved due to human rights thinking being blended into program management tools, rather than being forced into a new world of program management that they are not familiar with. The Regional Director for Asia notes that the little resistance experienced is largely because Oxfam GB has not pushed it very much and that resistance may increase if the organization pushes the approach more.

Oxfam GB has some soft-core resistance at the management or senior level. A key issue is that the organization has announced itself as an RBA organization, and some senior management of Oxfam GB do not think that Oxfam GB should engage in the advocacy work in developing international human rights standards. While some senior management holds that as a large and leading NGO working from an RBA, Oxfam GB should join with others NGOs in advocating for governments to adopt the Optional Protocol of International Covenant on Economic, Social and Cultural Rights (ICESCR), other senior management disagree and do not see any reason why Oxfam GB should go in such a direction. Two reasons stand out; one, that it is going to take a lot of time, another, that lobbying and advocating for the ratification of the Optional Protocol is not one of Oxfam GB's campaign priorities. This disagreement ends up with no action to support the Optional Protocol of the ICESCR, reflecting the triumph of the orthodox Equity RBA over a deviant. That is, for the Equity RBA to champion in "economic and social rights" means to work on "economic and social justice," which comes from subjective notion of social justice-legitimized through public campaign and the media, and not from international human rights norms and standards.

SC Sweden's Staff and its Classical RBA

Like ActionAid, Save the Children Sweden recruits new program staff with a human rights background. This is due to the demand of good knowledge and understanding of national and international human rights framework of the Classical RBA. Previously, it recruited program staff with development backgrounds, partly resulting in slow progress in mainstreaming its Classical RBA in the first half of the 1990s. It was only from 1994-1995 that SC Sweden recruited staff with a strong interest and commitment to human rights.

The new recruitment policy resulted in the co-existence of two groups of program staff members, the development people and the human rights people. The development people want to work on their own, focusing on implementing projects. They have less interest in human rights, compared to people with human rights backgrounds. The difficulty can be seen more in Stockholm than in country offices as many staff and partners still see SC Sweden as a development NGO that primarily works on implementing projects for children, rather than as an advocacy organization or supporter of local advocacy groups.

The new staff with human rights backgrounds have been directly assigned to the task of linking human rights and development. This new staff is expected to be more "outspoken" in addressing political and power relations issues, which the organization believes to be the root cause of child rights abuses. They are therefore required to have skills in communicating with the media, which was not a qualification before the adoption of an RBA. In other words, the new staff has to be both good community organizers and good communicators, particularly with the media.

SC Sweden's step-by-step change approach has brought the least resistance both at the headquarters and the country offices. The "soft-sell approach" of SC Sweden took the organization four to five years before the CRP became widely accepted by SC members and staff (Theis 2003). At the same time, resistance was reduced due to the slow pace of adoption, rather than to push staff to accept the Classical RBA. This "bottom-up" approach of SC Sweden has also helped staff with a variety of strategies chosen to promote children's rights in different country contexts.

A staff of SC Sweden writes: "an RBA requires that staff take positions on controversial issues. This may cause resistance from staff and partners who see themselves as welfare workers rather than rights activists" (Theis 2003, 8). In practice, there has been some soft resistance at the country level. Some program staff at the country level resist the RBA because they see it as abstract, complex, impractical, and too political. Trainings on Child Rights Programming have not helped lessen this resistance. It is suggested that less abstract and more practical program tools need to be developed for program staff, such as the Global Impact Monitoring (GIM) which simplifies what is seen as a complex approach into five simple questions (Theis 2003).

In sum, reactions of staff of the three NGOs are different, resulting from the different RBA interpretative frameworks and organizational change processes. The RBA interpretation framework determines the level of the needs for new skills and knowledge from staff relating to human rights and RBA. The organizational change processes affect how the organizations respond to the new needs, including whether a new recruitment policy is established.

The three organizations have provided little incentive for their staff to adopt RBAs. However, RBAs have emerged in the three organizations as a new way of working, which provides opportunities for fast learners to be more recognized and therefore promoted. In general, RBAs are welcomed by staff of the three organizations, although there are areas and spots of resistance. This resistance is an obstacle to the realization of RBA concepts, which would require full commitment from staff members in learning to work with the new methods. Resistance management and motivating staff to the new approach is a clear need of the three NGOs.

THE FAMILY FACTOR

All three organizations-ActionAid UK, Oxfam GB and SC Sweden-are members of alliances-ActionAid International, Oxfam International, and the International Save the Children Alliance-respectively. All three NGOs are key members who push their NGO families in adopting and transforming into RBA organizations. Their families now are in different stages in terms of RBAs. The families are not static, or simply the sum of their families members. Interestingly, all three families are moving towards a unilateral organization mode. That is, their members are willing to give up some of their autonomy to the centre. This is largely due to competition, funding, and donors. Within this context, this section will assess the effects that the NGO families have on RBA adoption of ActionAid UK, Oxfam GB, and SC Sweden, and vise versa.

ActionAid UK, ActionAid International and the Popular RBA

ActionAid UK has been known as ActionAid for a long time. In fact, the "UK" was only added in the name when the ActionAid Alliance was founded in 2003. ActionAid UK is one of the most influential members in the family. It played an important part in forming the ActionAid Alliance, initially situated in Brussels. In December 2003, ActionAid International was founded as part of the process of the "internationalization" of ActionAid (ActionAid International 2003).

Its office is located in Johannesburg, South Africa. One motivation for the move to South Africa was to be "politically correct" in not having its headquarters in a developed country. Another motivator was to start "the process of making all our country programs equal partners with an equal say on how we operate."

From its inception, ActionAid International has adopted "Fighting Poverty Together: ActionAid's Strategy 1999-2003," expanded to cover the period of 1999-2005, and developed by ActionAid UK, as its strategy. ActionAid International has a small policy team that engages directly with its RBA. The team works with 40 country offices. The link between the headquarters and country offices is carried out through regional offices. After ActionAid International was reformed in its move to Johannesburg, it has played more of a role in regional strategic directions as it now has directors overseeing regions, themes, and functional areas. This is a major change compared to the previous ActionAid Alliance, which had few staff and played a minor role, for instance, providing technical support in fundraising to country offices.

Within the family, members of ActionAid International have high autonomy in planning and implementing projects.

They are independent financially and can make decisions on the projects they wish to work on. As the most influential family member, ActionAid UK has been able to turn ActionAid International into a rights-based organization from its very inception. It is agreed among ActionAid members that the organization must move away from service delivery to the poor toward advocating to the duty bearers to provide services and other obligations to the poor. As ActionAid puts it, "rights-based approaches focus on not allowing the duty bearer to escape its responsibility for service delivery. Rather than acting for the poor by providing direct services, rights work focuses on acting with the poor so that they can demand services from duty bearers themselves (ActionAid 2000a).

ActionAid International has little affect on ActionAid UK and its RBA. On the contrary, it is ActionAid UK that influences ActionAid International. This may change in the near future as ActionAid International is being restructured with more authority to make policy and provide frameworks for program delivery.

Oxfam GB, Oxfam International, and the "Equity" RBA

A meeting to establish Oxfam International (OI) was held in 1992, resulting in the development of a shared policy paper outlining the issues and needs. In 1994, Oxfam International was set up by Oxfam GB and Ireland and nine other relief and development agencies. The first joint strategic plan, "Towards Global Equity," was adopted in 2000.

Since its inception, OI has remained a weak central office with a limited role. It now has 25 staff members, working in 8 offices including advocacy offices in Washington, New York, Brussels, and Geneva. Recently, OI has played more of an advocacy role through its advocacy offices. This is in addition to its ongoing traditional work on networking and coordination, particularly on humanitarian work and its work in communications and facilitation, such as, assisting new organization members in capacity building.

One of the reasons for these limited roles is that key organization members, including Oxfam GB, are reluctant to give up more autonomy and resources to the International Secretariat. Oxfam GB believes that OI should remain small, continue in its current role, and retain a confederation relationship with affiliates. Their view is that if OI has more work, it should be conducted by using the resources of Oxfam's affiliates. Oxfam GB also proposed that the Oxfam family should not be too large, as it would be difficult to get agreement on policy and could result in a loss of efficacy due to increasing organizational transaction costs (Oxfam GB 2003f).

Plan and common positions on advocacy work. However, Oxfam GB does not agree with the idea of "moving towards an ever closer union."

In 2002, Oxfam International initiated a review process of its organizational architecture. The Executive Directors and Board members began the discussion in November 2002. Oxfam GB participated in the initiative focusing on its collaboration with OI. Using McKinsey Consultant's findings, Oxfam GB posited that the Oxfam family's different areas of focus need different types of collaboration. To Oxfam GB, global advocacy and campaigning offers the greatest potential for collaboration. Their priority, then, is integrating advocacy and campaign work at the regional level. For international humanitarian work, Oxfam GB sees the need for greater collaboration and proposes a humanitarian consortium model. In essence this would mean that only a few Oxfam members would take the lead in humanitarian response on behalf of all Oxfams, and would be accountable to them (Oxfam GB 2003f).

Country and regional programs, where a human rights-based framework can largely apply, are the areas where Oxfam GB does not seek to unify the work. Its position is that Oxfam members can work in the approach they believe in, and improve the learning and sharing of knowledge and experience from the field (Oxfam GB 2003f).

Oxfam GB is an influential member in OI. Of the two, Oxfam GB exerts greater influence on OI than OI does on Oxfam GB. There are Oxfam members that still largely practice relief work, although to a lesser degree when compared with to Save the Children and ActionAid. Being the largest and traditionally most influential member, Oxfam GB has played a crucial role in bringing Oxfams together and directing them towards an RBA network. While there is room for improvement, Oxfam GB does not seek to push other Oxfam affiliates further toward a stronger commitment to an RBA. The organization states that it does not wish to change other Oxfam members' approach and that it sees the diversity of the different Oxfam as a strength (Oxfam 2003f).

After the first Save the Children organization was founded in London in 1919, the Save the Children Union was officially founded in 1920. During the early years, the Save the Children family started off with one body to make decisions over all of its operations in the 1930s and swung to the other way by becoming completely separate, independent organizations by the 1970s. In 1977, a number of Save the Children formed the Save the Children Alliance, a network that works mostly to coordinate international advocacy work from Geneva. (ISCA 2005). The movement toward a stronger central authority began again in the 1990s when it developed a weak umbrella coordination in 1993 to cope with problems of maintaining standards. In 1997, efforts continued as members met to project a common brand name and strengthen quality standards. Save the Children then entered the confederation stage with the establishment of the International Save the Children Alliance (ISCA) in 1997. The current intention to move forward to a federation stage is not easily implemented in that member organizations have developed their work in different directions, with different emphases and working methods.

The ISCA is home of 29 Save the Children members, which operate in 120 countries. There are, however, other Save the Children agencies in numerous countries that are not members of the ISCA and who do not necessarily endorse the ISCA's policy and goals.

The ISCA itself plays a limited role. It has about 25 staff, working to serve its 29 members. It has focused the work around building fundraising capacity for individual members, including helping organize fundraising events such as the World Sailing Race (Lindenberg and Bryant 2001). Another role of the

Alliance is to coordinate with its members. There have been successful cases, such as in Kosovo, when the alliance completed its negotiated agreement among alliance members. However, in general, the coordinating role has been rather limited, as members, including those that work in the same country of operation, tend to have their own priorities, networks, and capacities to carry out the work. This also leads to a rather limited role of the alliance in strengthening quality control and preventing duplication (Lindenberg and Bryant 2001).

Despite a new mission statement in human rights terms, Save the Children has not been able to form a new set of common strategies shared by all of its members. Many SC members pushed for a joint RBA strategic plan, but they ended up having a "five-year plan of action" and a "Common Framework of Operation," aiming primarily to map out all the work that SC members do in particular countries. The key objective of the paper is a coordinating one-to avoid overlapping and to work together more effectively-not an agreement on strategies or attempts to integrate human rights into development programs. In general, there are still little external forces to move away SC members from existing work or to develop common positions or strategies shared by all members. That is partly why there are still little substantial outcomes of dialogue on developing a common strategy among SC members, though there are some positive signs, as the Chair of ISCA assures that the ISCA is "investing considerable time and effort in the development of a strategy to ensure that Save the Children can achieve much more for children in the year ahead. Every Member of the Alliance has contributed to the development of a long-term strategic plan" (ISCA 2003, 19).

The "second attempt" at an RBA instrument within the family aimed primarily to develop a common framework to a rights-based approach. The ISCA set up a Coordinating Group on Child Rights Programming. The group consists of members of SC Sweden (convenor), SC Norway, SC Denmark, SC UK, SC Canada, and the Alliance Secretariat in London. One of the major products of the Group was a handbook of Child Rights Programming (CRP), published in 2002. The handbook provides a comprehensive introduction to an RBA and child rights programming and serves as an official guideline to the Classical RBA. Although the CRP is a handbook, and not a joint strategic paper, it is expected that it will pave the way to a joint strategy of ISCA members. At least it is the first concrete confirmation of the commitment to RBA of the ICSA, pushed forward by these seven SC members.

Unlike Oxfam, SC members do not have common strategic directions. The absence of shared strategies leads SC members to a great diversity in their commitment to its RBA. Several factors have intensified this variation. First, the ISCA is a confederation organization. Its members are independent organizations. The "plan of action" is only a set of guidelines that leave plenty of room for members' discretion. The ISCA does not have any incentives or pressure to get its members to come up with agreed-upon plans. For instance, SC US has a seat at the ISCA's Board, which approves the Five-year Plan of Action, but it has not taken steps in a rights-based direction.

Secondly, the ISCA does call on its members to adopt an RBA, but the result of the call depends on the intention and interests of its members. Although there is a forum for all members to meet and exchange experiences, this forum does not function as a decision-making body.

Third, different members tend to have different cultures in working with other organizations. SC Sweden has a stronger culture of working with others, compare to SC UK or SC US. This is a supportive factor of the adoption of a rights-based approach, which tends to require working with others. Other SC members may not have such characteristics.

Fourth, some thematic issues are more closely related to human rights, making it easier for NGOs to adopt an RBA, and vice versa. For instance, SC US focuses on children's health and nutrition issues, which are traditionally relief-oriented, while SC Sweden works on child protection, which is more human rights-oriented.

Finally, members of ISCA have different development backgrounds and work in different contexts. Although they work on the same children's issues, some of them do largely relief work and some work through government funding, making it hard for them to lobby governments on development issues. SC US, for instance, has acted as a government contractor and is not motivated to become an RBA NGO. It finds itself with "has more in common" with other organizations like CARE USA than it does with Save the Children Sweden (Lindenberg and Bryant 2001,133). In addition, SC US works under different US charity laws, in a society that is less friendly to an RBA commitment, compared to that of Europe.

In sum, the loose structure of ISCA, the lack of joint strategies, the lack of pressures or incentives from the ISCA, as well as diversity in working themes, cultures and working environments, all leave the ISCA with about 7 out of 29 members that are committed to the classical RBA. These members include SC Sweden, Norway, Denmark, UK, Australia, New Zealand, and Canada.

The Effects of the Family on the Adoption of RBAs

From three case studies of NGOs and their families, the following can be concluded: First, NGO families have limited influence on the adoption of an RBA of large NGOs. Large and influential NGOs like ActionAid UK, Oxfam GB and Save the Children Sweden have interests in adopting RBAs due to their own causes, and not because of the family. In an opposite way, the three NGOs played active roles in pushing and turning their respective alliance networks into RBA networks, which may influence other alliance members to a greater level of commitment to RBAs.

Second, NGO families can give positive reinforcement for the adoption of an RBA by family members. That is, a strong alliance network with a commitment to an RBA can strengthen the commitment to RBA adoption by its members. Oxfam International, for instance, has its members sign up to a shared strategic paper, which governs key directions of programs. Member organizations that traditionally do not show a strong interest in a human rights-based approach, such as, Oxfam Hong Kong, have gradually added more human rights elements in their programming work. Three, a joint strategic paper is a key in mainstreaming RBA within a family. Without a joint strategic paper, an NGO family tends to have difficulties promoting the RBA within the alliance. For example, the ISCA has had difficulties promoting RBA among its members. The CRP handbook is finished, but it is no substitute for a joint strategy. Pro-RBA members of ISCA still have to develop a joint strategy. On the other hand, OI and AAI have joint strategic plans to strengthen commitment to RBAs by tying together the goals and strategic directions of other Oxfam and ActionAid members. Two factors are found to strengthen this tie to a strategic paper. The first is the level of obligation derived from signing the strategic paper. Oxfams, in a confederation structure, have taken the compiling of a strategy more seriously, compared to ActionAid in its federation structure. The result is that there is less diversity in strategic directions among Oxfam members. The second is the level of articulation and sophistication of the strategic plans. Oxfam's "Toward Global Equity" has gone further in turning a goodwill and aspiration statement into achievable and measurable goals, compared to ActionAid's "Fighting Poverty Together," which is still relatively broad and less practical.

TRAININGS AND OTHER ORGANIZATIONAL LEARNING POLICIES

Training and organizational learning policies are an important organizational dimension of the interpretation of the three types of RBAs and the organizational change processes. In this study of the three NGOs-ActionAid UK, Oxfam GB, and Save the Children Sweden-trainings are used to achieve the goals of becoming a Popular, Equity, and Classical RBA respectively. These trainings also interact with the experimental, the blueprint, and the step-by-step approaches of the change processes respectively.

ActionAid UK's Learning and Training Policy on RBA

ActionAid UK has an organization learning strategy, stating that it aims to become a learning organization and a "knowledge leader" in six areas, including an RBA area. In practice, the

RBA learning process of ActionAid UK can be described as on-going and "learning by doing." Organizing training workshops is one of the key tools that ActionAid UK has used in promoting its RBA. In fact, the organization has organized numerous training workshops on RBA, starting with RBA trainings on selected themes. Food rights was one of the earliest training issues, before ActionAid UK moved to a broad range of issues covering the first five out of six types of RBA trainings: (1) human rights principles and standards (e.g. non-discrimination, particular treaties); (2) rights-based tools (analysis, planning, monitoring, and evaluation); (3) advocacy skills (lobbying, campaigning, and media); (4) mobilizing skills (participation, partnering); (5) thematic human rights (e.g. education, HIV/AIDS, and food); (6) specific professional training (e.g. to police, prison guards, and military personnel). These trainings were co-organized by the headquarters, regional offices, and country offices.

In general, ActionAid UK's training is less structured and focused, allowing greater flexibility for participants to raise and discuss issues. The positive side is that the training encourages participants to voice their concerns. However, the down side is that its trainings touch on many issues at a surface level, leading to the most frequently found problem of RBA trainings-participants find RBA interesting and get motivated, but do not know what and how to do things when they get back to their home countries. In the other words, the hard part of the trainings is not to understand the policy or concepts, but rather to implement the RBA policy. In response, ActionAid UK has developed case studies on its RBA in order to fill in the gap between policy and practice. The Asian regional office in Bangkok, for instance, hired consultants from Mahidol University in Thailand and Harvard University in the US to conduct the implementation of a rights-based approach, comparing RBA experiences in Vietnam and India (Petcharamesree and Rosenblum 2003).

ActionAid has yet to fully use trainings as a tool to achieve its Popular RBA goal. The challenges of power relations at the grassroots and local levels are only minimally reflected in its

RBA trainings. The framework, difficulties, and experiences of grassroots empowerment are not yet the central points of workshops. Rather, its training activities-which cover most of the possible training issues-reflect its "experimental" change process. As the organization continues experimenting and trying to find its direction, training workshops also reflect the void of a core training strategy. It is therefore a challenge for ActionAid UK to identify training priorities and to strategize its training and learning activities in ways that maximize the learning and knowledge gained from its numerous experiments.

Oxfam GB's Learning and Training Policy on RBA

Oxfam GB has a long history of experience in institutionalizing the sharing and learning of development work. Specifically, it has produced a well-respected journal, "Development in Practice," and has initiated a "Cross-Program Learning Fund" to create more space for learning with relatively few resources (Roche 1995). However, when it comes to the learning and training on its Equity RBA, Oxfam GB has invested very little in new planning and monitoring tools, or in training of staff and partners in human rights.

While other NGOs mainstream their RBA by rolling out a process of staff training in a human rights framework, Oxfam GB does not train staff on a rights-based approach or international human rights laws and standards. What Oxfam GB has done instead is to change the way it plans its work and the way it talks about its work. Now all the work has to contribute to changing of policy, practice, ideas, and belief.

In the absence of RBA trainings, Oxfam GB produces a simplified version of a learning tool, a Power Point presentation. It is aimed for staff to get an overview of what RBA means for Oxfam. The presentation explains what international human rights instruments mean, what the implications are, and how the organization might plan and evaluate its work. The presentation was developed by a staff of Save the Children and then adapted by Oxfam GB. This learning process, however, is voluntary, so there are no measurable outcomes associated with it.

Why has Oxfam GB not provided RBA trainings for its staff? On the surface, it does not make sense for a well-respected and leading NGO like Oxfam GB to fail to provide proper trainings and skills to complete its work. But on closer examination, it can be understood that Oxfam GB's Equity RBA puts together its five aims-based on international human rights standards-but it does not base its work and working methods on such human rights standards. With the tactical use of human rights in the Equity RBA, there is no need to retrain its staff, because there are little new human rights skills and knowledge needed in adopting the Equity RBA. The same reason applies to Oxfam GB not recruiting new staff with a human rights background as ActionAid UK and Save the Children Sweden have done. The Equity RBA does not require many new skills. As long as the program staff integrates campaigns-its major advocacy tool-into their development work and ensures that their work contributes to changes in policy, practice, ideas, and belief, development work will contribute to its RBA goals, the five aims. So, instead, Oxfam GB sees that the skills they need to build for staff are advocacy, communications, and campaigning skills, and not international human rights laws and standards.

A question remains to be answered in Chapter 7: Does Oxfam's GB Equity RBA work on the ground, given that the staff has no background, knowledge or skills in human rights?

Save the Children's Learning and Training Policy on RBA

Save the Children has a good track record in organizational learning. Similar to its change processes, its learning and training initiatives are largely driven by mid-level management with considerable support from top leadership, resulting in relatively slow progress in the first ten years of the adoption. Despite the slow start, SC Sweden has accelerated its training and learning initiatives on RBA since 2000. Compared to ActionAid UK, SC Sweden has invested more resources systematically and continuously on trainings. In the first six slow years of RBA learning (1989-1995), SC Sweden focused its learning around the legal framework provided by the CRC. This included the CRC monitoring and reporting mechanisms, and dissemination of the CRC reports. The trainings at this time covered basic knowledge of the CRC and the legal framework of this international human rights law. Starting in 1997, SC Sweden started to realize that the dissemination of information and reports of the CRC were not quite enough in pursuing its goals. The content of its RBA learning and trainings then shifted to the implications of the CRC with the intention to link the CRC with the existing work on the ground.

Since 1998, the SC Alliance started its rights-based learning process by organizing a series of meetings, aimed at helping organizations understand the meaning and implications of Child Rights Programming (CRP). The goal of clarifying CRP has been carried out through a number of CRP training workshops, introductory booklets, and experimental program work at the country level. SC Sweden actively participated in the process and co-led with SC UK in developing key CRP documents and training workshops. It was through this process of ongoing learning that CRP received acceptance on the country and regional levels.

Despite the lengthy time involved, a positive side of the process is that SC members and programming staff are engaged in the RBA learning process, which is a crucial component in the mainstreaming of an RBA. In the other words, these four to five years of "clarifying" and mainstreaming have both started and continued the learning process. By the time the CRP was widely accepted, staff had already progressed in learning and experimenting with the classical RBA.

A senior staff of SC Sweden notes that SC's rights-based approach has gone through three stages. The first stage clarifies the concepts, principles, and standards of an RBA, and is done through training consultative meetings, workshops, and publications. The second stage applies the concepts and principles into existing development and human rights frameworks. The third and ongoing stage moves rights-based thinking and practice beyond traditional development and human rights by finding simple and effective approaches, new forms of management, new tools from other fields, and moving beyond conventional sectoral work (Theis 2004).

SC Sweden has hired new staff to link the headquarters' policy to mainstream CRP and local training needs. Its work is to develop staff's capacity with Classical RBA work, including developing its own CRP training materials and conducting training workshops. SC Sweden's training workshops have high standards, tailor-made to fit the needs of its Classical RBA and local contexts. They are well structured, focusing on types 1 and 2 of RBA trainings: (1) human rights principles and standards (e.g. non-discrimination, particular treaties); and (2) rights-based tools (analysis, planning, monitoring and evaluation). In the early 2000s, it was found that the training needs of SC Sweden's staff had shifted from explaining to staff what human rights, RBA, and RBA tools are, to how to implement an RBA, how to work with children, how to do advocacy work, and how to work with the media.

A strong dimension of the training course is that participants can bring their own projects in and try to examine them within a human rights framework, starting from whether the objectives are broad enough; which human rights instruments are relevant; who the duty bearers are; why they have not done what they should have done; who can be influential; what are the root causes of the violations; how can the root causes be addressed; who is included; who is excluded; and what can be done to help the people demand their rights, to hold duty bearers accountable as well as to assist them achieve their obligations (Theis 2001).

Despite the well-structured training course, local staff still find it difficult to go back to the field and start a human rights-based project. Many find it hard to understand the concepts of human rights themselves, particularly the staff from countries with a weak culture of individual rights, such as China. The idea of challenging authorities in China, for instance, is a huge conceptual leap for local staff. In a country such as Burma, where there are widespread human rights violations, there is also good awareness of human rights. This is similar to the Philippines and Cambodia. In contrast, staff from China,

Vietnam, Malaysia, and Laos-where the political and state ideology are hostile to human rights-find it harder to understand and interpret the concepts, and transform them into practice.

Training materials are developed by a Senior Advisor on CRP and his team. SC Sweden provides training courses for staff of other SC members and partners. At the beginning, trainings were conducted separately by other SC members who do similar types of training. Recently, there have been efforts to develop a common course on RBA programming, drawing on experiences from all SC members. A pool of trainers was also brought together by SC members in hopes of developing and promoting joint trainings on RBA.

In conclusion, from the study of the three cases, no "import" learning has been found. For ActionAid UK and SC Sweden, trainings have been used as key tools in building staff's capacity with their RBAs. While ActionAid UK offers training on a broad range of issues with loose structure, reflecting its experimental organizational change process, SC Sweden uses its step-by-step approach in delivering focused and well-structured trainings on selected issues.

Oxfam GB does not use the training mode in mainstreaming its RBA, as its Equity RBA does not require new human rights-related skills.

What ActionAid and SC Sweden have in common is that their training workshops have proved insufficient in the transfer of RBA thinking to local staff. This is because core learning activities largely rely on four to five day training workshops, which have carried a number of functions and purposes. First, they had to provide knowledge and a framework of human rights principles and mechanisms. Second, they had to have been persuasive to local staff-persuasive enough for the staff to go back home and start implementing their RBAs. Third, the workshops had to have been able to demonstrate how to transform a rights-based policy into practice. These objectives of transferring the knowledge, stimulating interest and commitment, and developing skills tend to be too much for a four to five-day workshop. When local staff returned to their field of operations, it is not always clear whether the local staff will act differently. Typically some may come up with new initiatives, some will not change the way they do business, while others will try to change but won't be able to.

The well-developed rights-based frameworks from Stockholm and London are therefore far from being automatically able to create fundamental change in development practices. The commitment to implement RBAs still depends very much on the effectiveness of the workshops, the interest and commitment of local staff, and the struggles to initiate RBA programs within diverse contexts.

Finally, concerning an RBA learning concentration, the ActionAid UK learning process is led by several groups of policy staff at their headquarters, regional offices, and country office. For Oxfam GB, there have been attempts to spread the learning into the working regions; however, its learning is still concentrated around the head offices and key senior management. For SC Sweden, policy staff and new CRP advisors are at the centre of the CRP learning process. It is still unclear how much local staff is familiar with the CRP, especially those in human rights-hostile countries. Compared to ActionAid UK and Oxfam GB, the learning of SC Sweden spreads further to different parts of the organization. This is due to a less centralized structure of the organization and a policy to facilitate the learning at the regional level.

CONCLUSION

From the study of organizational changes of three NGOs, we can make the following conclusions.

First, organizational changes of the three NGOs are yet another managed anarchy. To the question of whether organizational changes in the context of RBA adoption are planned changes or chaotic changes, the answer is that they are managed anarchy. In all three cases, each NGO has done some planning for organizational changes, particularly from the headquarters, including making changes in visions and missions to reflect their beliefs and development framework. But the planned changes at the headquarters quickly turned out to be rather chaotic at country offices where the scheme used is to organize the anarchy and keep it at an acceptable level. Oxfam GB was the least chaotic with the most limited changes that it actually planned to make for its Equity RBA. SC Sweden was devoid of the leadership to properly plan and manage organizational change towards its Classical RBA. The task of mainstreaming RBA is left to mid-management who rely on cooperation with other staff, resulting in a step-by-step approach.

ActionAid UK, in contrast, has mostly used the "science of muddling through" (Lindblom, 1959). Its decentralized structure with weak central change plans leads to a situation where staff can experiment in a variety of ways, resulting in the loss in focus of its Popular RBA.

Despite the variation of anarchy of the three NGOs, the conclusion on organizational change of this study confirms the findings of DiBella (1992) that organizational change of NGOs is closer to "organized anarchy" than "planned change."

Second, an organizational change in the context of an RBA adoption is not an organizational transformation although it may seem to be. To measure organizational changes of the three NGOs against the three types of organizational changes: (1) transformational change-the total and radical change, involving a completely new context and configuration of behaviours, roles, attitudes, motives, beliefs, and values; (2) transitional changeless radical, referring to organizational change that evolves slowly through many transitional steps during which the organization is neither what it once was nor what it aims to be, and similar to transformational change, seeking to replace ways of doing things; (3) and organizational development-the most minor change, aimed to improve skills, methods and other conditions in order to meet current expectation, and not to change the ways of doing things.

In this study, none of the three organizations is close to a transformational change. There is no plan to radically change their organizations, the roles of staff, attitudes, beliefs, or values, although there are attempts to integrate human rights values into the systems, but with no concrete or systematic plans.

SC Sweden's organizational changes are closer to transitional change than the other two types of change. Its step-by-step approach evolves the organization slowly. Yet it has changed the foundation of its roles and its work. The ways SC Sweden makes intervention in the development world has changed from direct assistance and relief to poor children, to working to protect children's rights through several means, including advocacy and research. Over a decade, SC Sweden changed from a community development organization in the 1980s to a children's rights organization. The Classical RBA interpretation plays an important part in going beyond a quick grasp and superficial use of human rights concepts to including international human rights standards, mechanisms, and principles in the new development framework. Among the three NGOs, Save the Children Sweden has made the most organizational change. Yet, the organization still falls short of what its own interpretation would require, a transformational change, to instead deliver a transitional change.

Oxfam GB never wanted to go beyond a developmental change. Its Equity RBA leads the organization to use human rights concepts and principles selectively. The Equity RBA of Oxfam GB is, in essence, not a human rights-based development framework, but a tool with a social justice development framework. It aims primarily to improve Oxfam GB's coherence, its effectiveness, and its ability to leverage change. Organizational changes are therefore limited to an improvement mode with some "do more of" what already exists. Among the three NGOs, Oxfam GB is the only organization that can deliver organizational changes that are required by its own RBA interpretation. That is, Oxfam GB's organizational change in the context of the adoption of RBA is developmental change, as its Equity RBA suggests.

ActionAid's Popular RBA suggests a rather radical organizational change, including a totally new configuration of roles, values, attitudes, and motivation in empowering the poor to claim their rights. The organization has goodwill and the intention to "doing things differently." But organizationally, it has not yet been able to arrange itself to go beyond using human rights principles for the improvement of its traditional approach to development work. Combined with the "add-on" and "experimental" approach, ActionAid's organizational change in the context the adoption of an RBA is limited to developmental change, rather than transformational change as its Popular Interpretation would suggest.

The gap between organizational changes required by RBA interpretations and what is actually happening have been explained in this chapter with an understanding of the internal factors of each organization, such as the lack of centrally-planned change and experimental approach in the case of ActionAid and the lack of leadership in the case of SC Sweden.

However, it should be noted that another explanatory factor influencing organizational changes in the three cases is the tendency for all three to want to keep their traditionality, which likely makes them hold on to core expertise, maintain constancy of practices, and make calculated and selected "customization of changes."

Third, Nadler and Tushman's typology of change is one of the few typologies useful in establishing the understanding of NGO's organizational changes in the context of the adoption of RBAs.

In general, it is more difficult to manage change when the need for change is urgent (Hayes 2002). Although there have been increasing questions about NGOs' effectiveness and accountability and calls for improvement, the creation of RBAs occur when there is no immediate requirement to change.

The three NGOs adopted RBAs in anticipation of better ways of achieving their strategic visions. They have taken their time in going through their change processes. They therefore can be categorized in Nadler and Tushman's anticipation group.

SC Sweden adopted an RBA largely because of the vision of the leadership. It has, over a decade, created its own Classical RBA, using international human rights standards as its development framework. With this interpretation, it has gone further than the other two NGOs in a fundamental redefining of its strategies, roles, and values.

SC Sweden has sought not only to "do things better"-which the other two organizations largely do-but also to "do things differently." This is why SC Sweden's organizational change can be categorized as "reorientation."

Oxfam GB and ActionAid UK adopted their RBAs as a result of strategy reviews in the second half of the 1990s. Both organizations acted largely for strategic reasons, aiming to improve the results of their work without completely re-vamping their organizations. Oxfam GB, despite its five aims stated in human rights terms, has not moved beyond its traditional social justice development framework.

The Equity RBA is a process of adapting, modifying, and emphasizing certain aspects of work-such as campaigning and media work and not an attempt to work completely differently or to move itself into a new category of development NGOs. Similarly, while Oxfam GB has quickly grasped RBA values, built its own Equity RBA brand, and incorporated RBA values to strengthen its campaign orientation and its advantage of global leverage, ActionAid UK has been conducting a number of multidirectional experiments, resulting in a slow progression of grasping RBA concepts and tools to strengthen its grassroots work.

In sum, organizational changes resulting from the Equity and Popular RBAs, are "incremental." The organizations employing them seek mostly to improve their development work by "selective use" and by "adding on" to their existing work, and not to produce a new product or new kind of product to the market.

Fourth, the change process of NGOs that adopt RBAs is non-linear. Gemmil and Smith (1985) theorize four basic processes of change: disequalibrium conditions, symmetry breaking, experimentation, and reformulation processes.

The three case studies show that there was not a "symmetry breaking" aspect to the change process as the usual process associated with the system was not breaking down. Similarly, the unfreeze-moving-refreeze model of Kurt Lewin (1975), or the seven-step processes of Kolb and Frohman (1970), have little relevance in explaining the behaviours of organizational changes of the three NGOs.

This is largely because the organizational change in the context of the adoption of RBA is not quite planned change, rather it is managed anarchy with some degree of vagueness for most people involved. This vagueness is partly due to the complexity of the concepts of RBA. Within that complexity, all three NGOs did not create a fixed master plan of organizational change, but instead, played it safe and kept it flexible by deploying the experimental, the blueprinting out, and the step-by-step approaches to mainstream their RBAs into their organizations.

Fifth, we can conclude that, as expected, NGOs' staff are not trained to deliver RBA programs. They tend to have limited knowledge about human rights and RBA, especially local staff in rural areas. The three cases of NGOs confirm that RBA interpretative frameworks and organizational change processes exert influence on: the needs for new skills and knowledge on human rights and RBA; staff dynamics; staff resistance, all of which in turn affect the success of the RBA adoptions.

ActionAid has gone through the most disrupted changes with a number of development staff leaving the organization. The Popular RBA framework does require good knowledge and skills of human rights and RBA. ActionAid UK has responded by developing a clear policy to recruit new staff with backgrounds in human rights. While this policy is not applicable to some country offices, it pressures staff in some national offices into leaving the organization.

The two groups of staff-the new ones with human rights backgrounds and the remaining staff with development backgrounds are yet to be integrated. In addition, some staff in rural areas remain ignorant about the RBA. Oxfam GB neither has staff leaving due to the adoption of an RBA, nor does it have a policy to recruit new staff with a human rights background.

This is because the Equity RBA framework, without a strong human rights component, does not ask for human rights skills from staff. The integration of selected human rights principles into organizational goals, objectives, and especially program management tools, not only reduces the need for new skills, but also increases positive acceptance of the new approach as it leads to more relevance and effective programs. In addition, the more gentle approach towards the implementation of the RBA by the management reduces staff's resistance and increases their positive attitude towards the new approach.

SC Sweden's Classical interpretation framework demands strong human rights knowledge from its staff, which could have raised the level of pressure to staff with development background. But SC Sweden's soft-sell approach, expanding the concept over a decade has softened this pressure, while allowing the new staff with human rights background and old staff with development background to integrate well.

Sixth, three conclusions can be drawn regarding the family factor. First, NGO families have limited influence on an RBA adoption of individual NGOs. Large and influential NGOs like ActionAid UK, Oxfam GB and SC Sweden have interests in adopting RBAs due to their own causes, and not because of their NGO family. On the contrary, the three NGOs have all exerted influence on their family in becoming RBA families. Second, NGO families can give positive reinforcement for the adoption of an RBA by family members.

A strong RBA alliance can strengthen the commitment to RBA of its members, such as the case of OI and Oxfam Hong Kong. Third, a joint RBA strategic paper is a key factor in mainstreaming RBA within a family. Without a joint strategic paper, an NGO family tends to have difficulties promoting the RBA within the alliance. By contrast, an NGO family that has a joint RBA strategy can move forward much faster in turning a policy into practice.

Finally, training workshops on human rights and RBAs as an organizational learning tool can be useful, but have limitations and are far from sufficient in solving the problem of the lack of knowledge on human rights and RBAs. This is largely because most of training workshops are one-time events with participants expected to learn human rights concepts and

RBA tools, return to their countries or rural areas, and start to articulate and develop RBA projects. A long-term, two-way, and on-going learning approach is needed for RBA NGOs, including for Oxfam GB, which does not use training on human rights and RBA for their staff and partners.

To put it all together, how much do organizational dynamics weaken the strength of RBA concepts? The answer is in the difference between the level of organizational change required by their RBA interpretations and the level of organizational change that actually takes place. In addition, a full realization of RBA concepts is held back at the organizational level by resistance from the staff, inactiveness from the NGO family, and the lack of knowledge of human rights and RBA, and the dependence on training sessions as a learning tool. More importantly, organizational processes can hurt RBA concepts the most when there is a failure to pick up key principles of human rights, such as accountability and non-discrimination, and mainstream and integrate into its programs.

10

The Paradoxes and Researches

This chapter sums up the findings of this research and discusses emerging issues in the adoption of RBAs. The first section summarizes key findings of this research, including factors influencing the adoption of RBAs, and how a new paradigm-shift concept like a human rights-based approach became weakened and devalued into an add-on instrument of traditional development through the three-step process of the interpretation of RBAs, organizational changes, and the implementation of RBAs.

From the second section onwards, discussions focus on four RBA paradoxes, which lead to dilemmas and challenges in future RBA implementation. The second section looks into the paradox of the use of human rights language in non-human-rights-friendly countries. On the one hand, human rights language gives development NGOs legitimacy and a moral and legal ground. On the other hand, the language can irritate repressive governments, resulting in the closing of the door to good relationships and productive cooperation.

The third section discusses the omnipresent paradox of RBAs, as there are increasing claims that many development NGOs adopt RBAs, regardless of whether they actually do or not. The positive side is that there is increasing interest in joining the RBA movement, which may result in an increased use of RBA tools. However, a negative side of such claims is that to be an RBA organization without adopting key human rights principles may weaken the RBA movement as a whole. The fourth section discusses the dilemma of issue choosing. The choice of working on sensitive issues may get to crucial problems, but it may hurt the NGO-government relationship.

The choice of working on non-sensitive issues can maintain good relations with government, but it may not solve key development problems in the country. The fifth section analyzes the co-operational and confrontational approaches in terms of changing power relations. The co-operational approach of RBAs, as opposed to a confrontational approach of human rights NGOs-such as the naming and shaming approach, can be a key vehicle to a productive engagement between RBA NGOs and governments, but the question remains: Can RBA NGOs stop human rights violations with the co-operational approach? Can they change power relations between the poor and the government with this approach? The last section assesses what they all mean to the development enterprises.

Factors Influencing the Adoption of RBA

As stated in the literature review, there has been an increasing amount or writing on why development NGOs should adopt an RBA, but a gap remains in answering why development NGO actually adopt or do not adopt RBAs.

This research answers parts of these questions by testing possible factors that may affect the behaviour of RBA adoption. The test is aimed primarily to identify risk factors of RBA adoption. A set of samples is drawn from the top 30 NGOs in terms of total annual incomes, which can partially demonstrate the level of influence of NGOs.

Fifteen factors are measured to test their relationship with the adoption of an RBA. These factors are categorized into six groups:

(1) Percentage of annual revenue from governments;

(2) Number of NGO members in the family;

(3) Country associated (country where the NGO was founded and country in which the central office is located);

(4) Religious association;

(5) Working methods (work on advocacy, work on empowerment, work on campaigns, work with the UN);

(6) Issue areas of work (work on IFIs; work on HIV/AIDS; work on women's issues; work on children's issues; and work on trade, debt, or aid.

The finding from the logistic regression analysis is that there are seven risk factors to RBA adoption. These include two negative risk factors: countries where NGOs were founded and religious association. These two factors increase the risk of not adopting an RBA to 9 and 3.28 times, compared with the group that does not have such factors. The other five factors that have positive relationships with RBA adoption are:

(1) Government funding (16-40%);

(2) NGO member (6-15);

(3) Work on advocacy;

(4) Work on campaigns; and

(5) Work on trade, debt, and aid.

The risk ratios are 8.889, 6.333, 40, 63, and 9 times, respectively.

This means that, first, NGOs that receive a medium amount of funding from governments (16-40%) are more likely to adopt RBAs than NGOs that receive government funds over 40% or less than 16%. The chance of finding NGOs receiving the medium amount of funding from government and adopting RBA is 8.8 times higher than the chance of finding NGOs receiving higher or lower amount and adopting RBAs. This contradicts the notion that the more NGOs receive money from the government, the less they are going to adopt RBAs, and to a further extent, the less they are going to work against it.

Second, NGOs that have between six to fifteen family members are more likely to adopt RBAs than those having more than fifteen or less than six family members. The chance of finding NGOs with medium family size that adopt RBA is 6.3 times higher than the chance of finding NGO with large or small family size that adopt RBAs. This means that size does matter.

Medium-sized NGOs adopt RBAs more than other groups as they are small enough to be flexible when adopting a new approach, and large enough to have different views and dynamics within families. Small-sized NGOs have the flexibility to adopt RBAs, but tend not to due to being a religious association and being founded and based in the US.

Third, the chance of finding NGOs that use advocacy as a working method that then adopts an RBA is forty times higher than the chance of finding those that do not use advocacy and adopt RBAs. Fourth, the chance of finding NGOs that use campaigns as a working method and adopt an RBA is 63 times higher than those that do not use campaigns and adopt an RBA. Finally, the chance of finding NGOs that work on trade, debt, and aid that adopt RBAS is nine times higher than those that do not work on the issues and adopt RBAs. This says that advocacy, campaign, and trade, debt, and aid-as an issue area are bridges to human rights spheres of development NGOs.

The test of correlations shows that seven factors, in addition to the risk factors mentioned above, have significant negative and positive relations with the adoption of RBAs. The factors that have negative relationships with the adoption of an RBA are the US as the country where the NGO central office is located, the percentage of government funding (less than 15%) and the NGO family size of less than five members. The factors that have positive relationships with the adoption of RBAs are: the UK and Belgium as the countries where NGO central offices are located in, work on IFIs, and work on HIV/AIDS.

The Interpretation of RBAs

Development agencies increasingly claim that they too are rights-based organizations, or their development work too contributes to human rights. This research examines their claims by assessing their human rights-related development framework against four indicators: development goals, development processes, development programming, and use of human rights instruments. As a result, an RRA is one of the four types of interpretations of the relationship between human rights and development. The four types of conceptual frameworks of the interconnection of human rights and development have been identified. First, the "Apolitical

Assistance" type sees that human rights and development goals and processes are different. Human rights and development are in separated spheres and have little to do with each other, although parts of civil and political rights can contribute to development. This first type rarely uses international human rights instruments. Examples of this group are the World Bank, Asian Development Bank, and AUSAID.

Second, "Democratic Governance" sees that human rights and development have different goals. Some human rights tools are used in development programs, emphasizing civil and political rights, election mechanisms as key political participation, and democratic institution building. Like the first type, Democratic Governance does not use or refer to international human rights standards and instruments. Examples of this group are USAID, CIDA, and JICA.

The third type is the Caesar's Salad. Development agencies of this type hold that human rights and development have shared goals. Some human rights principles are applied in development programs, although the use of international human rights instruments is still limited. This group tends to add new concepts to its previous ones and tries to mix them together. Examples of this group are UNDP, SIDA, and the EU.

The last type-RBA-believes that human rights and development goals are largely the same goals. Organizations in this group apply a variety of human rights principles and tools in their development work. Human rights consist of civil and political rights and economic, social, and cultural rights. They make reference to international human rights standards and use some instruments. Examples of this group are DFID, CARE, and ActionAid.

Within the same RBA type, NGOs interpret RBAs differently in important ways, resulting in a variety of policies, strategies, and programming. More importantly they interpret the concept of RBAs in ways to fit their organizational background and expertise, rather than trying to capture a full meaning of what an RBA could mean. Three variant of RBA are identified: the Popular RBA, the Equity RBA, and the Classical RBA of ActionAid UK, Oxfam GB, and SC Sweden, respectively. This means that although it seems that there is consensus of what an RBA should mean at international forums and conferences, in reality development NGOs interpret the concept of RBA differently in important elements.

The three types of RBAs distinguish themselves in conceptual frameworks, policies and strategies, and the use of international human rights standards. ActionAid interpretation leads to the "Popular RBA," featuring a local-to-global analysis, strong empowerment of the poor and the marginalized, the "add-on" human rights principles in programming, "local-up" advocacy, and a limited use of international human rights instruments. The Popular RBA addresses power relations from the local upward by strengthening people's capacity at the grassroots level, particularly by understanding and claiming their rights.

Oxfam GB's interpretation forms the "Equity RBA," featuring a selective use of human rights norms and instruments to legitimize and mobilize people and resources in challenging power relations at the global level with its global campaigns. In direct contrast to ActionAid, Oxfam GB has a global-to-local analytical framework. Oxfam's brand also features its five Aims, based on international human rights norms and linking together three types of intervention. Campaigning is a key advocacy tool for the Equity RBA, especially at the global level, where Oxfam GB has been more effective, compared with the local level.

Save the Children Sweden introduces the "Classical RBA," featuring a comprehensive use of international human rights norms and instruments. It states its goals within a human rights framework, compared to a poverty framework of the Popular and Equity RBAs. It deploys a variety of human rights and development tools in strengthening the protection and promotion of children's rights within the framework of its Program Areas. Advocacy work is a key tool both on the international and national levels, although grassroots work has been limited.

The finding of these three types of RBA interpretations tells us that the international community agrees upon one type of interpretation-the original and ESCR-oriented interpretation of the HRCA-is not true. This ESCR type of RBA interpretation, is not comfortably adopted by relief and development NGOs. In fact, development NGOs praise it, but do not actually adopt it. This is not because of human rights frameworks or principles, but rather because of the many implications that come with the adoption of an ESCR framework involve working methods, tools, and expertise that are outside the comfort zone of development NGOs, such as monitoring of laws, policies, and practices that are against international standards, addressing discriminations, and the use of respect-protect-fulfil to analyze situations on the ground. The HRCA interpretation of RBAs also has a downside, that is, it uses international human rights standards as the starting point of RBAs, and not NGOs' existing programs, expertise, and working methods. As a consequence, while development NGOs endorse the HRCA RBA-because of its compelling and logical interpretation of the ICESCR-they do not intent to do everything they give a nod to, as they have to start from existing organization working methods, culture, and traditionality.

The 2000 Stockholm workshop, which Frankovits and Earle facilitated, was a good example. Although the workshop concluded in the first recommendation "that ESCR should be an integral part of any human rights approach" (Frankovits and Earle 2000), this is not happening among development NGOs that adopt RBAs, including the three models of RBAs. Similarly, other recommendations that get the nod, but on which no action is taken are: "Violation of economic, social, and cultural rights should guide programming" (Frankovits and Earle 2000, 22).

This is rarely practiced by development NGOs, and none of the three NGOs use violations of ESCR to guide their programs. An interesting note is that while a violations approach was a recommendation from the workshop, most development NGOs, never be willing to take such a confrontational approach, are instead in favour of a co-operational approach without the emphasis on violations. Finally, a recommendation reads: "Development actors should use the General Comments and Concluding Observations of all the UN human rights treaty bodies and the reports of the Special Rapporteurs" (Frankovits and Earle 2000, 8). Among the three NGOs studied, only the Classical RBA has made use of these international human rights instruments.

In sum, the Popular, the Equity, and the Classical RBAs do not follow the early version of RBA interpretation by the HRCA, which is largely operationalizing ESCR. The closest to an ESCR-oriented RBA is the Classical RBA of Save the Children Sweden, which use international human rights framework, standards, and principles as the foundation of the interpretative conceptions-although Save the Children Sweden emphasizes the CRC, while the HRCA emphasizes the ICESCR. However, the HRCA interpretation receives warm welcome from the development community for its compelling, provoking, and ideal interpretation. Yet, development NGOs do not actually adopt the ESCR version of RBA, but develop its own conceptual framework, based on organizational expertise, existing missions and working methods, and organizational traditionality.

The Popular, the Equity, and the Classical RBAs can be seen as results of the struggles for what the ESCR-oriented RBA could not offer. The three RBAs show us that theoretically one can build up an RBA framework based on international human rights laws alone, but the three models of RBA show us that NGOs do not adopt all aspects of RBAs, rather they choose some of the concepts, standards, and principles that can best fit, sharpen, and improve the work, in which they already have expertise, working methods, tools, and mandates. ActionAid's long time engagement with people at the grassroots level conforms to the Popular RBA, emphasizing empowerment of the poor.

Oxfam GB's long experience in campaigns on structural inequality at the international level leads to the Equity RBA interpretation, which strategically uses human rights to legitimize and mobilize its campaigns, and create the five Aims to strengthen coherence of development work at the country level. Save the Children Sweden's engagement with international children's rights standards help formulate the Classical RBA, characterizing by the use of a variety of international human rights principles and instruments in strengthening the promotion and protection of children rights at the national level.

RBA and Partnership

It is assumed that by adopting an RBA, an NGO adopts a set of human rights goals, which are ambitious and comprehensive. These goals are simply too large for any one organization to accomplish all by itself. Everyone has to work together toward these same human rights goal, resulting in greater partnership. Others argue that RBA brings greater partnership because an RBA would trigger solidarity among NGOs and generate choices of new partners. This research finds that these arguments for greater partnership are not true. In practice, NGOs work to achieve their own goals, not a set of shared human rights goals. They may work together on projects, mostly short-term and one-time events. But NGOs that adopt RBAs run into problems clarifying their version of RBA, causing confusion among partners. Despite its necessity, working with partners proves to be a disconcerting experience. "Too much time spent," "too slow" and "not going according to plan" are some of the reflections of working with partners.

Partnership and relationship with stakeholders is a key area where interpretation of an RBA leads to different outcomes. The Popular, the Equity, and Classical RBAs all agree that RBA adoption creates greater needs for partnerships, and with more of a variety of partners, including human rights groups. A more controversial interpretation is whether an RBA means more cooperation or confrontation with governments. When faced with a clear-cut challenge to take sides, ActionAid takes a strong strand on the side of the poor and chooses to confront with governments when necessary.

The Equity RBA acknowledges unequal power relationships. With more experience working on political issues, Oxfam GB aims to address power relation issues and confront governments and international institutions at the global level through its global campaigns. The Classical RBA is of a view that the merit of cooperation and confrontation is not absolute, but a relative one. It finds that constructive cooperation can accelerate the progress towards the realization of children's rights, while confrontation can be appropriate to address certain policies and practices that undermine human rights.

RBA and Organizational Change

The second step of a process that results in a weakening concept of RBAs is the organization dynamics of NGOs. The three case studies show us that none of the cases underwent a transformative organizational change, which the concept of RBA would require. Only Save the Children Sweden manages to produce a transitional organizational change, using new working methods to replace traditional child relief work. The other two cases-Oxfam GB and ActionAid UK-only produce a development change, aiming to improve the same working methods.

Organizational process is an important part in understanding an RBA adoption. This research finds that NGOs attempt to made organizational changes from the top level, in terms of vision and mission statement, to the operational level on the ground. But these changes are insufficient to deliver the full spectrum of an RBA meaning. More importantly, these changes are aimed to improve effectiveness within the same way of working, rather than changing the way of working, as a transformational change would suggest. While organization process helps turn some human rights principles into practice, this process has diluted the strength of the RBA concept, as it left out some human rights principles such as non-discrimination. NGO families play important roles in accelerating and slowing down efforts toward becoming a rights-based NGO.

In greater detail, the findings of organizational change in the context of the adoption of RBAs can be summarized as follows.

First, organizational changes in the context of the adoption of RBAs are managed anarchy. It is neither planned changes nor chaotic changes alone, but a mixture of the two. In all three cases, each NGO has done some planning for organizational changes, particularly from the headquarters, including making changes in visions and missions to reflect their beliefs and development framework. But the planned changes at the headquarters quickly turned out to be rather chaotic at country offices where the scheme used is to organize the anarchy and keep it at an acceptable level. Oxfam GB was the least chaotic and with the most limited changes that it actually planned to make for its Popular RBA.

SC Sweden was devoid of the leadership to properly plan and manage organizational change towards its Classical RBA. The task of mainstreaming RBA is left to the mid-management who relies on cooperation with other staff, resulting in a step-by-step approach. ActionAid UK in contrast has mostly used the "science of muddling through" (Lindblom, 1959). Its decentralized structure with weak central change plans leads to a situation where staff can experiment in a variety of ways, resulting in a loss of focus in its Popular RBA. Despite the variation of anarchy of the three NGOs, the conclusion on organizational change of this study confirms the findings of DiBella (1992) that organizational change of NGOs is closer to "organized anarchy" than "planned change."

Second, organizational transformation has not been the type of organizational change experienced in the context of an RBA adoption, but rather it has been organizational development and organizational transition. Transformational change refers to total and radical change, involving a completely new context and configuration of behaviours, roles, attitudes, motives, beliefs, and values. Transitional change refers to a less radical organizational change that evolves slowly through many transitional steps during which the organization is neither what it once was nor what it aims to be, and similar to transformational change, seeking to replace ways of doing things. Developmental change refers to the most minor change, aimed to improve skills, methods and other conditions in order to meet current expectation, and not to change the ways of doing things. None of the three organizations has experienced anything close to a transformational change. Although there has been no plan to radically change these organizations, the roles of staff, attitudes, beliefs, or values, there has been an attempt to integrate human rights values into the systems, but with no concrete or systematic plan.

Organizational changes within SC Sweden are closer to transitional change than the other two types of change. Although its step-by-step approach evolved the organization slowly, it has changed the foundation of its roles and its work. This has resulted in changes of ways that SC Sweden makes intervention in its development work, from direct assistance for poor children to working to protect children's rights through several means, including advocacy and research. In over a decade, SC Sweden changed from a community development organization in the 1980s to a children's rights organization. The Classical RBA interpretation plays important parts in going beyond the superficial use of human rights concepts to include international human rights standards, mechanisms, and principles in this new development framework. Among the three NGOs, Save the Children Sweden has changed its organization most significantly-a transitional change-although its Classical RBA seems to suggest for a transformational one.

Oxfam GB's organizational changes are the least among the three NGOs. The organization never wanted to go beyond a developmental change from the start. Its Equity RBA leads the organization to use human rights concepts and principles selectively and strategically.

The Equity RBA of Oxfam GB is, in essence, not a human rights-based development framework, but a tool with a social justice development framework. It aims primarily to improve Oxfam GB's coherence, effectiveness, and ability to leverage for change. Organizational changes are therefore limited to an improvement mode with some "do more of" what already exists. Among the three NGOs, Oxfam GB is the only organization that can deliver the organizational changes that are required by its own RBA interpretation. That is, Oxfam GB's organizational change in the context of the adoption of RBA is developmental change as its Populist RBA suggest.

ActionAid's organizational change has been limited to development change, despite its willingness to go further. The

Popular RBA suggests a rather radical organizational change, including a totally new configuration of roles, values, attitudes, and motivation in empowering the poor to claim their rights. The organization has goodwill and the intention to "doing things differently." But organizationally, it has not been able to arrange itself to move beyond the use of human rights principles for the improvement of its traditional approach to development work. Combined with the "add-on" and "experimental" approach, ActionAid's organizational change in the context the adoption of an RBA is limited to developmental change, rather than a transformational change as its Popular interpretation would suggest.

Third, by using Nadler and Tushman's typology of change, it is found that SC Sweden's change is of a "reorientation," while Oxfam GB and ActionAid UK's changes are of "tuning." Although there have been increasing questions about NGOs' effectiveness and accountability, the adoption of RBAs took place when there was no immediate requirement to change. The three NGOs adopted RBAs while seeking to find better ways of achieving their strategic visions. There was no time-pressure factor. They all have taken their times in going through their change processes, and therefore are categorized in the anticipation group.

The vision of the leadership was a key factor in the adoption of an RBA by SC Sweden. It has, over a decade, created its own Classical RBA, using international human rights standards as its development framework and adopting the CRC as the foundation document of the organization. With this interpretation, it has gone further than the other two NGOs in a fundamental redefining of its strategies, roles, and values. SC Sweden has sought not only to "do things better"-which the other two organizations largely do-but also to "do things differently." This makes SC Sweden's organizational change a "reorientation" change.

Both Oxfam GB and ActionAid UK adopted their RBAs as a result of strategy reviews in the second half of the 1990s. The adoptions were largely for strategic reasons, aiming to improve the results of their work without completely changing the ways they had worked. Despite its SCOs stated in human rights terms, Oxfam GB has not moved beyond its tradition social justice development framework. The Equity RBA is a process of adapting, modifying, and emphasizing certain aspects of work-such as campaigning and media work-not an attempt to work completely differently or to move itself into a new category of development NGOs. Similarly, while Oxfam GB has quickly grasped RBA values, built its own Equity RBA model, and incorporated RBA values to strengthen its campaign orientation and its advantage of global leverage, ActionAid UK has been conducting a number of multidirectional experiments, resulting in slow progress in grasping RBA concepts and tools to strengthen its grassroots work. In sum, organizational changes resulting from the Equity and Popular RBAs are "incremental." They seek mostly to improve their development work by "strategic use" and by "adding on" to their existing work, and not to produce a new product.

Fourth, the change process of NGOs that adopt RBAs is non-linear. This is largely because the organizational change in the context of the adoption of RBA is not quite a planned change, rather it is a managed anarchy, resulting from the complexity and ambiguity of the concepts of RBA.

With these limitations, none of the three NGOs create a fixed master plan of organizational change, but instead, played it safe and kept it flexible by taking time in deploying the experimental, the blueprint, and the step-by-step approaches to mainstream their RBAs into their organizations.

Fifth, NGOs' staff is not trained to deliver RBA programs. The tendency is that they have limited knowledge about human rights and RBAs, especially country offices' local staff in rural areas. The three cases of NGOs confirm that RBA interpretative frameworks and organizational change processes do have an effect on: the needs for new skills and knowledge on human rights and RBA; the pressure put towards staff; and the resistance from staff, which in turn affects the success of the RBA adoptions.

ActionAid has experienced dramatic changes with a number of development staff leaving the organization. In response to the requirement of the Popular RBA framework that its staff have good knowledge and skills of human rights and RBAs in order to help people be aware and claim their rights, ActionAid UK develops a clear policy to recruit new staff with a human rights background. While this policy is not applicable to some country offices, such as Vietnam, it pressures staff in some national offices into leaving the organization.

The two groups of staff-the new human rights background and the old development background are yet to be integrated. In addition, some staff in rural areas are ignorant of its RBA. In contrast to ActionAid, Oxfam GB neither has staff leaving due to the adoption of an RBA, nor does it have a policy to recruit new staff with a human rights background.

This is due to the Equity RBA framework, as it does not consist of a strong human rights component, pressuring for the new human rights skills from staff. The integration of selected human rights principles into goals, objectives, and especially program management tools helps reduce the sharp need for new skills and increase positive acceptance of the new approach, as it leads to more relevance and effective programs. In addition, the not-too-strong push on the RBA by the management reduces staff's resistance and increases their positive attitude towards the new approach.

SC Sweden's Classical interpretation framework demands strong human rights knowledge from its staff. But the organization can cope with the demand of its interpretation well, as it has continuously built its staff capacity on international human rights laws over the decade without pushing or pressuring staff. The soft-sell and step-by-step approach, which expanded over a decade has softened this pressure, especially on staff with development backgrounds. The step-by-step approach also allows the new staff with human rights backgrounds and old staff with development backgrounds to integrate among one another well.

Sixth, the interactions of NGOs with their families regarding the adoption of RBA help us draw three conclusions. First, NGOs families have limited influence on an RBA adoption of individual NGOs. Large and influential NGOs like ActionAid

UK, Oxfam GB, and SC Sweden have interests in adopting RBAs due to their own causes, and not because of the family. On the contrary, the three NGOs are rather influential in turning their family into RBA families.

Second, NGO families can give positive reinforcement for the adoption of an RBA by family members. A strong RBA alliance can strengthen the commitment to RBA of its members, such as the case of OI and Oxfam Hong Kong. Third, a joint RBA strategic paper is a key factor in mainstreaming RBA within a family. Without a joint strategic paper, an NGO family tends to have difficulties promoting the RBA within the alliance. On the contrary, an NGO family that has a joint RBA strategy can move forward much faster in implementing its RBA development policy.

Finally, training workshops on human rights and RBAs as an organizational learning tool prove to be useful, but have limitations and are far from sufficient in solving the problem of a lack of knowledge about working on human rights and RBAs. For many development NGOs, most training workshops are one-time events where participants are expected to learn about human rights concepts and RBA tools, and then to go to their countries or rural areas, and start to articulate and develop RBA projects. A long-term, two-way, and on-going learning approach is needed for RBA NGOs, including Oxfam GB, which does not use training on human rights and RBA for their staff and partners.

The Implementation of RBAs

RBA implementation is found to be another process that weakens and softens the radical concept of RBAs. Development NGOs adapt and compromise their implementation in order to receive acceptance and cooperation with the government at the country level. This research examines the hypotheses in regards to the implementation of RBAs by using the case of the three NGOs in Vietnam. Since the late 1980s, these three NGOs have worked in the country, and from the late 1990s, ActionAid Vietnam, Oxfam GB, and SC Sweden started their Popular RBA, Equity RBA, and Classical RBA, respectively. They have earned important achievements. At the same time they have encountered many difficulties. Yet, several lessons can be drawn from these experiences.

The three NGOs conducted situational analyses based on their RBAs. The Classical RBA's analysis framework, based heavily on human rights assessment, proves to be more effective than the poverty analysis frameworks of Oxfam GB and ACTIONAID in terms of identifying groups of the vulnerable, the marginalized, and people at risk of human rights violations. This is to say, in practice, NGOs conduct little human rights situation analysis. Rather they practice traditional situation assessment for development projects. In Vietnam, only SC Sweden uses some thematic human rights-situation analysis. This limited use of human rights analysis is due to the complexity and comprehensive nature of human rights analysis. A human rights situation analysis requires a good knowledge of human rights and human rights-based approach to assess the situation on the ground with human rights lens. This capacity is yet to be built by staff of the three NGOs, especially that of Oxfam GB and ActionAid UK.

For SC Sweden, the Classical RBA analysis framework gives the organization the opportunity to work with a pool of marginalized children. However, only some of them get selected within its Program Areas. In priority setting, Oxfam GB is largely guided by its five Aims and SCOs, where target groups are selected to fit program priorities. Similarly, ActionAid Vietnam sets its priorities based on its expertise and other factors, before choosing target groups to work with. That is, the most marginalized people are not prime target groups that the three NGOs are working for, as they all have their already set priorities, except for SC Sweden who works for some of the most marginalized children.

All three organizations have made substantial progress in applying their RBAs in planning and evaluating their work. Oxfam GB has taken important steps in integrating human rights principles into its program tools, resulting in a greater potential for strengthening state accountability and improvement of people's access to services, resources, and opportunities. SC Sweden has developed a human rights-based planning framework and its Program Areas, focusing particularly on strengthening capacity to implement the CRC, making it relatively easy for program staff to plan according to local situations. ActionAid Vietnam has strengthened people's involvement in the planning and evaluation process of its own development projects, reflecting a strong belief that participation in itself is empowerment.

The three NGOs in Vietnam, however, have not completely moved away from service delivery to policy advocacy, although they all increasingly engage with the national government on a variety of policy issues. This is a new phenomenon in the country. ActionAid Vietnam has halved its direct services, although it intends to keep the other half, helping it retain influence over local governments and partners. Oxfam GB ceased its service delivery work in 2001, and instead advocates for quality of services. It has developed several advocacy projects focusing on trade, livelihoods, and budget for social services, such as education. SC Sweden stopped its service delivery work before the other two NGOs. It has advocated for greater awareness and acceptance of several children issues, including inclusive education for children with disabilities, children's right to voice and participate, and children with HIV/AIDS. It also advocates for the amendment of a labour law so that it complies with the CRC.

The implementation of RBAs of the three NGOs are largely affected by their own interpretation of RBAs, their organizational changes-particularly change processes, and the preparation for delivery of RBA programs-particularly the development of strategies and RBA analytical, planning, and evaluation tools. ActionAid's Popular RBA interpretation leads to work with a strong component of empowerment and participation of the people. The experimental change process and the lack of RBA planning tools open up an opportunity for its program staff to try out different tools for change, including changes of roles in the grassroots level and the use of campaigns at the national level. Oxfam GB's Equity RBA interpretation leads to the focus on the improvement of social services, trade, and pro-poor policies in the country. Its blueprint organizational change process and the new-developed planning and evaluation tools help contribute to both the focus and progress of its RBA programs. SC Sweden's Classical interpretation steers its focus towards the protection of vulnerable children in Vietnam. The human rights situation analysis helps identify these children's groups, while its Program Areas solidify its projects in fighting inequality and discrimination.

The RBA implementation of these three NGOs in Vietnam is greatly restricted by limitations of civil and political rights, especially in terms of the operations of these NGOs, which are strictly controlled by government agencies. PACCOM is a government mechanism that both monitors and "approves" NGO projects before they are implemented. The new "Grassroots Democracy Decree" has legitimized people's participation at the local level, although it still has limitations in several dimensions in practice, and it has had little impact on people's participation in national policies. The lack of a participation culture obstructs the development process of NGOs. People still see government officials as "the authorities" to whom they should show respect and do what they are told, rather than ones who are obliged to fulfil their human rights. The culture of children's participation is also weak, affecting programs of SC Sweden.

In practice, partnership, as experienced by the three NGOs, does not confirm the expectation that after adopting RBAs NGOs will work more closely together towards shared human rights goals. Rather, NGOs work independently towards different goals, based on their organizational missions, expertise, working methods, and traditionality. They occasionally work together mostly on one-time and short-term specific projects, rather than a continuous, long-term commitment, or with shared goals and strategies. Moreover, working with partners becomes one of the problems development NGOs encounter after the adoption of RBAs. They face difficulties communicating with local partners they are working with. There are also no human rights NGOs for international development NGOs to work with in the country.

This framework consists of three RBA principles-accountability, empowerment, and equality and non-discrimination. Each principle has implications on strategies and actions. Among the three principles, holding the state accountable is the weakest area of the three NGOs. Although Oxfam GB and Save the Children Sweden have designed and used programming tools, holding the state accountable proves to be an area of great difficulty for development NGOs.

The staff of the three NGOs also has limited experience in the work. However, there have been initiatives to put children rights issues on the public agenda and continuing work to amend laws by SC Sweden; to call for people's supervision of poverty reduction programs and the monitoring of the CPRGS by Oxfam GB; and to improve people's participation in grassroots development work on the village level by ActionAid Vietnam.

Empowerment is the area where all three organizations have made substantial gains. Empowering the people is a key facet of ActionAid Vietnam's work with its Popular RBA projects. The organization has substantially reorganized its work to involve people's participation in the development process. However, its work to support people in claiming their rights is still limited, due to its organizational culture of serving people and of being less critical and political, as well as the limited knowledge of human rights and RBAs.

Oxfam GB has supported, organized, and mobilized people to have better access to the market, services, and resources, while allowing less people participation in its own development projects. SC Sweden does not aim to empower people directly, but its human rights education has helped empower different groups in Vietnamese society. Putting it all together, participation is the RBA instrument that is most used by the three NGOs, followed by the process of organizing and mobilizing people to have better access to services and resources, as a part of the scheme to support people to claim their rights.

Finally, equality and non-discrimination is a weak area for the three organizations. It receives limited attention in terms of operationalizing the principle into development programs.

Only SC Sweden has managed to transform this principle into its working language. Its work in promoting equality and non-discrimination is evident in its inclusive education and juvenile justice programs, as well as in its work on HIV/AIDS for street children. ActionAid Vietnam and Oxfam GB lack tools for human rights analysis to identify marginalized groups of people who are discriminated against in society. However, the two organizations help ethnic minorities gain access to resources and services.

In sum, the three NGOs have not directly steered their work towards changing power relations, resulting in very limited changes in the power relationships between the Vietnamese government and the Vietnamese. The three NGOs have helped the poor, improved many aspects of their lives, given them better access to education, healthcare, market, resources and services, but their work still has limited impacts, in terms of setting up legal, political, or social guarantees of those human rights. There has been even less impact on changing power relationships, or the structure of inequality in the country. Government officials are still "the authorities," rather than "duty bearers," as international human rights laws affirm. Without clearly aiming to change power relations, or establishing legal, political, and social guarantee of rights, most of the work of the three NGOs only contributes indirectly and in a limited way to changing power relations, except for some direct work with clear aims, particularly Oxfam GB's plan to improve accountability and access, ActionAid Vietnam's scaling up its people participation, and SC Sweden's work for marginalized children and on HRE for duty bearers.

THE HUMAN RIGHTS LANGUAGE PARADOX: LEGITIMACY THAT COMES WITH PROBLEMS?

The human rights language that comes with RBAs has become a paradox in the implementation of RBAs in developing countries. On the one hand, human rights language gives development NGOs legitimacy they need to refer to governments' human rights obligations. On the other hand, it makes things more difficult for development NGOs, as human rights are not goals, framework, nor development strategies of most developing countries. Moreover, a demand for rights is not usually what governments want to hear from NGOs.

In repressive regimes, human rights language often becomes a minority language, raising people's eyebrows rather than serving as magic words that bring about positive change. More and more development practitioners now ask: Can and should we do a rights-based approach without saying that it is a rights-based approach, or without referring to human rights? Supporters of a "non-human rights language RBA" argue that doing it in this way-using human rights frameworks and principles in all parts of development processes without referring to human rights-achieves the same results of an RBA, while helping reduce frictions with the authorities. Less friction means more likelihood of success of programs. In addition, not many people-whether they be government officials, development NGOs, or the people-understand how to turn human rights language in development into practice. Non-supporters, on the other hand, argue that doing an RBA without stating it explicitly reduces legitimacy and power that comes with human rights, particularly state obligations, as Sidoti and Frankovits (1995) point out. Acknowledging there might be possible irritation of the authorities, this group believes that the use of human rights language will be of more benefit in the long run, as it repeatedly calls for responsibility from the authorities and strengthens the culture of accountability, which otherwise would not be cultivated.

The emergence of a "non-human rights language RBA" debate reflects frustration and the sense of risks resulting from speaking human rights language, particularly in countries run by relatively repressive governments. This is especially true for cases where the authorities, who are not positively disposed to the obligations that comes with the language. This reminds us of Swift (1999)'s argument that for an RBA to be a successful approach, one of the four conditions that have to be met is that human rights has to be fundamental and universal. In the case of Vietnam, it is true that the lack of a human rights culture does to a certain degree alienate human rights language, and turns what seems to be normal human rights-endorsing statements in the western world into slightly more aggressive or somewhat challenging statements for repressive governments.

The human rights language does make it more difficult to work with the Vietnamese government. This leads development NGOs in Vietnam to at least three choices: first, postpone the RBA development policies and programs in the country until it positively changes its human rights culture; second, continue implementing RBA development policies and programs but without or little referring to human rights, unless necessary; and third, continue to implement RBA development policies and programs, using human rights language explicitly, and applying additional tools to manage and strengthen the relationship with the government.

The human rights language paradox of RBAs is a big problem that still receives little attention. A few strategies and actions to improve the situation include: first, a large-scale human rights education in prioritized sectors in the country. This does not refer to workshops introducing human rights to some 15 to 25 participants at a time. Rather, it means the development of national human rights education plans, covering formal and informal education, and including curriculum development that take into consideration local culture and contexts, and trainings of trainers. Second, donors have a key role to play in creating a human rights culture in a country. Human rights education is a "promotional" side of human rights work, involving less confrontation, compared to the "violation" side.

The declaration of the UN Decade of Human Rights Education legitimizes this area of work, enabling donors to more easily step in and set up national HRE strategies and plans. Third, regional human rights bodies can help lessen the human rights language paradox. Mainstreaming human rights education in their member countries is a priority area that most countries welcome, as it normally does not entail exposure of human rights violations. However, there is a great difference in the progress of regional human rights institutions. For example, the European human rights mechanisms have developed human rights courts, while the establishment of ASEAN human rights mechanisms has limited progress. Finally, development NGOs need to create lobbyists and advocacy strategies targeting southern countries. In the past, most advocacy work of international NGOs focused on the governments of developed countries. RBAs call for the change of this focus. They call for significant changes in working relationship with southern governments. That is, to change from being receivers of aid or development assistance to ones that are held accountable to their human rights obligations through the mixture of advocacy and pressure, while maintaining productive working relationship.

THE OMNIPRESENCE PARADOX

This paradox of RBA is that some development NGOs and their staff believe and claim that they are implementing an RBA, regardless of whether they do it or not. In other words, everything one does is a rights-based approach. On the one hand, such claims may help increase discussions on human rights and human rights-based approach among the development community, and may bring in new organizations into the RBA movement, which may result in an increasing use of RBA tools. On the other hand, such claims of adopting key human rights principles without actually adopting them may weaken the RBA movement as a whole. This is because rhetorical adoption, intentional or not, benefits the status quo, obstructing experiments and learning of the development and implementation of RBA development policies. Moreover, over-claims of being RBA hurt the RBA movements as a whole, as overusing of human rights language makes human rights values and principles lose their meanings-which undermines the values, the beliefs, and principles underling and shared by development NGOs that adopt RBAs.

Claims of adhering to an RBA to development NGOs and staff can be seen as a rhetorical level of the adoption of RBA. Many social scientists hold that there is difference between adopting human rights language and not adopting at all. It is believed that the adoption of the human rights language is a first step towards actual practices of the language, which is "better" than not saying anything at all. However, there is also a possibility that the adoption of human rights language can be an instrument for not taking the organization any further than the rhetorical level. This claims, as argued by Uvin (2002), can benefit by putting adherents on the moral high ground and able to avoid criticisms, and maintain the status quo.

Examples of the omnipresence of RBAs are on the rise. These can be categorized into two types. First, service delivery is an RBA instrument. In Vietnam, some interviewees of this research call their relief efforts and other direct services RBA work, as direct services contribute to "the fulfillment of human rights." Type two is gaining popularity among old, southern-based NGOs and grassroots networks. These organizations sincerely believe that their organizations have been RBA ones for a long time without calling it as such, because they too have used "participation," "empowerment," "advocacy," "calling governments to be accountable" and "focusing on the disadvantaged." Both types believe that they too are RBA organizations without having to change the ways of working.

During their trip to India, ActionAid's consultants also recorded type one omnipresence: "there is a strong belief among ActionAid staffs that "everything" they do is human rights because, after all, it concerns elements essential to those rights-including education, housing, health, food, shelters, etc. The challenge is to make a distinction between provision of rights-or simply providing education, food, etc.-and facilitation for the realization of rights. It requires a change of mind-set."

A few people have already suggested ways to differentiate RBA work from other, which will not be discussed again here. However, two ways can be noted. One is a long and complex version, using the ESCR framework of the obligations to respect, protect, and fulfil human rights. This first method is recommended by the ESCR school of RBA, including the HRCA and FIAN. Another way is to see if the development work lead to the arrangement of a long-term social guarantees of human rights in ways that people can continuously enjoy their basic rights.

THE PARADOX OF ISSUE CHOOSING

Choosing issues to work on in Vietnam is a dilemma in the implementation of RBAs. In general, working on less sensitive issues means more government cooperation and a better relationship with the government. These less sensitive issues include vaccinations, malnutrition, and water for children. On the contrary, working on more sensitive issues can lead to worsening relationships with the authorities. These issues usually involve national security, civil and political rights, and issues relating to political freedoms, press freedoms, ethnic minorities, and refugees. In Vietnam, development work taking place near national borders is also seen by the authorities as sensitive, particularly near the border with Cambodia.

Besides issues concerning national security and civil and political rights as such, sensitive issues in Vietnam also include themes on economic, social, and cultural rights, which may make the Vietnamese government loses its face. Examples are child labour and child prostitution. International NGOs have learned that if they work on such issues, they have to be especially cautious, as such groups of people in the society may make the government feel ashamed in the presence of foreigners, particularly on the issue of child labour. The Vietnamese government used to deny the existence of child prostitution. It has just recently accepted it, meaning that NGOs can now work on the issue. Although street children still sounds like a face-losing issue, the government finds it acceptable to talk about it. The bottom line of choosing sensitive issues is that "if an NGO starts to pick on one of these projects, then the door might be closed."

The three NGOs have chosen the strategy of starting on less sensitive issues, in hopes to slowly expand to more sensitive ones. To date, they have tended to stay or move from one less sensitive issue to another. SC Sweden works on children's participation, focusing on awareness raising and sensitization, an important area and yet being seen as less threatening. Its education, HIV/AIDS, and trafficking programs are all in the safe zone. ActionAid Vietnam has retained service delivery in rural areas, as well as in the agricultural sector, which is technical in nature and therefore less sensitive. ActionAid Vietnam and Oxfam GB have increasingly worked on people's participation, taking advantage of the Grassroots Democracy Decree. They are working with care, and trying not to cross the line the authorities have drawn.

A more sensitive issue in the country, for example, is human rights violations of the Montagnard ethnic minority. The groups have been so systematically and seriously deprived of their rights to religious beliefs, livelihoods, and land rights that many have had to flee their homes and seek refuge status in Laos, Cambodia, and Thailand (Amnesty International 2005 and Human Rights Watch 2005).

These violations involve both civil and political rights and economic, social, and cultural rights, which could be a good opportunity to human rights and development NGOs to work together. Unfortunately, no development NGO appears to work with this minority group, although some dimensions of violations against the Montagnard minority fall into their organizations' missions. This may be due to the fact that the denial of ESC rights do not take place in the development areas that the three NGOs are allowed to work in. Another possible reason is that the scale of abuses is so severe that it increases the level of sensitivity, reaching the point where it turns this "human rights" and "development" issue into a "national security" one, which is not a business of relief and development NGOs.

Nevertheless, development NGOs do have options of choosing which issues to work on. CARE International's rating scale of the fulfillment of CARE International Program Principles differentiate levels of RBA strength, reflecting choices in how far NGOs would want to challenge power relations and the risks that may come with it. A "considerable" RBA means that "we are willing to work with various actors and at various levels, as long as it doesn't put our organization or others at risk." A "strong" RBA thinks: "we work at various levels and are willing to tackle thorny issues, even if it puts us in conflict those in power." Against this scale, no programs of ActionAid Vietnam, Oxfam GB, or Save the Children Sweden falls into the "strong" RBA categories. The three organizations are more likely to be in the "basic" degree of RBA, meaning that they may work on any issues, but "if working on these issues might risk our funding source and have other negative impact implications for the organization, we back off."

The question here is whether or not "less sensitive issues" that development NGOs choose to work on are in fact priorities for their organizations and for the people in this country, or whether or not they are concerned with some of the most vulnerable and marginalized groups of people? If not, then the three NGOs may have not fulfilled their mandates to work with the most marginalized people.

On the other hand, if the three NGOs choose to work on sensitive issues, they risk hurting positive and productive relationships that they have long built. One sensitive issue may irritate the authorities, affecting cooperation on other non-sensitive issues, or in the worse case, development NGOs may be asked to leave the country. Choosing issues to work on is a dilemma for development NGOs in Vietnam. Yet, the choices are there for them to choose, as Oxfam GB's SCOs, SC Sweden's Program Areas, and ActionAid UK's strategic plan are all broad enough to fit both sensitive and non-sensitive issues.

THE COOPERATION PARADOX

The tradition of cooperation with governments has deep roots among development agencies. It has deep effects on various fronts ranging from choices of working methods to choices of issues on which to work. In general, development NGO's cooperation, friendliness, and avoidance of conflict with governments becomes greater as government control over NGOs becomes greater. Government control over NGOs often becomes greater, as the need for NGOs to stay out of certain issues become stronger.

This need for NGOs to stay out of certain issues often becomes stronger when the level of human rights violations that the government commits becomes graver. That is, the graver human rights violations a government commits, the more cooperative development NGOs would be with the government. This logic sounds wrong, but true.

The cooperation paradox starts with the idea that the adoption of an RBA enables development NGOs to see the world through a human rights lens. Through this lens, human rights violations may be seen. Yet, development NGOs are quick to point out that there are at least two ways to react to new pictures of human rights violations: confrontation and cooperation (Jones 2000).

A confrontational approach consists of documentation of human rights violations and the use of such documentation to mobilize pressure targeting those responsible for the violations. This approach is widely known as the "naming and shaming" method, widely used by large human rights NGOs, such as Amnesty International and Human Rights Watch. The "violations approach" of ESC rights monitoring (Chapman 1996) is also often seen as part of the confrontational scenario.

Most, if not all, development academic and practitioners believe that development NGOs should leave the confrontation/violations approach to human rights NGOs. The logic behind this belief tends to be because: (a) development NGOs have different professional backgrounds, traditions, criteria of success, and professional ethics than human rights NGOs; (b) development and human rights NGOs work in a different political and social environment; (c) development NGOs "stay longer on the ground, work more closely with much larger numbers of local partners"; (d) development NGOs are more dependent on state collaboration (Uvin 2004, 149); (e) a violations approach tends to lead to antagonism and risks, which local employees of development NGOs do not want to take more than that of human rights NGO staff (Uvin 2004); (f) development NGOs work in "a world of trade-off, of community and government ownership, of small, incremental change", which a violations approach does not fit into well; and lastly, (g) development NGOs actually avoid the "hot potato" of human rights, because it is likely to lead to more confrontation with states (Uvin 2004, 48).

Uvin proposes a "lite" violations approach, consisting of three components:

(1) conducting human rights impact assessments;

(2) applying non-retrogression principle; and

(3) holding NGOs' own processes and practices to human rights standards (Uvin 2004).

While the three methods are crucial and useful for both development and human rights NGOs, they do not tend to sufficiently redress the shortcomings of the lack of documentation and assessment of practices against human rights standards (of the violations approach), or of direct calls for those responsible to be accountable to their human rights obligations (of the confrontational approach).

Before further discussion, it is useful to look at the degree of NGO control in Vietnam and the practicality of the cooperation and confrontation approaches of the three NGOs.

The Cooperation of Control: Experience from Vietnam

A dimension of the relationships of NGOs and government in Vietnam is control--a key issue in the implementation of an RBA in the country. The availability of political space, rather than level of economic development, affects the ability of ActionAid Vietnam, Oxfam GB, and SC Sweden in the implementation of their programs. In Vietnam, with a poor human rights record, especially in terms of civil and political rights, the three NGOs have faced much difficulty. In large part, the three NGOs accept the situation and try to work within the given space, rather than trying to change it. Nevertheless, the Vietnamese government has affected the work of three NGOs in several ways.

First, the government affects NGO's priority and target selection. Oxfam GB, for example, wanted to work in districts that its team has identified as the poorest communities. But the government did not allow the organization to do so for these areas are the borders of Cambodia. Other prohibitions prevented Oxfam from following up its research work, such as in the central highlands areas in the north.

Second, the Vietnamese government acts as if it were the Board of the International NGOs (INGOs). This is done through the People Aid Coordination Committee (PACCOM), the

Vietnamese government agency that is responsible for coordinating and controlling about 400 INGOs registered with it. The committee is designed to monitor INGOs and their activities, including watching the move of political NGOs. In practice, PACCOM is more than a paper tiger-it is serious about checking NGOs. It requires progress reports from INGOs every six months. More importantly, it requires that all action plans be sent to its offices prior to implementation. Plans cannot be implemented without its approval. The committee also determines provinces that NGOs can and cannot work in.

The cases of the three NGOs in Vietnam indicate that a confrontational approach is not being practiced in the country. Ironically, even if a confrontational approach is chosen, it must be approved by the government! All three NGOs avoid confrontation with the government, as all informants of the three NGOs agree that confrontation is the number one thing to stay away from in Vietnam. It "would not change anything"; it would "stop them from listening" and "the door would be closed." Instead, the three NGOs have adopted a cooperative mode. ActionAid Vietnam works harder on its homework in presenting to the authorities what, why, and how it wants to change. Oxfam GB identifies supportive individuals, and tries to influence policies and practices through such engagements. SC Sweden plays by the rules, presenting its work as "social development", which is the only role of NGOs that the Vietnamese seem willing to accept-"nothing more than that".

Four RBA NGOs in Vietnam, Oxfam GB, Actionaid Vietnam, SC UK, and SC Sweden have organized meetings to learn experiences from one another. They confirm the importance of avoiding confrontation, in favour of building trust and consensus (Van Ngoc, 2003). Although this approach is certainly useful in some situations, using it in all cases raises a few questions: Can consensus between NGOs and government always be found in the struggle for the realization of all human rights in Vietnam? What can be done, if consensus cannot be found? Will the NGOs drop their position, or pursue other approaches? More importantly, will the approach lead to a stronger accountability in Vietnamese society? Given that human rights are minimum guarantees of human dignity, obliging the state and other duty bearers, how can they be negotiated, or bargained in search of consensus?

Changing Power Relations with Cooperation?

A cooperation approach can be costly, yet it may not be able to change power relations. In Vietnam, the price that development NGOs pay for this approach is to not work on sensitive issues, in which many poor and marginalized people may be involved. From the cases above, we see that in order to maintain a good relationship and to be able to work in the country, NGOs have to accept the government's approval of their own their project plans and working areas. To maintain "good cooperation", they avoid sensitive issues, in favour of more easily-accepted ones.

Yet, the work of the three NGOs in changing power relations are limited, as steps needed to be taken to strengthening accountability are not always conflict-free or pressure-free. The choices made by ActionAid Vietnam, Oxfam GB, SC Sweden in balancing these priorities are not unique. A workshop on RBA organized by SC Sweden in Stockholm concluded that one of the main criticisms among development actors (NGOs, bilateral development agencies, and UN development agencies) was that they "in general were seen to refrain from pressuring Governments about specific rights violations, for fear of risking their legitimacy and future program activities". (SC Sweden 2003, 2)

The CARE RBA rating scale, one of the few well planned and progressive thinking pieces in the RBA business to date, also reflects reluctance to do oppositional work, as it risks worsening relationships with government. The "minimum" scale (level 1) to "ensure accountability and promote responsibility" reads: "We maintain a low profile and do not challenge any power holders." A step stronger, the "symbolic" scale (level 2) suggests: "We identify conditions that need to change, but don't talk in terms of responsibilities, because we aren't a political organization." While the low (weak) level of engagement is really low, the high (strong) level is not as high.

The "strong" scale (level 5) only reads: "When appropriate, we are willing to risk loosing donor support because of the stands we take." However, on "addressing discrimination", CARE's "strong" RBA scale becomes much stronger: "Discrimination is a way for those in power to maintain control and perpetuate poverty. Poverty can only be overcome by challenging those power structures that are discriminatory." On how to challenge power structures, CARE answers: "We not only analyze the existing patterns of discrimination, we also find out where this discrimination is rooted (e.g. policies, rules norms, structures, institutions) and proactively work to confront these factors." (CARE International 2005) An interesting note about this scale is that it identifies two types of risks in adopting an RBA. The first risk is stated explicitly, that is, the risk of doing things with which donors may disagree; which may result in loosing donor support. The other risk is not stated clearly, but involves challenging "power holders", or the state.

The Promotional Side of a Cooperation Approach

Perhaps, human rights violations are not the only pictures available through a human rights lens. There is other work for development NGOs to contribute constructively through a co-operational approach, such as helping fulfil certain economic, social, and cultural rights. This is the case for most development NGOs. Instead of violations and confrontation, or the "lite" violations approach, most development NGOs pursue a cooperation approach. This approach focuses on the positive side of progress of achieving development goals, rather than on the negative side of correcting human rights violations. The Millennium Development Goals (MDG) campaign is one of the major works on the cooperation approach. The campaign has built up leadership commitment from developed and developing countries, as well as international organizations and NGOs, and shifts the focus to specific development goals, reflecting some priorities in the global south.

As NGOs continue to work towards the MDG, they have started to realize that they need to strengthen their own work to influence southern government's policies, laws, and practices and keep governments' commitment towards development goals; as opposed to targeting its advocacy at northern government as in the past (Oxfam GB 2002a; 2002b; Lawson, no date). This is where a human rights framework can contribute to the movement, to hold governments accountable to their obligations. Oxfam GB recently established a new position, a global advisor on institutional accountability, to advise its national staff in policy influencing and advocacy strategies, as well as to make use of a human rights framework in its Aim 2--especially in regards to health, education, and HIV/AIDS. In sum, after putting on a human rights lens, addressing human rights violations is not the only option in RBA work. Oxfam GB and other NGOs, therefore, have chosen to hold governments accountable, through influencing both the policy environment and advocacy work regarding pro-poor laws, measures, and practices.

How effective is the cooperation approach alone in addressing some of the key RBA goals, namely (a) to stop human rights violations, deprivation, denials, and discrimination; and (b) to strengthen accountability and change power relations? Will the initiative and support of good policies, without opposing bad ones, be enough to achieve these goals? In which conditions does a cooperation approach become more effective, and in which conditions does it become less effective?

In general, a cooperation approach and consensus building are effective in a non-violation situation, such as when NGOs and government work together towards fulfilling a human right. In the case of human rights violations and efforts to change power relations, however, a cooperation approach has not proved to be effective. This is shown in the Vietnamese cases where, under a cooperative and good relationship mode, NGOs have failed to address human rights violations and have minimally changed power relations.

There is a risk for the development NGOs to move closer to development UN agencies, which work mostly on issues that receive government cooperation, and further from grassroots organizations, which often work against governments' policy and practice and adopt a confrontational approach. The "play it safe" type of RBA NGOs may simply be generating a mutation of new non-governmental UN agencies.

The Dichotomy of Cooperation and Confrontation

One of the most dangerous trends in the current RBA business is the dichotomous thinking of cooperation and confrontation, leading the development community to think "either/or"-either confrontation or cooperation. What Offenheiser and Holcombe (2003, 286) call "carrots and stick", also falls into this dichotomy trap. The dichotomy leaves the development community with no choices, but to say: leave the confrontation of human rights violations with Amnesty International, and we, the development community, will pursue a cooperation approach.

Interestingly, the 2003 meeting of development agencies in Stockholm started to question the existing approach, as the meeting report notes: "There was widespread agreement that other approaches should be used in conjunction with the RBA, so long as organizations put the individual at the centre of these approaches." (SC Sweden 2003, 1) It was not clear from the meeting report what the "other approaches" were. But it is argued here that one "other approache", that should be added and integrated with a cooperation approach, is the confrontational approach-or a challenging approach.

It is argued here that confrontation and cooperation do not constitute and an "either/or" issue. In fact, both approaches help one another in realizing human rights and development goals. The cooperational approach alone is to say only "yes" to governments on service delivery, or certain policies, laws, and practices. On the contrary, the confrontational alone is to only say "no" to governments on policies, laws, and practices. An RBA NGO needs to learn when and how to say either "yes" or "no" to governments, including saying "no" to human rights violations-in all forms of laws, policy, and practices.

Human rights NGOs have used both cooperation and confrontational approaches, both together and separately, for quite some time. Amnesty International, one of the best-known organizations for the "name and shame" or a "say no" method, has a long history of using both confrontational and co-operational approaches with governments. The organization has developed both strategies and tools for promotional and opposing work. Promotional strategies and tools include human rights education, human rights awareness, public campaigns, and promotional media work.

Opposing strategies include research on human rights violations, the use of media, and the mobilization of its 1.8 million members around the world to campaign for change. But this is little news to both development and human rights communities, who generally see Amnesty International as an organization that only confronts governments by documenting human rights violations and then shaming them. The reason for this misunderstanding is that the confrontation side usually gets more publicity both by the media and because of NGOs' intention to mobilize pressure against violating governments. The unseen cooperation side includes working with governments in the reform of the administration of justice, jointly developing and training government officials on human rights education, and public awareness and campaign on a variety of human rights issues.

Even the largest human rights NGO, best known for confronting governments, develops both co-operational and opposing approaches in its own work. The good side of employing both approaches is that it gives an RBA a balance of (a) working together with governments to develop policies, social protection, and service provision, and (b) challenging them when they fail to respect or protect people's rights.

Confrontation and cooperation can co-exist. In fact, its co-existence is a key element in having a good human rights relationship with governments. Amnesty International Thailand, for instance, has used AI's fact finding report on torture in prisons to organize a meeting with the Heads of the Corrections department (confrontation). AI's delegation briefed authorities, gave them a copy of the full report, and discussed possibilities to improve the human rights situation (work based on the fact). As a result, AI Thailand and the Director General of the Corrections Department agreed to jointly organize human rights training workshops for all commanders of the 133 central prisons in the country (cooperation).

In addition, the agreement included AI Thailand's work to integrate training sessions on human rights standards into orientation workshops for all new staff of the Corrections Department, and AI Thailand's training for ten trainers of the department. Another example is AI's Business and Human Rights Network (BERN), whose work has focused on holding companies accountable to their human rights obligations.

Some European sections of AI use a cooperational approach to meet the objective, such as lobbying, organizing lunch meetings with companies, running roundtables, and providing training sessions for companies. The US section uses confrontational campaigning against abusive companies. It should be noted also that it is not only human rights organizations that document human rights situations, many development agencies such as Save the Children also document children's rights situation.

This is to say that discussions on human rights NGO's confrontation or "naming and shaming" approach and development NGO's cooperation approach, have been misplaced. These discussions allow development NGOs to feel good about maintaining their relationships with governments, by avoiding speaking about human rights violations, claiming that a confrontational approach should be reserved for only human rights NGOs. Both types of NGOs need both approaches so that they can appropriately use and mix them together when necessary. A co-operational approach of RBA, that does not challenge human rights violations, or in development terms, impoverishment, is not likely to change power relations, structure of equality, and human suffering.

In sum, this section argues that first, there is a contradiction of NGO cooperation with government, as they tend to cooperate more and oppose less with violating governments which tightly control them, such as is the case in Vietnam. Second, a cooperation approach can contribute greatly to the development world, such as with policy influencing and advocacy, but the approach alone is insufficient in: (a) stopping grave human rights violations or impoverishment, and (b) changing power relations. Third, there is a risk of this dichotomous thinking of cooperation and confrontation, which turns the nature of working with governments into an "either/or" issue-either be friend or enemy, either support or oppose governments. Fourth, the best way to work with governments is to adopt both cooperation and confrontation in given situations. That is, RBA NGOs have to learn when and how to "cooperate" and "challenge". They should articulate strategies and develop tools for both methods and learn to balance them, while maintaining their credibility, legitimacy, and effectiveness, so that they can be in a better position to actually make poverty history.

Bibliography

Aptekar, Lewis. *Street children of Cali,* Durham, Duke University Press,1988.

Gabriel, Marie Cruz: *Children of the street,* New York, Penguin Books, 1994.

Global Policy Forum: *NGOs and the United Nations,* New York, Global Policy Forum, 1999.

Harry J. Steiner: *Diverse Partners: non-governmental organizations in the human rights movement,* Cambridge, Harvard Law School and Human Rights Internet, 1990.

John Ehrenberg: *Civil Society: The Critical History of an Idea,* New York, New York University Press, 1998.

John Foster with Anita Anand: *Whose World is it Anyway? Civil Society, the United Nations and the multilateral future,* Ottawa, United Nations Association of Canada, 1999.

Julie Fisher: *The Road from Rio: sustainable development and the nongovernmental movement in the Third World,* Westport, Praeger, 1993.

Kees Biekart: *The Politics of Civil Society Building: European Private Aid Agencies and Democratic Transitions in Central America,* Utrecht, International Books, 1999.

Marcos Arruda: *NGOs and the World Bank: Is It Possible to Collaborate Critically?,* Rio de Janeiro: PACS, 1995.

Paul J. Nelson: *The World Bank and NGOs: The Limits of Apolitical Development,* New York, St. Martin's Press, 1995.

Peter Willetts: *Pressure Groups in the Global System,* London, Francis Pinter, 1982

Thomas G. Weiss & Leon Gordenker: *NGOs, the UN & Global Governance,* Boulder, Lynne Riener, 1996.

Index

□□□